The New York Times

NEW COMPLETE GUIDE TO HOME REPAIR

The New York Times

NEW COMPLETE GUIDE TO HOME REPAIR

BERNARD GLADSTONE

Quadrangle/The New York Times Book Co.

Book design: Beth Tondreau

Illustrations by Hank Clark

Library of Congress Cataloging in Publication Data

Gladstone, Bernard.
   The New York Times new complete guide to home
repair.

   Includes index.
   1. Dwellings—Maintenance and repair—Amateurs'
manuals. I. Title. II. Title: New complete guide to
home repair.
TH4817.3.G55 1976   643'.7   75-13756
ISBN 0-8129-0599-7

CONTENTS

INTRODUCTION

These days more and more people from all walks of life are doing their own home repairs and taking care of most of the routine maintenance around their homes and apartments.

Some do it because they enjoy the satisfaction and the sense of achievement that comes from not having to depend on others. Others do it because the high cost of hiring a professional painter, carpenter, plumber, or electrician, coupled with the scarcity of this type of help in most communities (and the difficulty encountered in trying to get them to come when *you* want them, especially if it is only a small job), often leaves homeowners with only two alternatives. They can either learn to fix things for themselves; or they must get used to living with leaky faucets, sticking doors, squeaking floors, lamps and doorbells that don't work properly, and all kinds of other minor (and sooner or later major) nuisances.

Because an increasing number of people have in recent years chosen the more sensible first alternative—that is, learning to fix things for themselves—there has been a steady demand for up-to-date, accurate, and easy-to-understand "how-to" information which today's handyman or handywoman can use as a guide.

Homeowners and apartment dwellers alike want to know how to take care of their own repair problems—which in many cases involves working with products or pieces of equipment that were either unknown or seldom encountered years ago—problems that have not been covered in many previous books on home repair and maintenance.

For example, until recent years few homes or apartments were equipped with single control faucets (often called "one arm" faucets), so few, if any, of the how-to volumes available tell the do-it-yourselfer how to repair these. Compact room air conditioners are another modern development, so maintenance of these is also seldom covered. And ten or fifteen years ago latex paint was still a comparatively new development and was only suitable for limited indoor use; today it is widely used on the outside as well as the inside and comes in almost every type of finish—so people want to know when and how to use these popular coatings.

In my weekly Home Improvement column which has been appearing in Sunday editions of *The New York Times* for twenty years (and is now nationally syndicated), I am constantly writing about these and other new products and materials, and I am continually having to update the information that I pass on to my readers because of the rapidity with which the technology keeps changing.

Homeowners always want to know the latest—how they can use new adhesives to make previously "impossible" repairs; how they can use newly developed space-age sealants to save time and money and often make repairs that previously might have called for expensive replacements or major overhauls; or how they can update their noisy, leaking toilet tanks by installing newly developed fill-valves and modern "flappers" to replace the old-fashioned rubber balls which most tanks have on the inside.

This book has been written to answer the demand for this kind of up-to-date information, as well as to cover many home repair projects that are often ignored in other volumes: how to fix overhead garage doors and sliding cabinet or closet doors; how to repair masonry and brickwork; how to replace a damaged piece of clapboard siding; and what to do about such persistent problems as peeling paint or damp basements.

In simple, nontechnical language that is meant for *anyone* to understand, the text and detailed drawings explain how to do all of these money-saving repairs, as well as almost every other type of home repair or maintenance job. Also included are a wealth of shortcuts and timesavers that will be of equal value to beginners or experienced home handymen alike, plus many "tricks of the trade" that I have gathered from years of practical experience in the home improvement and maintenance fields.

Repair projects are logically grouped by category into separate chapters so that the reader can quickly find the answer to any home maintenance problem by simply checking the contents page for the appropriate heading. Numerous cross-references are inserted in the text to direct the reader to other pages or illustrations that will prove helpful, and in the back there is a complete index to provide a more detailed and explicit listing of subjects that can't be quickly located.

Primarily written for those who are interested in doing their own home repairs, this book will prove just as valuable to those who plan to do little or none of the work themselves. By learning how and when repairs *should* be undertaken they will be able to deal more effectively with contractors and tradesmen, and will be able to learn how to avoid being high-pressured by unethical contractors, or fleeced by unscrupulous repairmen.

Bernard Gladstone

The New York Times

NEW COMPLETE GUIDE TO HOME REPAIR

Chapter one
TOOLS AND MATERIALS

It would be virtually impossible for anyone to make up a complete list of all the tools and materials you should have on hand in order to meet all household emergencies. Therefore, some people recommend that you not buy *any* tools or materials until the need for them arises. This may be one way to avoid spending a lot of money on a large assortment of tools, but if carried to the extreme, it means that you will be forever running to the local hardware store. Furthermore, you are bound to get stuck without a necessary tool in the middle of a job on some weekend or evening when all the stores in the neighborhood are closed.

BASIC TOOLS

The middle course is actually the wisest one: Assemble a basic assortment of good quality hand tools and frequently used supplies that almost everyone will need at one time or another, then add to these as you gain experience and as the need for other tools arises.

When buying your tools, remember that even the best quality hand tools are comparatively inexpensive, and in normal use most of them will probably last a lifetime. It is foolish economy, therefore, to buy "bargain basement" tools. Not only will cheap tools need replacing more often, they also will make every job much harder and more tedious to complete—and they are also more likely to cause accidents (blades break, handles come off, and jaws slip).

This chapter will list basic tools which should be included in every home tool kit or workshop, along with some pointers on selecting and working with each of these tools. The list is by no means all-inclusive, but it should prove a good starting point for every do-it-yourself homeowner or apartment dweller.

SCREWDRIVERS

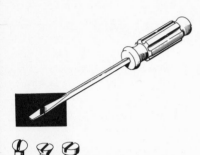

Standard flat-blade screwdriver

Screwdriver with Phillips-type blade fits Phillips-head screws

There are two basic types or styles of screwdrivers—flat and Phillips. The conventional flat blade fits ordinary slotted screws, and the Phillips-type, or cross-slot blade, fits Phillips-head screws. Most of the screws you're likely to buy at your local hardware store will have the more common slotted heads, which require only a conventional flat blade screwdriver. Phillips-head screws and bolts are frequently used by manufacturers for assembling appliances, furniture, toys, and other items which you may have occasion to take apart or repair. Therefore, both types of screwdrivers should be included in even the most basic of home tool assortments.

Actually, you'll need several sizes of each type: at least three or four screwdrivers with flat blades of varying sizes (plus a very narrow blade model for tiny screws), and two Phillips-head screwdrivers, one with a standard size tip, and one with a small tip.

In addition to variations in the size of the blade, screwdrivers also vary in length, with lengths usually increasing as the blades get thicker and heavier. Although the six screwdrivers mentioned above will handle over 90 percent of your home-repair problems, you'll soon find that there are other specialized types which are indispensable for some jobs and which will prove worthwhile additions to any tool kit. One of the most popular, usually referred to as a "stubby," has a very short blade (about 1½ inches) which will enable you to reach into tight places where a conventional long-handled screwdriver would not fit (between shelves that are spaced close together or under a short-legged piece of furniture). Stubby screwdrivers come with various size blades and in both Phillips and flat-blade models, but as a start one medium-

Stubby screwdriver

size, flat-blade stubby driver, plus one with a
Phillips-type tip will probably solve most of your
problems.

Another type of screwdriver that will prove in-
valuable on certain jobs is the type commonly referred to as a "screw-holding" driver. There are
several versions of this tool, but the most common
style is the one which has little spring claws. These
can be pushed out past the tip of the blade so as
to grip the head of the screw firmly with the blade
pressed inside the screw slot. This enables you to
insert screws in tight spots which you cannot reach
with your hand, as well as in awkward corners
where it would otherwise be impossible to hold the
screw while starting it.

For tight spots where even a stubby screwdriver
will not fit there is another type which most experienced home mechanics soon acquire—the offset
screwdriver. As indicated in the accompanying
drawings, these come in two models: one has a
blade bent at right angles to the handle (one
blade at each end, usually at 90 degrees to each
other); the other consists of a flat handle with a
ratchet-operated short blade that sticks out at one
end. (On some models there is a blade on both
sides of the handle.)

When using a screwdriver, try to choose one with
a blade that most nearly fills the slot of the screw
and is about the same width as the screw head.
A blade that is wider than the screw head will
mark up the surface of the wood when you drive
the screw all the way in, and a blade that is too
narrow will tend to twist and chew up either the
tip of the blade, the screw slot, or both. Also remember that screwdrivers with longer handles or
blades will normally enable you to apply more
leverage than those with shorter ones.

One final word of caution: screwdrivers are made
for only one purpose—to drive or remove screws.
Don't use them as pry bars, punches, or chisels. The
tip of the blade should always have a square, blunt
end which will sit firmly in the screw slot. Blades
that have become worn and rounded should be
filed or ground to restore their original shape.

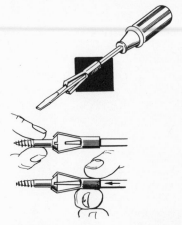

Common type of screw-
holding driver

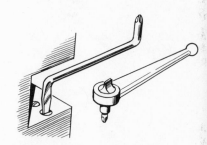

Two types of offset screwdrivers: one has fixed blade
bent at right angles (left);
other has ratchet-operated
blade

PLIERS

Slip-joint pliers

Channel-type pliers

Needle-nosed pliers

Diagonal wire-cutting pliers

If you want to keep your tool collection to a bare minimum, you can probably get by with just one pair of pliers—slip-joint pliers, similar to the ones illustrated. They should have jaws that meet smoothly, with minimum excess play in the pivot joint. The slip joint enables you to shift the relative position of the handles so that the pliers will open to grab objects of large diameter, although in this position its grip won't be quite as strong. Some models have built-in wire cutters which can come in handy on many jobs.

An even more versatile type of slip-joint pliers which experienced mechanics prefer for many jobs is the channel type which has longer handles and comes with offset jaws. Sometimes called mechanic's pliers or water-pump pliers, these come in various sizes (lengths), with the 10- or 12-inch models being the most popular. The jaws can be set for larger size widths or openings, and the offset handles permit greater leverage than would be possible with conventional slip-joint pliers. In addition, the angled jaws permit reaching into places where it might be awkward to use an ordinary pair of pliers. They are particularly handy for plumbing repairs when large packing nuts or retaining rings are often encountered.

In addition to the slip-joint pliers described above, you'll also find a pair of needle-nosed pliers valuable for reaching into tight corners, particularly while doing electrical work. They also are handy for holding small nails and brads (small wire nails) while starting them, as well as for many other jobs where an ordinary pair of pliers will not fit. For maximum versatility, buy a pair that also has built-in wire cutters since this will be useful when doing electrical work. You can use the pointy nose for bending the end of a wire to fit around terminal screws, while the built-in cutter will enable you to do a neat job of snipping off excess wire.

A specialized type of pliers which does an even neater job of cutting off wires, and is useful for stripping insulation off electric wires as well as for clipping off small brads and nails, is a pair of diagonal cutting pliers (often called "dikes"). Although not essential for the beginner, these enable you to cut close to the surface because of the curve of the jaws, and their offset angle also enables you to apply much greater cutting leverage than is possible with the built-in wire cutters of conventional pliers.

HAMMERS

You'll probably need only one hammer for most of your repair jobs around the home—a carpenter's claw hammer of medium size and weight (10 ounces is a good weight). Make the one hammer that you buy a good one; it should be well balanced, with a polished steel head to minimize the possibility of accidentally bending nails or banging a finger (on a good hammer the head is less likely to slide off the top of a nail if your blow is not dead center). The claws should have sharp ends and inside edges to facilitate pulling out nails even when the nail's head is almost flush with the surface.

Carpenter's claw hammer

If you do much woodworking or furniture repairs, you'll find another type of hammer handy—a wood or plastic mallet. This is used for driving chisels (a metal hammer may cause the handle of the chisel to split or "mushroom") and for pounding on surfaces where a conventional hammer would cause dents or other damage, for example, when assembling snug-fitting wood joints.

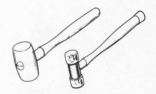

Mallets: wood (left) and plastic-faced (right)

WRENCHES

You'll need several different wrenches in various sizes for gripping nuts and bolts with hexagonal or square heads. In addition, you'll need at least one pipe wrench for gripping pipes and other round objects.

For tightening or loosening nuts and bolts, you can start out with two adjustable Crescent-type wrenches (Crescent is the brand name of the company that first produced this type of wrench). One

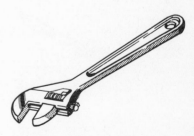

Crescent wrench

Open end wrench

Combination wrench—open wrench at one end, box wrench on the other

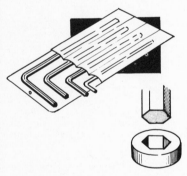

Allen wrenches have hexagon-shaped ends (detail).

Pipe wrench

should be a small, 6-inch model and the other should measure 8 to 10 inches in length. However, if you do much mechanical work, you'll also find it handy to buy a set of open-end wrenches. These have fixed jaws with different sizes at each end. They are faster and more convenient to use than adjustable models are, since you don't have to reset the jaw openings. Also, they will reach into places where an adjustable wrench won't, since the open ends are smaller and narrower.

Instead of open-end wrenches, experienced mechanics often prefer combination wrenches which have an open-end wrench at one end and a box wrench to fit the same size nut or bolt head at the other end. The advantage of a box wrench over an open-end wrench is that it wraps completely around the nut or bolt and thus insures a much firmer grip. Furthermore, it has a comparatively narrow rim that will reach into tight places where an open-end wrench might not fit.

Because many appliances, toys, and power tools often have pulleys and other parts that are secured with setscrews which have hexagon-shaped recesses in their heads, you'll also need a set of Allen wrenches. Though you won't need them very often, when you do need them there is nothing else that will do the trick. Consisting of a hexagon-shaped steel rod that has a short bent section at one end, these come in various sizes (diameters) to fit different size setscrews, and are usually sold as sets in handy plastic pouches or envelopes.

Pipe wrenches, also called Stillson wrenches, have two serrated jaws—one fixed and one movable. They are specially designed to grip round objects firmly by tightening automatically as more pressure is applied to the handle. For most repair jobs around the home, one 10-inch wrench will do the trick, but if you do much plumbing work you'll soon find that for many jobs you'll need two wrenches, one to hold the pipe and the other to turn the fitting or another length of pipe when two parts are being screwed together. If you're going to buy two pipe wrenches, buy them in different sizes for maximum versatility—a good choice would be an 8-inch wrench and a 10- or 12-inch one.

There is one other type of exceptionally versatile wrench which is really not a wrench at all—it is a cross between a wrench and a pair of pliers, and has unlimited uses that overlap the functions of both these tools. Like most multi-purpose tools, it's good, but not as easy to use as those designed specifically for one purpose. Usually referred to as locking pliers, this tool looks very much like a pair of pliers. However, a compound-lever mechanism enables you to close the jaws with a powerful grip many times stronger than you could apply by hand, and also keeps it locked into the work so that you can use it as a portable vise, a twisting tool, or a clamp, as well as in place of a pipe wrench, adjustable wrench, or conventional pair of pliers. Most brands also have powerful wire cutters built in that are strong enough so that by gradually increasing the pressure on the jaws (there is an adjustable screw that enables you to do this with very little effort) you can cut small bolts, large nails, and heavy wires.

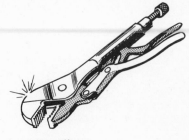

Locking pliers

SAWS

If you're planning to do only those repairs that are absolutely necessary, and have no intention of getting involved with large woodworking or carpentry jobs, then chances are that you won't need a full-size carpenter's hand saw. But you will need at least one small wood saw for such jobs as trimming moldings, as well as some type of hacksaw for cutting metal. For beginners the least expensive solution is to buy an all-purpose utility saw set similar to the one show here. This usually consists of a single handle with two or three interchangeable blades, one of which may be used for cutting metal. The other blades will be for cutting wood. They usually will include a small blade that comes to a point and has fine teeth (commonly called a keyhole saw or compass saw), used for cutting curves or cutting out holes and inside openings in paneling and plywood, and a larger blade with coarser teeth that serves moderately well for conventional wood cutting.

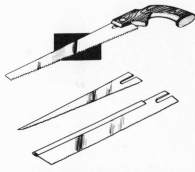

Utility saw set with three blades

However, as you become more experienced, you'll soon find it advisable to buy a conventional carpenter's hand saw. These come in two basic styles—crosscut saws and ripsaws. As the names imply, a crosscut saw is for cutting across the grain while the rip saw is designed for ripping, that is, cutting parallel to the grain. Most home carpenters can get along with just a crosscut saw, since it can be used for occasional ripping. The ripsaw, however, is not very satisfactory for crosscutting, and crosscutting is what you will do most often.

Although the metal-cutting blade of the utility saw set mentioned above may be adequate for the novice, a regular metal-cutting hacksaw is a much more useful tool. This comes with a replaceable blade in various degrees of coarseness (fine for cutting thin tubing and soft metal, coarse for cutting harder and thicker metals, steel pipes or bolts) and the rigid frame will enable you to cut metal almost as easily as you do wood.

Hacksaw

WOOD CHISELS

Wood chisels come in a variety of sizes and styles, but local hardware stores normally stock only the most popular type which has a 9- or 10-inch-long blade that is beveled along the sides and

Crosscut saw (left) and rip saw. The teeth on these saws are slightly different.

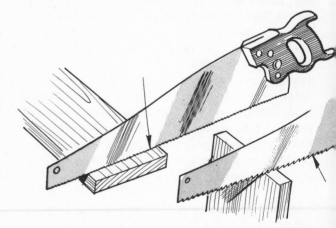

on the cutting edge. Most brands have tough plastic handles which won't split when hammered, but as a rule it's still best to use a wood or plastic mallet rather than a conventional hammer, since there's less likelihood of slipping, and blows are easier to control.

Although chisels come in widths that vary from as little as ¼-inch to several inches, most home repair jobs can be handled with just three or four sizes. You can buy these in sets (½ inch, ¾ inch, and 1 inch) or you can buy them individually as you need them, starting with a ¾ inch chisel and then adding larger or smaller widths as needed. (One advantage of buying the chisels in sets is that they usually come in a handy plastic pouch which not only keeps them together, but also protects the cutting edges against accidental damage when stored in drawers or toolboxes.)

For light, paring cuts only the hands are used: one hand gripping the handle while the other grips the blade near the tip to guide it. For deeper cuts you tap the handle lightly with a hammer, keeping your eye on the chisel blade and not on the hammer or chisel handle. Most paring cuts (without a hammer) are made by moving the blade with an angular slicing action so as to shave the wood off in thin layers. For most chiseling jobs, such as cutting recesses for door hinges, the chisel is used with the beveled side up. To keep the chisel from digging in on very shallow cuts, the blade is turned so the beveled side is down.

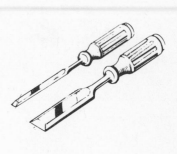

Wood chisels

PLANES

A wood plane has a blade similar to that of a wood chisel; it is held firmly at an angle to the base of the tool, so that its cutting edge projects down a fraction of an inch below that base. The amount of projection can be controlled to set the depth of the cut and to determine how much wood will be taken off with each stroke. There are various models and sizes available, but you'll need at least one small plane for such jobs as trimming door edges,

Block plane

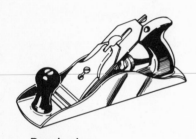

Bench plane

moldings, shelves, and other wood surfaces, as well as for smoothing rough pieces when making repairs or additions.

There are two basic types of planes which are used by do-it-yourselfers: block planes and bench planes. Block planes are small (generally one standard size) and probably the most useful for home repairs. They can be held with one hand, and are ideal for trimming moldings and for spot planing of edges on all kinds of wood doors and drawers.

However, if you intend to tackle larger jobs such as building cabinets, trimming paneling, or installing new doors, you'll probably find a bench plane faster and more convenient. It will also enable you to do more accurate work since it is hard to plane a long edge accurately with a small block plane. As shown here, bench planes are not only longer, they also have two handles—a knob at the front end and a curved wooden handle at the back end. When using a bench plane it is essential that the piece being worked be firmly held or gripped in a vise, clamp, or other device, since you'll need both hands for working the plane.

When using any plane, it is best to set the blade for a thin cut since it's easier to control the amount of wood taken off in this way. Setting the blade too deep may cause gouging and scratching of the wood as the blade tries to dig in. At the beginning, it's best to experiment: start out with the blade barely projecting, then readjust as necessary until the desired depth of cut is achieved. If you have trouble with the blade digging in too much, no matter how fine the adjustment, try planing in the opposite direction. Wood grain is seldom exactly parallel to the edge or surface, so that while planing in one direction will keep the blade from digging in, planing in the opposite direction will tend to make the blade follow the grain and thus dig deeper. When planing end grain, always plane from each edge in toward the center; never allow the blade to go past the opposite edge as this will almost certainly result in splintering.

FILES

You won't need a file very often (nor will you need many of them), but when the need for a file arises, nothing else will do the job.

Files come in many different shapes—square, round, flat, half-round, and triangular—but one 6-inch or 8-inch flat file will take care of most of your needs. In addition to varying in size, files also vary in coarseness and type of cut (that is, in the kind of teeth it has). The teeth on a file slope at an angle across the face and there may be just a single row (single-cut) or a double row (double-cut), which has two rows of teeth crisscrossing each other in opposite directions. Single-cut files give the smoothest finish; double-cut files cut faster but do not leave as smooth a surface.

Flat file and triangular file

For smoothing off rough edges on metal your most useful file will be a flat combination file which has single-cut teeth on one side and double-cut teeth on the other. In addition, a small triangular file will come in handy for reaching into tight spots where a conventional flat file won't fit, as well as for cutting grooves when starting cuts with a hacksaw. A large flat combination file will also be needed for sharpening tools such as rotary lawnmower blades, small hatchets, and garden tools. Round files are handy for working inside curves, enlarging holes, or removing burrs on inside openings.

Round file

MEASURING AND LEVELING TOOLS

Although some professional carpenters and mechanics prefer folding wood rulers, chances are that you'll find a flexible steel tape the most convenient to use—it's light and strong, it slips into your pocket easily, and you can buy it in lengths which extend anywhere from 6 to 50 feet. A 12-foot steel tape should prove long enough for most measuring jobs around the house, yet be compact enough for carrying. Some models have extra-wide blades that are rigid enough to support themselves when ex-

Flexible steel tape

tended outward for several feet, and some have 16-inch markings to simplify locating and measuring for studs (the 2 x 4's inside the wall).

In addition to a tape measure, you will also find a metal or wood yardstick handy as a straightedge for those jobs when you have to draw long straight lines.

You'll also need at least one other type of basic measuring tool—a square. Squares come in various types, but one of the most useful all-round versions is a combination square similar to the one shown here. This is not only an accurate measuring tool (fractions of an inch are engraved on the blade's edge), but it also enables you to measure right angles—as well as 45-degree angles—for mitering. In addition, most models have a built-in bubble level on the handle which can be used either as a level for checking horizontal surfaces, or as a tool for checking vertical surfaces and edges to make sure they are plumb (exactly vertical). To use a combination square as a plumb gauge, hold its long blade against the vertical surface; if the surface is perfectly plumb the bubble of the spirit level in the handle will be dead center because the handle is exactly at a right angle to the blade.

For larger projects such as putting up shelves, building cabinets, or making room additions, you'll need a 24-inch-long spirit level to provide added

Combination square

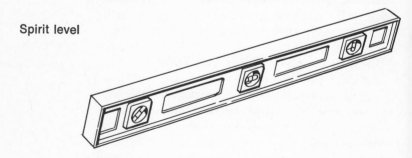

Spirit level

accuracy when plumbing and leveling. This tool normally has two sets of bubbles, one parallel to the length of the tool and one at right angles to it, so they can be used to check whether vertical surfaces are plumb and horizontal surfaces level.

DRILLS

There are many repair jobs for which you'll need a drill, particularly for making pilot holes (starting holes) before driving screws. Chances are that for a large percentage of these you can get by with an inexpensive hand drill, such as one of the push-pull types (you just pump up and down on the handle to drive the bit into the wood), or a rotary hand drill. The push-pull drill usually comes with a set of special bits which are stored inside the end of the handle, while the hand drill uses regular twist drill bits which usually come in sets that vary from $\frac{1}{32}$ to $\frac{1}{4}$ inch in diameter (some hand drills also come with a set of these bits stored in the handle).

Push-pull drill

Although an electric drill costs more than a hand drill, sooner or later you'll want one. These portable power tools are surprisingly light, compact, and inexpensive, and they are useful for many other jobs besides drilling holes. You can equip them with special bits for boring holes in metal, brick, and masonry; or you can add attachments that will enable you to use your drill for sanding and buffing, or driving and removing screws.

The most popular size electric drill is the $\frac{1}{4}$-inch model (the size is determined by the capacity of the drill chuck—a $\frac{1}{4}$-inch drill will hold bits and accessories with shanks up to $\frac{1}{4}$-inch in diameter). However, many companies produce $\frac{3}{8}$-inch drills which are only slightly larger than their $\frac{1}{4}$-inch models and cost only a few dollars more. These not only will enable you to use larger drill bits, but they are more powerful, and well worth considering when making an initial purchase.

Electric drill

The most popular models are those known as "shock-proof" models, which have special nonmetallic housings and internal wiring that eliminates the need for a three-prong plug or three-conductor extension cord. These provide maximum protection against shock and are particularly useful when the drill is used outdoors or in damp locations.

Another feature worth considering when shopping for a new electric drill is variable-speed control. This means that the harder you pull on the trigger, the faster the drill goes; the less pressure applied, the slower it goes (all without a loss of torque, or turning power). Variable-speed models enable you to slow the drill down when using large-diameter drills, hole saws, or boring bits, and when using it for driving screws. Variable speed control is also ideal for starting drill bits when working on very smooth surfaces where the bit tends to skip around at the beginning if started at full speed.

MISCELLANEOUS TOOLS

In addition to the basic tools described on the previous pages, your home repair kit should include a number of other tools which will be necessary to meet various emergencies and repair problems. This list, again, is not all-inclusive, since you will undoubtedly want to add other tools as experience and needs dictate. However, the following are essential for beginning:

A sharp *utility knife* of the kind that uses disposable razor-sharp blades and normally stores extra blades in the handle.

Two *putty knives*—a stiff one about 1½ to 2 inches wide, and a flexible one at least 3 or 4 inches wide. The stiff one will be used for scraping and prying jobs, as well as for light duty masonry patching, while the wider, more flexible model will be needed for patching cracks and holes in interior walls and ceilings when applying spackling compound, patching plaster, or gypsum board seam compounds.

A plumber's *force cup*, also called a "plumber's friend" or plunger. This bell-shaped rubber cup

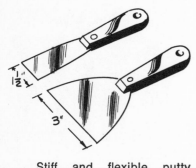

Stiff and flexible putty knives

with a wood handle is used for unclogging sinks or toilet drains. It is an indispensable tool for every homeowner or apartment dweller, and will often save the price of an expensive visit from a plumber —as well as eliminating the inconvenience of being stuck without sanitary facilities (overnight or over a weekend) while waiting for the plumber to arrive.

Plumber's force cup

A *plumber's snake,* or drain auger, is used for stubborn clogs that can't be freed up with the force cup, or that occur in a waste line in places where the force cup's action will not be effective. (A force cup is most effective in freeing up clogs which occur directly below the fixture or immediately beyond its U-shaped trap.) Plumber's snakes come in various types and consist, essentially, of a long flexible steel wire or springlike coil which can be poked and twisted into the waste pipe or trap to break up or remove accumulations of solid waste and other foreign objects which obstruct the pipe. Most models have a tapered coiled spring at the working end with a sharp point to help them penetrate. Some also have off-set handles at the other end to simplify twisting and turning the snake as you force it forward into the pipe.

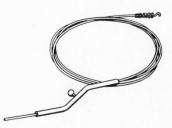

Plumber's snake

A *nailset* which, as its name implies, is primarily designed for setting nail heads below the surface of the wood. This tool is useful on carpentry jobs where you'll want to recess nail heads so that you can then cover them with putty or crack filler. It is also handy for driving small nails in tight corners where a hammer head won't fit, or where a poorly aimed blow might cause damage to surrounding surfaces. Nailsets can also be used as a punch on light-duty jobs, as well as for pushing nails completely through wood without splitting it when you want to remove strips of molding that can't be replaced easily (in old houses, for example).

Nailset

One or two *clamps* in different sizes which can be used for holding parts together while gluing or assembling; these often are essential when repairing furniture, toys, and play equipment. The most popular, and probably the most versatile, type of clamp is the so-called standard C-clamp. It comes

C-clamps

in various sizes, from tiny ones that open to only 1 inch to large models that open to 10 or 12 inches For most home repair jobs a medium-size model with jaws that open to about 4 inches will be adequate.

When you are ready for a second clamp, get a larger size that will handle work up to 6 or 8 inches thick. Eventually, you will want to add a long bar clamp, similar to the one pictured here, since this will be needed for repairing furniture or cabinets when you will be gripping objects which are wider than the capacity of any C-clamp. The most versatile type of bar clamp is the one which uses a length of ordinary pipe (threaded at one end) for the "bar." Hardware stores sell only the clamp end—the length of pipe is bought separately and can be as long as you like. One advantage of this is that you can buy several pieces of pipe in different lengths so that you can assemble any length bar clamp you want simply by changing the pipe.

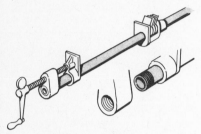

Bar clamp fits on ordinary pipe.

A *combination oilstone* (fine grit on one side, medium on the other), will be necessary for keeping chisels, knives, plane blades, and other tools sharp. These inexpensive sharpening stones are used by holding the cutting edge of the blade flat against the top of the stone and then rubbing back and forth with parallel strokes. They are called oilstones because you keep the surface coated with oil while sharpening, to lubricate the whetting action and to keep the stone itself from becoming clogged with metallic particles. An oilstone will take care of most sharpening needs since a properly cared-for chisel or other cutting tool should seldom need grinding—periodic honing or whetting on the oilstone will keep a keen edge on the blade indefinitely.

STORING AND CARING FOR YOUR TOOLS

Regardless of how many tools you have when you get started, chances are that you will be adding to your collection as time passes and as your experience grows. If possible, plan to keep all your tools in one place, so you can find them easily when needed. You can hang them up on wall clips or on perforated hardboard racks in your basement or garage. You can also store tools in a couple of drawers, or keep them in one or two portable tool boxes of the type that are widely available in hardware stores and lumber yards.

One advantage of keeping tools—especially frequently used ones—in a portable box is that you can pick up the box and carry it with you, instead of carrying loose tools in your hands or pockets. However, if you do buy a toolbox or carrier, be careful you don't buy one that is too large or heavy—when loaded it could be impossible to carry around easily. That is why many prefer two, or even three, smaller boxes, keeping the most frequently used tools in one, and the ones that are needed only occasionally in the others.

Whatever your storage system, remember that for working convenience, as well as for safety, all tools should be kept clean and in good repair with sharp edges protected against damage. A loose or greasy handle on any tool is a hazard because it may slip and cause you to lose your grip. Cutting tools with sharp blades are actually safer to use than those with a dull edge since dull ones require more pressure and are more likely to slip. That is why chisels and similar tools should have edges protected when stored with other tools, either by keeping them in canvas or plastic pouches, or simply by wrapping the edges with adhesive tape when not in use.

Chapter two

PAINTING AND PAPERING

More people do their own painting and finishing than almost any other form of do-it-yourself home maintenance, probably because they find that painting is one of the simplest and most gratifying of home repair chores. Results are instantly seen for everyone to admire, and modern paints and finishes have been so vastly improved that almost anyone can accomplish a professional-looking job with little or no previous experience. In addition, professional painters are now so expensive—and so hard to find—that many people have no choice; if they want part or all of the house painted they either have to do it themselves or do without.

However, in spite of the fact that today's paints are more foolproof than ever before, you still cannot be certain of getting good results on every surface unless you use the right kind of paint. While it is true that some brands are advertised as being suitable for practically every purpose, there is still no such thing as a truly "all-purpose" paint that can be used everywhere and under every condition. That is why every reputable manufacturer makes a variety of different kinds of paints in a choice of finishes, and why you must know something about the various types that are available if you want to select the one that best meets your particular needs.

CHOOSING INTERIOR PAINT

Interior paints can be divided into four broad categories, depending on their amount of gloss and the uses to which they will be put:

Flat paints have little or no sheen and are most often used on walls and ceilings. Flat finishes make bumpy and wavy areas less obvious, but they are not very stain-resistant and will not take as much abuse as paints which dry with a glossy finish.

Semigloss paints, also referred to as satin finishes, are midway between high gloss and dead flat when dry. They are most often used on woodwork such as windows, doors, and trim where you may not want a high shine, but you do want a finish that is more washable and stain-resistant than a flat. Semigloss finishes are often used on the walls and ceilings of kitchens, bathrooms, and laundry rooms, since they will stand up better when exposed to dampness and hard wear, and are less likely to be stained by splashing or accidental spills.

High-gloss paints, usually referred to as enamels, give a hard shiny, finish that will take more abuse than duller finishes. Enamels are generally used on surfaces which get very hard wear and are frequently washed—kitchen cabinets, furniture, toys, and appliances—but they require more care in application since brush marks are more noticeable on a glossy surface.

Primer-sealers or *undercoats* are designed to be used as a first coat or primer under one of the other finishes. They may be called by various names but are not intended to serve as a finish coat. You should use one of these only when the manufacturer of the particular paint you plan to use recommends it on his label, or when working on previously unpainted or badly worn surfaces.

You can buy all of these paints in latex types that thin with water, or in oil-base or alkyd types that thin with turpentine or similar solvent. Chances are that you'll find latex paints easier and less messy to work with—you can wash your brushes, rollers, or other tools in water, and you can clean off smears and drips with a damp cloth. (Of course you won't need any special thinner since these paints thin with water.) Latex paints dry much faster than oil paints so you can replace furniture, or apply a second coat if necessary, within an hour or two; in the flat finishes, latex paints are more stain-resistant and tend to cover better than solvent-thinned flats.

In spite of the conveniences offered by the use of water-thinned latex, there are still some cases when you will find solvent-thinned paints and finishes preferable, especially in gloss or enamel finishes. You can buy various brands of enamel with a latex base, but in most cases these are not available in as wide a range of sharp, bright colors as the solvent-thinned enamels are, nor are they as durable. In addition, latex enamels still do not cover as well (especially on one-coat jobs) as the alkyd enamels.

When choosing between latex and oil-base or alkyd finishes, remember that latex paints do not adhere properly to a glossy surface. Alkyd enamels are less finicky in this respect. However, all shiny surfaces should be dulled down by sanding or by use of a liquid deglosser before repainting.

On most indoor paint jobs, you won't need any special primer or undercoat if you're using a latex paint—unless you're working on new wood, metal, or plaster. In addition, if you're painting walls or ceilings where you've just done a great deal of patching, or if the new paint involves a drastic change of color, then a first coat of primer-sealer or undercoat is usually advisable. (The label on the paint can will provide specific recommendations as to which one to use.) When a primer or undercoat is required, remember that these base coats only come in white, so if your final color is going to be dark, it's best to tint the primer or undercoat to make it at least half as dark as the finish coat; otherwise you'll have quite a time trying to cover the white primer with one finish coat.

CHOOSING EXTERIOR PAINTS

Like interior paints, most of the paints required for use on the outside of your house are also available in either latex (water-thinned) form, or in oil- or alkyd-base formulations. As a rule, the latex types are easier to work with (they clean easily with water, are easier to spread, and no special thinner is needed). But for the weekend painter one of the biggest advantages in using a latex paint on the exterior is that the paint can be applied over surfaces which are still partially damp. This means that you can paint at any time—you don't have to wait a day or two after it has rained, nor do you have to wait several hours in the morning until the dew dries (you can actually apply a latex paint within minutes after the rain has stopped). In addition, since latex paints dry much faster than oil paints you can replace screens and storm windows on the same day and close windows within an hour or so after painting. You'll have fewer problems with bugs sticking to the wet surface and, if necessary, you can apply two coats on the same day.

Most of the paints that you will use on the outside of your house fall into one of six broad categories: house paints, trim paints, masonry paints, shake paints (also called shingle paints), deck paints, and primers.

House paints are those intended for use on wood siding, overhanging eaves, and other large areas on the body of the house. Oil-base house paints usually have a medium to high gloss; latex house paints are comparatively dull, and dry with a finish that varies from almost flat to a satin sheen.

Trim Paints are those intended for use on doors, shutters, windows, and other forms of outdoor trim. They dry to a harder, glossier finish that will take more abuse and will shed dirt more readily. They are available in bright, sharp colors you can't find in ordinary house paint. Trim paints should not be used on clapboard or other large surfaces—they are hard and brittle and thus are more likely to crack or chip when the wood expands and contracts.

Masonry paints are intended for use on brick, stucco, and concrete. They dry to a dull finish and are formulated to be more resistant to attack by excess alkali and moisture in the mortar, brick, or concrete (conditions often encountered).

Shake (shingle) paints are very similar to masonry paints in that they also dry dull, and are less prone to blistering or peeling when moisture seeps in behind the film (a problem on most masonry and shingle walls). Many companies make one paint which they recommend for use on both masonry and shingles, since the problems involved in painting both these surfaces are so similar.

Deck paints are, as the name implies, intended for painting decks and floors such as porches, patios, terraces, and steps. They are available in both alkyd-base formulations and latex types, and are specifically designed to withstand the abrasion and scuffing encountered when people walk on them. Latex deck paints (also called floor paints) dry to a dull finish which, when wet, is less slippery than a glossy finish. Moreover, on concrete slabs which come in direct contact with the ground, they generally stand up better than oil or alkyd paints. Alkyd deck paints dry to a glossier, harder finish and generally stand up better on wood decks, porches, and steps.

Primers are intended for use as a base or first coat on new or previously unfinished surfaces, on surfaces which have been scraped bare, or on those which have been so badly eroded that a foundation coat is needed before the finish can be applied. Primers come in a wide variety of types and formulations, depending on both the surface over which they will be be applied and the top coat that will be applied over them. To make certain that you use the right primer, read the specifications on the label. It is important that you try to use the product recommended by the manufacturer of the final coat you will be using.

As mentioned previously, all of these paints are available in both water-thinned latex types and conventional solvent-thinned oil- or alkyd-base formulations. One big advantage offered by many latex exterior paints is that one paint can be used on three or four different kinds of surfaces. For instance, the average good quality latex house paint is not only suitable for use on clapboard and siding, it is also an excellent masonry and shingle paint. Thus, if the exterior of your house is constructed of more than one material, instead of having to work with two or three different kinds of oil paint, the one latex paint may be used on every type of siding.

In addition to its easy-working and easy-cleanup characteristics, another advantage of latex exterior paint is that it dries with a permeable "breathing" film which lets moisture trapped inside the wood or masonry escape harmlessly without causing blisters and eventual peeling. Bear in mind that you get this extra benefit only when you're applying a latex paint over an unpainted surface, or directly over a coat of latex paint. However, when you put latex paint over an old coat of oil paint, the old paint can still blister and peel, taking the new paint off with it.

Always remember that outside paints have to stand up under a great deal of exposure and hard wear, so it's foolish economy to buy on the basis of price alone. Choose the best quality you can find and always read the manufacturer's instructions on the label carefully to determine what primer or undercoat (if any) is required and over what kinds of surfaces the paint can be applied.

PAINTING WALLS AND CEILINGS

For painting walls, ceilings, and other large flat surfaces, you'll find it easier and faster to use a paint roller than a brush. Roller covers are made of different kinds of synthetic fiber with naps or piles of different lengths. As illustrated (from top to bottom), short nap, mohair covers are used for gloss or semigloss finishes on extra-smooth surfaces. Those with a thicker ¼-inch or ⅜-inch nap are used for conventional flat paint on relatively smooth walls. For textured walls, use a ½-¾-inch nap, and if your walls have a very rough surface, like stucco or brick, you'll require a longer nap cover—one with fibers that are 1–1½ inches in length.

Although roller covers vary widely in price, it never pays to buy the least expensive ones, even if you plan to throw them away (rather than cleaning them) after the job is done. Even with the best paint, inexpensive, poor-quality covers make it almost impossible to get a smooth, uniform finish, and they inevitably cause a great deal of splattering,

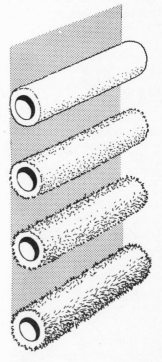

Roller covers range from those with short nap mohair (top) to those with deep pile, long naps (bottom).

Use a brush to paint around windows and in corners, before using roller.

dripping, and running. A densely fibered, close-napped, top-quality cover will feed the paint onto the surface at a uniform rate with less likelihood of skipping, streaking, and dripping, and the fiber will not mat or cake up as you work.

When painting an entire room, the usual sequence is to paint the ceiling first, the walls next, and the woodwork and trim last. Since you can't reach into the corners, or "cut-in" close to the woodwork and trim with a roller, you'll need a brush for these areas. As a rule, then, it's best to do all the brushwork on each wall first, then finish the large areas with the roller. The roller should cover as much of the brush work as possible so that any difference in texture will not be noticeable.

It is best to start applying the paint to the wall with a series of angled strokes so that the pattern forms a large upside down "V" on the surface. Then roll back and forth with parallel strokes to fill in the open spaces and eliminate ridges while spreading the paint uniformly. Bear in mind that for uniform coverage you must apply the paint liberally (especially when working with latex paint), so, instead of pressing harder when you start running out of paint, stop and pick up more paint immediately.

To make cleaning the paint tray easier, line the bottom of the tray with aluminum foil before pouring the paint in. Fill the tray only about two-thirds

Angle strokes to form a series of large, overlapping V's or W's.

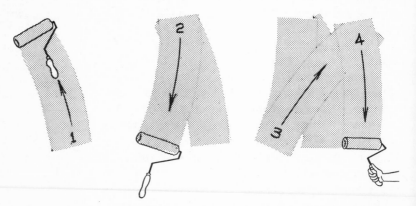

full, leaving a bare space at the top of the sloping section where you will be able to roll out the excess each time you dip the roller in. Always make sure the roller is uniformly saturated on all sides, and when painting walls make your first stroke with the fully loaded roller in an upward direction to avoid dripping. On a ceiling the first stroke should always be *away* from you. To simplify painting ceilings and to minimize the amount of ladder moving and climbing required, buy an extension handle for your roller—this will enable you to do the whole job (except for the brush work needed in the corners and around the edges) from the floor.

To clean a roller after the job is done, always remove the cover from its handle before the paint dries. If you leave it on, some paint may get inside the core and dry hard, making it almost impossible to remove the cover. With latex paint, cleaning is easy: simply flush in running water until the water runs clean. With oil paint, the simplest way is to roll the cover back and forth on a stack of old newspapers, peeling off the top sheet as it becomes saturated and continuing on through the pile until no more paint rolls out. Then rinse in a small amount of paint thinner placed in the bottom of a pan. Work the solvent into the fibers with your fingers (wear a plastic glove to protect your hands), then pour the thinner out, replace it with fresh solvent, and rinse again. Finally, rinse in a warm detergent solution, and finish by rubbing with a rag until the fibers are dry.

PAINTING WOODWORK AND TRIM

Although you could use a roller on flush doors, you'll have to use a conventional paintbrush on most of your other woodwork and trim. But remember, even in the hands of the most skilled painter, an inexpensive, poor-quality brush will make it almost impossible to do a good job. So instead of buying cheap "throw-away" brushes which you'll have to replace repeatedly, invest in one or two good brushes with plenty of flagged

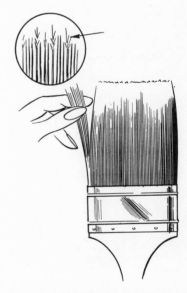

Lots of flagged tips are one sign of a good brush.

bristle tips. As with rollers, washing out brushes is no longer the laborious chore it once was, since with modern latex paints all you need is plenty of running water, and even with oil paints you can wash your brushes effortlessly if you use one of the liquid brush cleaners that are designed to emulsify oil paint so that it becomes soluble in water (after you agitate the brush in the liquid you can then wash it out in water).

Another frequent mistake is selecting a paintbrush that is too narrow for the work at hand—either because it costs less than a wider brush or because a narrow one would just fit into the opening in a small can of paint. Actually, for proper and thorough mixing, the paint should always be poured out of the original can into a larger pail or bucket (you can buy disposable paper buckets, or save your old coffee cans for this). That way you'll have room to mix without slopping paint over the sides, and you'll be able to dip in a brush of adequate size. A wider brush will require fewer brush strokes and will finish the job quicker, with less chance of brush marks or streaks on the surface. As a rule, it is best to choose the widest brush that you can handle easily on the surface being painted (except on very narrow moldings where you're more likely to use the brush edgewise).

A 2-inch sash brush (the kind that has a long handle) will work best on windows, while a 2½- or 3-inch trim brush is good for baseboards, door frames, cabinets, and other built-ins. In the 3-inch width this same type of brush is also good for doors —although as you progress you may find that a 4-inch brush will get the work done quicker.

When dipping your brush into the paint, never dip it to more than one-third its bristle length. Dipping it any deeper will only load the heel with paint and will eventually ruin the brush's working qualities, in addition to making it much harder to clean. Apply the paint with a moderate amount of pressure—but never scrub or rub it on.

Always start on a dry, unpainted area and brush back into the fresh paint. To avoid ridges or visible brush marks try to "feather" each stroke by ending

To avoid leaving brush marks, paint toward the already painted area and lift brush gradually at the end of the stroke.

with a gradual lifting action during the final smoothing, making certain you start in a freshly painted section and end up in a previously painted area, lifting up gradually.

PAINTING WINDOWS

Amateur painters seem to have more trouble painting windows than they have with almost any other part of the house; yet, with a little practice there is no reason why you can't do a neat job without having to spend hours cleaning paint smears off the glass.

To paint the window moldings and frame without also painting the glass, you can either use one of the various aids or accessories that are available for the purpose, or you can learn to "cut in" neatly with the brush the way a skilled professional does.

The most popular accessory for keeping paint off the glass is a metal or plastic shield that looks like a piece of venetian-blind slat. You hold it so that its edge is pressed against the molding while you're painting, sliding it along with the brush so that it keeps the bristles from coming into contact with the glass. With one of these gadgets you can do a neat job quickly and easily. Remember, however, that each time you dip the brush into the paint you should also wipe off the edge of the shield with a rag or else the accumulated paint will smear onto the glass.

Masking tape provides another method for pro-

Dip bristles into paint only an inch or so, then remove excess by patting against the side of the can, above the level of the paint.

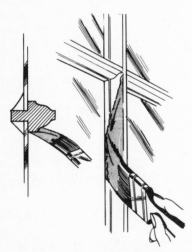

Direct a slow, steady stroke toward the pane so that bristles fan out and then just touch the pane as the stroke continues.

tecting the glass, but unless it's put on carefully so that the tape does not overlap the wood you may wind up with unpainted edges in some spots. Most people find that putting the tape on accurately takes so long that it's hardly worth the trouble; you might just as well apply the paint as best you can, and later scrape off any smears with a razor-blade. If masking tape is used, make sure you pull it off before the paint is completely hard, otherwise you're liable to peel off some of the paint with the tape.

If you have a good quality sash brush with springy bristles that come to a nice sharp edge, there's no reason you can't learn to "cut in" or trim a window neatly by just working free-hand. Dip the brush in no more than an inch or so, then tap lightly against the inside rim of the can above the level of the paint. (Never wipe your brush across the rim of the can to remove excess since this takes too much paint out and also creates bubbles that make it hard to get a smooth finish—especially when working with varnish.)

Touch the bristles to the wood molding so that they are slightly away from the glass, then press down lightly, with a mild twisting action so that the bristles "fan out" to a sharp chisel-like edge. Now move the brush along with a slow but steady stroke while gradually bringing the edge of the bristles up to the glass; then keep moving it along in a straight line with the bristle tips just contacting the glass until the brush starts running out of paint. Stop and pick up more paint before continuing. In each case start out the same way—touch the brush to the wood an inch or so away from the glass, then fan out the bristles and work them in gradually until they touch the glass.

In addition to trying to paint the sash frames without painting the glass, there is another common problem—trying to figure out what sequence to follow or, how to paint all parts of both the upper and lower sash frames without skipping and without getting paint all over your hands as you try to move them up and down.

The simplest way to do this is to raise the bottom

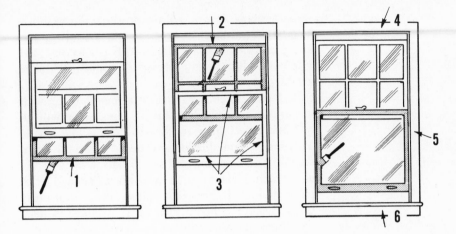

Paint the two sash frames of double-hung windows in the sequence shown here. Shaded areas indicate where paint has been applied.

sash as high as it will go, then lower the top sash as low as it will go. Now, following the sequence illustrated here, first paint the bottom half of the upper sash as shown, then move the two sashes back to their normal positions—the upper one at the top and the lower one at the bottom, but don't close them all the way—leave each one open slightly. Next, finish painting the rest of the upper sash frame, then paint all of the lower sash frame, in each case painting the narrow moldings between the glass first and finishing the outside of each frame last. When you have finished both sashes, paint the window channels and the frame on each side, then the trim around the window, doing the window sill last.

WORKING WITH VARNISH AND ENAMEL

Varnishes and enamels are similar in composition, the main difference being that varnish is clear while enamel has pigment added to give it color and make it opaque. Since they are both applied on furniture, cabinets, and similar surfaces where you want an extra-smooth finish, you should expect to spend a little extra time and care in applying them.

Varnish is transparent, so you'll have to be especially careful in preparing the wood underneath because every flaw will show up through the finish. Thorough sanding is necessary to remove stains and blemishes. Always finish with a very fine grit to remove all scratches left by the coarser grades of sandpaper.

A clean surface is a must for a smooth finish with varnish or enamel; dust left on the surface will inevitably result in a rough-looking, "sandy" finish. This means you should be especially careful about dusting and cleaning the wood. One way is to use a vacuum cleaner, then a cloth moistened with paint thinner. Better yet, wipe with a special tacky cloth (usually called a tack rag), available in most well-stocked paint stores.

For a smooth finish you'll also need a good quality, fully stocked brush with plenty of flagged bristles (see drawing on page 27). Dip the brush into the varnish or enamel no more than one-third its bristle length, then flow the varnish or enamel on liberally with only a slight amount of pressure on the brush. Ideally, you should first apply the finish with short strokes that go across the grain, then lightly with long strokes parallel to the grain.

As you dip the brush into the can each time, remember *not* to wipe the excess off by dragging the bristles across the rim. Instead, tap the bristle tips lightly against the inside of the container above the surface of the liquid to remove the excess. The idea is to remove no more liquid than necessary to prevent dripping as you carry the brush from the can to the work. Wiping across the rim will not only remove too much liquid, it will also cause tiny bubbles to form in the material that runs back into the can—and this will make it impossible for you to get a smooth finish as you keep working. You can also get air bubbles by pressing too heavily on the brush or by an excessive amount of back-and-forth brushing. That's why it is so important to brush lightly using long strokes.

Wherever possible, when finishing furniture or small pieces, try to lay the surface on which you are working in a horizontal position. If you have to work on vertical surfaces, start by brushing across (horizontally), then cross-stroke vertically to eliminate brush marks and spread the finish out uniformly. Keep checking back every few minutes to make certain that no sags or runs have developed. If any are noticed, brush them out immediately before the paint gets too tacky to permit smoothing.

On furniture or cabinets, always remove all hardware (knobs, handles, etc.) before starting—it is almost impossible to do a neat job of brushing around obstructions of this kind. Chests or cabinets with drawers are best painted by taking the drawers out and standing them up so that the front is horizontal. If more than one coat will be required (with either varnish or glossy enamel) thin the first coat with about 10 percent paint thinner, then put the second coat on as it comes from the can. In each case, allow the finish to dry completely hard, then sand lightly with very fine sandpaper between coats. After sanding, don't forget to remove all the dust before brushing on the next coat.

When buying varnish or enamel, keep in mind that these finishes come in varying degrees of semi-gloss or satin gloss, as well as in the traditional high gloss. The semigloss finishes save you the job of rubbing down a high gloss on those surfaces where you don't want a shiny finish, but as a rule they are not quite as durable or as tough as the high-gloss finishes. If you are painting or varnishing something that will be used outdoors or exposed to the weather, chances are you'll have to use a high gloss—few, if any, of the semigloss varnishes or enamels are suitable for exterior use. The working techniques are, however, similar in each case.

USING WOOD STAINS AND SEALERS

A wood stain is more like a translucent dye than an opaque paint—it is designed to soak into the wood and change its tone without hiding the original texture or grain, and without completely obliterating the original color. Wood stains are made in both latex and oil-base formulations, but with one or two exceptions, they are not actually finishes—they are merely a means for coloring or darkening the wood before you apply a clear, protective finish (varnish, shellac, lacquer, etc.) over it.

One exception to this is a penetrating wood sealer. While this is actually a transparent finish, it also comes with pigment or color added. Made with either a wax base or a processed-oil base, it is designed to soak into the wood and leave little or no surface film. However, it provides a finish that protects the surface, so it is both a stain and a finish in one application.

Because these penetrating sealers actually soak into the fibers of the wood there really is no surface film to scratch—although you can, of course, scratch the wood itself. Penetrating finishes of this kind are popular on floors where you want a dark tone without having to worry about scratches showing up, or where you want a low-sheen wood floor that will be easy to maintain. The same kind of penetrating finish is also used on furniture and shelving for pieces on which a low-lustre "oiled" or "Danish" type finish is desired instead of the built-up look of a high-gloss varnish or lacquer.

When you go shopping for any type of wood stain—regardless of whether it's a penetrating stain-sealer or an ordinary oil stain over which you will later apply varnish or shellac—remember that, unlike paint, the color samples that you see in the store are not necessarily an accurate indication of the color you will get on the wood in your home. Paints are opaque, which means that as long as you apply enough coats to cover completely, the color underneath has no effect on the finished color and the paint sample you see in the store is exactly what you should get at home. But wood stains are transparent, so the color of the wood underneath will affect the finished color of the stain. If your wood is redder than the wood used for the sample, then the finished effect will be redder than you expected. By the same token, lighter woods will come out lighter and darker woods will come out darker. Thus, the only sure way to know what color you will get is first to try a sample of the wood stain on exactly the same kind of wood, or on an inconspicuous corner of the actual piece being worked on.

Since wood stains must soak into the surface, the porosity of the wood will also affect the color—soft, porous woods come out darker, while hard woods generally come out lighter because the stain doesn't soak in as much. Cheap grades of wood with uneven porosity and sappy streaks will, therefore, come out uneven or blotchy. One way to prevent this, when you have to stain soft wood, is to apply a very thin coat of clear penetrating sealer before the stain. Thin the sealer with 25–30 percent turpentine, then apply it uniformly over the wood. Wipe off the excess with a clean rag, and allow it to dry before staining. If the wood feels fuzzy, sand *very lightly* with very fine sandpaper and dust thoroughly before applying the stain. This technique partially seals porous wood enough so that the stain will "take" uniformly without creating the blotchy appearance that often results when a poor grade of wood is stained.

SPRAY PAINTING

There are many paint jobs, such as finishing wicker furniture, wrought iron railings, fences, and other hard-to-paint objects, where the fastest and easiest way to do the job is to apply the paint by spraying it on rather than by brushing it on. You can either use a spray gun (which you can rent or buy) or you can buy paint in an aerosol spray can. A regular spray gun is faster and less expensive on all but the smallest jobs. It enables you to buy your paint in bulk instead of having to pay the high price involved in buying aerosol cans (each can holds only a few ounces of paint, the rest of its volume being taken up by propellant gases).

Aerosol cans are much more convenient for small jobs. They eliminate the problem of cleaning out the spray gun and its canister when the job is finished. However, spray guns provide more control. Guns permit adjusting the size and "wetness" (proportion of air to paint) of the spray, so that after a little practice you can do a much better job, especially on large projects.

Aerosol paint in spray cans is available in almost every kind of finish—flat, enamel, stain, varnish, lacquer, and shellac—and in a wide variety of colors and materials. Before using an aerosol can it is important that you shake it thoroughly, making certain you hear the little metal ball on the inside rattling around (this ball acts as an agitator in all aerosol paints, except for clear finishes which have no pigment). If you don't hear the ball rattling around when you shake the can, try rapping the bottom sharply against a solid surface to dislodge the ball, then shake again.

It is always best to do your spraying outdoors on a calm, windless day or in an open garage where you are protected from the wind. If you must spray indoors, make sure that the room is well-ventilated. Cover nearby floors and other surfaces to protect against drift or "overspray." Make certain the surface you are painting is clean and free of wax, oil, grease, dirt, or peeling paint, and remember: two thin coats will always do a better job than one heavy one.

Regardless of whether you are using a spray gun or can, there are certain techniques that should be followed if you want to insure uniform results and a smooth finish:

1. Try to hold your spray can or gun in a vertical position and hold it so that the spray tip is about 8 to 10 inches away from the surface.
2. At all times, keep the nozzle at a constant distance from the surface. Move the sprayer in parallel back-and-forth strokes that overlap each other by about one-third. Never swing your arm in an arc—this will bring the can or gun closer to the surface at the center of the stroke than it will be at the end—resulting in a heavy layer of paint at the center and an excessively thin one at each side.
3. Keep the spray gun or can moving at all times while paint is coming out. Start the stroke while aiming slightly off to one side of the object and don't shut off the spray until you have passed the edge on the other side.
4. When spraying horizontal surfaces such as a table top or chair seat, start spraying the part that is closest to you first, then keep moving away from your

body. This will eliminate the danger of "overspray" settling as a fine mist over a previously sprayed area —an error that often causes pebbly, uneven finishes.

5. When spraying tables, chairs, and similar pieces of furniture, always spray the undersides and other hard-to-reach areas first. Leave the easiest-to-reach and most noticeable sections (seats, backrests, table tops, etc.) for last.

6. Wherever possible, remove all hardware (knobs, handles, etc.) before starting to spray. This will eliminate the need for masking and will insure a continuous application. If masking is required, use a razor blade to trim the tape off so it does not overlap the surface to be painted. Peel the tape off before the paint dries. If you let the paint dry until hard, you might pull off strips of paint when you remove the tape.

7. If you don't use up all the contents of an aerosol spray can at one time, be sure to clean out the nozzle tip after finishing the job to keep it from clogging. To do this, turn the can upside down and spray out any

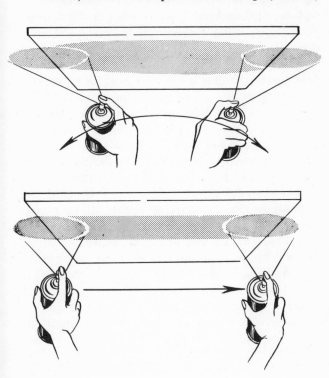

Don't wave the can in an arc (above). Bend the wrist as shown (below) to keep can at same distance from surface at all times.

paint that remains in the tube or nozzle (after a second or two, only gas will come out). Then wipe the tip of the nozzle with a clean piece of rag to remove any paint that is in or around the opening.

USING PAINT REMOVERS

There are many painting and finishing jobs for which you'll find it necessary to remove all of the old paint or varnish before you can apply a new finish. In some cases this will be necessary because the old paint is badly chipped, blistered, or is peeling. Or you may want to get down to the original wood, so that you can bleach it or apply a stain or other natural wood finish. You can remove old paint and varnish in one of four ways—by scraping the old finish off with a hand scraper, by sanding it off with an electric sander, by burning it off with a torch, or by using a prepared chemical paint and varnish remover.

Hand scraping is by far the most difficult of the three methods and it is only practical for taking off small patches of peeling paint where the finish is already loose and flaky. Sanding with an electric machine, using a disk or belt sander, is easier and faster. Disk sanders should only be used for comparatively rough work around the outside of your house because they tend to gouge the surface and leave swirl marks—they should never be used on furniture or interior paneling. A belt sander works fast and will leave a smooth finish, but these machines are rather heavy to handle, especially when working on vertical surfaces or overhead. (Both belt sanders and disk sanders can be rented from local hardware stores or tool rental agencies.)

Although professional painters frequently remove paint from the outside of a house by burning it off with a torch, this is a rather dangerous procedure which the amateur is well-advised to avoid. There are electric "torches" which have special quartz lamps that develop a very high heat, but these are also likely to scorch the wood and can start a fire if you're not careful. They are easier to control than a conventional torch, although they work a little slower.

Prepared chemical paint and varnish removers which are sold in all paint and hardware stores are the safest and easiest materials to use. However, using these often costs more than using any of the other methods. Removers come in different types (described below), but all work in basically the same manner—when you spread them over an old finish they soften and blister the paint or varnish so that you can scrape or wash it off easily.

Removers come either in liquid form or in a semipaste, which has a much thicker consistency, something like heavy cream. Liquids may run off vertical surfaces before they soften the old finish. Although cheaper to buy than the semipaste, a liquid remover is more volatile and evaporates more quickly, so you'll need more of it to do the same job. Since a remover only works until the solvents in it evaporate, liquids do not penetrate as thoroughly as semipastes when applied over heavy coats of finish. Semipaste removers are also generally more effective because they can be applied in thicker layers and stay wet longer—hence, they keep on working longer. The special ingredients added to thicken the solution so it won't run also form a film over the surface that keeps the air away and retards evaporation, another reason why the solvents in this type of remover work longer. In some forms of remover these added ingredients have a wax base that leaves a residue on the surface which must be neutralized or washed off with paint thinner or similar solvent before a new finish can be applied. To eliminate the need for this, many of the newer removers are of the so-called "no-wash" type—they do not contain wax and need no after-rinse.

One of the most popular types of removers is one that is water-washable. This is a remover that contains special emulsifiers so that you can wash it off with water. Hence, you can flush off the softened old finish with water—which is simpler and quicker than scraping it off or washing with paint thinner.

This water-wash feature is particularly handy when working on carved or grooved surfaces—all

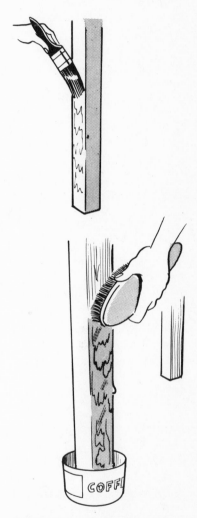

Water-wash remover is brushed on (top), then the softened finish is scrubbed off with brush and water (bottom). The can catches the residue when working on furniture legs.

of the softened finish can be washed off by simply scrubbing with a stiff brush dipped into water or even by flushing the finish off under a faucet or with a hose. In most cases these methods will leave a cleaner surface than if you had to scrape, but remember, you must be careful with old furniture because water might harm the glued joints or loosen the veneer.

Chemical removers also vary in combustibility. Originally they were highly inflammable but now many formulations are nonflammable. These cost more but are much safer to use indoors—particularly if there is likely to be an open flame nearby or if anyone may be smoking.

Regardless of the kind of remover you choose, remember that it should only be used outdoors or in a well-ventilated room. Wear plastic gloves to protect your hands. If any of the chemical accidentally gets splashed onto your skin, wash it off immediately. If you have to work overhead, or if you are going to work where there is a chance of splashing, wear goggles to protect your eyes.

To do its job properly, every remover must be applied liberally and with a minimum of back-and-forth stroking. Once you've brushed it on, don't disturb the finish until it's time to scrape off the softened material. Brushing again, or disturbing the film in any way while the remover is working, only lets air enter and speeds evaporation of the solvent, thus slowing up or stopping the softening action.

Allow the remover to soak into the surface for anywhere from 15 to 30 minutes (according to the specific instruction for the product being used and on the thickness of the old paint film). Then, if the surface is fairly flat, scrape off the remover with a dull putty knife; be careful to avoid scratching the wood. If the surface is not flat, use coarse steel wool or a stiff scrub brush instead of a putty knife. In grooves you can use an old toothbrush or a pointed stick although with a water-wash remover the simplest method is to scrub with steel wool or a stiff brush, dipping repeatedly in water.

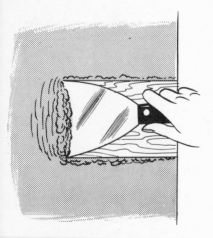

After old paint is softened by the remover, carefully scrape both off with a dull putty knife.

Ideally, every remover should be applied in a thick enough layer and left on long enough to soften up all of the old finish down to the bare wood in one application. Practically speaking, this doesn't always work, so you'll find it easier to apply a second equally heavy coat directly on top of the first one if the first few scrapes indicate that your old finish is not soft all the way through. Even after doing this, a second, and sometimes a third application may be required in some places to remove all of the old finish completely.

PROBLEMS WITH PEELING PAINT

When it peels, most people tend to blame the paint itself. Yet, in the vast majority of cases it is not the paint that is at fault.

Probably the most frequent cause of paint peeling is moisture—water seeping in behind the paint film to saturate the wood, plaster, or masonry over which the paint has been applied. This can happen on the inside as well as on the outside. Water can seep in from the outside through cracks and open joints in the siding or trim. It will then run along the beams or structural members inside the wall until it finally works its way into the back of a painted surface, which can be an outside wall, an inside wall, or a ceiling.

How do you know if peeling is caused by moisture? If it happens on the inside, one sure indication is that plaster will develop a yellowish or brownish stain (something like rust), or will start to crumble and powder away. On the outside, if moisture is the culprit, the paint will peel right down to the bare wood or masonry—not just the top coat or two. When this happens, the first thing you should do is check for leaks. Inspect all the caulking around windows and doors; look for cracks in siding or open joints in the corners; check the flashing above each window, around dormers, and in roof valleys; and look for any other place around the outside where water could conceivably enter.

If the peeling problem is on the outside and all layers are coming off down to the bare wood so that moisture is suspected—yet there is no sign of a leak anywhere—then chances are that you have a condensation problem inside that wall.

In order to combat a condensation problem (which occurs most frequently in houses with clapboard siding) you have to understand what condensation is. It develops when warm, moisture-laden air comes in contact with a cold surface, much in the way that a pitcher of ice water "sweats" on a summer day. During the winter the air inside your house is warmer than the outside and will have much more moisture vapor in it. This vapor can penetrate solid materials such as wood, plaster, or wallboard, and always tries to find its way to drier air—in this case the outside air (cold air is almost always drier than warmer air).

As the moisture vapor enters the hollow spaces inside the outside walls, it comes in contact with the back of the exterior siding which is normally much colder than the inside wall. This causes the moisture to condense out and form drops of water which soak into the back of the wood siding and then push their way through to the drier air on the outside. As they work their way through the siding, these drops cause the paint on the outside to blister, and then peel off completely. To prevent this, good construction practice calls for all insulated outer walls to have a vapor barrier installed on the inside, usually as part of the insulation. This vapor barrier (usually a sheet of foil or plastic, or a special impregnated paper attached to the inside of the insulation) must be continuous with no holes or tears in order to be fully effective.

In addition to a vapor barrier in all outside walls and in the roof or attic, it is also important to provide for ventilation in the peak of the roof above the insulation, as well as in all crawl spaces under the floor of a house that has no basement.

Attics can be ventilated with louvered vents at each end (up near the peak), or with a combination of vents under the eaves and a ventilator installed near the peak. These vents should provide for at least 1 square foot of opening for every 300 square feet of attic floor area. But remember, if the vent is louvered and covered with wire mesh, only about half the opening is available, so you will have to double the total size of the vents installed.

If your house has an unfinished crawl space instead of a basement, moisture may be seeping up from the ground and working its way into the hollow wall spaces. To prevent this, cover exposed dirt floors with a layer of heavy roofing felt or with sheets of heavy polyethylene plastic, overlapping the edges of each sheet along the edges by at least 12 inches. In addition, the crawl space should be ventilated with openings near each corner of the building foundation. These openings should provide 1 square foot of free opening for every 600 square feet of floor area (assuming the soil is covered as described above). These vents, as well as the attic vents mentioned above, should be left open all year round.

Sometimes, in spite of proper venting and the installation of vapor barriers, a house will still have an exterior paint-peeling problem that is caused by condensation—especially if the house is covered with clapboard siding or vertical wood siding on the outside. In cases such as this, the only cure is to install a series of miniature louvered vents directly into the siding from the outside in order to allow the trapped moisture vapor to escape harmlessly. Various types of siding vents which you can use are sold in paint stores and lumberyards, but the most effective ones are those that require drilling a hole in the siding and then forcing the vent in from the outside. To be fully effective, you'll need a vent between each stud, so that you will have to space them about 16 inches apart in the area where peeling is most serious.

When only the last coat or two of paint is peeling, leaving the old coats underneath still adhering firmly, chances are that the paint was applied over a dirty surface—one that had a film of wax, grease, dust, moisture, or other foreign material on it. This substance kept the new coat of paint from bonding firmly to the old one.

On the inside, this condition frequently occurs in kitchens and laundry rooms where walls, ceilings, and trim almost invariably require a thorough washing before painting because exposure to cooking fumes and steam has soiled the surfaces. It can also happen on kitchen cabinets where wax or polish may have been used and not completely removed before the new paint was applied.

On the outside, surfaces normally exposed to wind and rain are usually fairly clean by the time the need for a new paint job rolls around. However, where parts of the house are sheltered from the elements this may not be true. For example, the underside of an overhanging eave or a front entrance that is sheltered by a porch roof or other enclosure will get very little weathering, and after several years will become coated with a greasy, dirty film. Painting over this is a guarantee of peeling, so it is essential that these surfaces be scrubbed down first with detergent or wiped with paint thinner before new paint is applied. The same thing may hold true when painting under a covered porch, as well as in some parts of the house that may be protected by large shrubs or overhanging trees.

Sometimes a top coat of paint will crack and peel for an entirely different reason—the new coat may have been applied over a hard, shiny finish that did not provide enough "tooth" for the new film to bond properly. Often this condition starts out when the new paint begins to "alligator" (the paint checks or cracks so that it looks like an alligator's skin), but in other cases it will merely flake off in large sections. To avoid this, always remember to sand or otherwise dull down all glossy finishes before a new coat of paint is applied, especially if you are going to be applying a latex (water-thinned) paint. Latex finishes do not penetrate as much as oil paints and are more susceptible to peeling when applied over a very glossy finish, or when applied over a dusty or chalky film such as is frequently encountered on outside surfaces.

HANGING WALLCOVERINGS

Because so many of today's wallpapers are actually made of plastics or fabrics, most dealers and manufacturers now refer to them as wallcoverings rather than wallpapers.

At one time all wallpaper came with a selvage which had to be trimmed off before the paper could be hung, but today most wallcoverings are factory trimmed to make handling easier. Trimming the selvage requires a long straight edge which many people do not have, and since this is often one of the trickiest parts of a paper-hanging job, the beginner is well-advised to try to stick to only those papers which come factory trimmed.

In addition to buying wallcoverings that are pre-trimmed you can also buy wallcoverings that are prepasted. These have paste already applied to the back so that all you have to do is wet them before hanging. As a rule, you wet the back by dipping the entire strip into a pan or tray of water which you place on the floor at the base of the wall. Special trays for the purpose are sold by most dealers.

For papers that are not prepasted, there is a variety of pastes or adhesives, and it is important that you select the one recommended for the particular brand you are hanging. The heavier-weight vinyls, for example, will require special adhesives which are resistant to mildew and which will bond vinyl plastic and fabric. Some pastes come ready mixed, while others come in dry form and must be mixed with water before use.

Normally, strips of wallcovering are hung in sequence, starting in one corner of a room and then continuing all the way around until you wind up at the original starting point. Since it is likely that there will be no match where the last strip meets the first one, the least conspicuous spot in the room should be chosen as the place for this last seam— usually right next to the door at which the room is entered.

When cutting strips to length for each wall, always cut each one at least 4 inches longer than the total height required to allow for an overlap at the top and the bottom. The excess material is allowed to lap onto the ceiling (at the top) and the baseboard (at the bottom). This is trimmed off after the strip is hung, using a razor blade or a pair of sharp scissors. This is the only way to insure a neat fit at the top and the bottom—it is impossible to cut strips accurately to length beforehand since baseboards and ceiling joints are never exactly straight and horizontal. Before cutting a strip to length, be sure to unroll it on the wall and hold it next to the strip just hung to make certain that the pattern will match.

Paste is applied to the back of each strip while it is laying face down on a smooth table at least 5 feet long (a sheet of plywood placed on top of two sawhorses or on a smaller table will do). When brushing out the paste, make sure you cover every spot since dry spots or areas that have too little paste may blister or bubble later on. Be certain you spread paste right out to the edges, since failure to do this is a common reason for paper peeling away at the seams after it dries. To keep from getting paste all over the table (when you smear the paste on out to the edges) experienced paperhangers normally leave two or three extra strips underneath the one being pasted (also face down) so that any paste that runs out past the edge will be smeared onto the back of the next strip, rather than onto the table top where it might cause smears on the face of the pattern.

As shown, the near edge of the strip should be even with the edge of the table. Apply paste to as much of the strip as is laying on the table, then fold the strip over back-to-back so that you have the pasted side on the inside with the pattern side out. Now slide the strip lengthwise along the table so the pasted portion hangs over one end with the unpasted section on the table. Continue applying paste to the rest of the sheet, after which you fold it back-to-back in the same way so that all of the pasted area is now covered (on the inside of the folds) and the total length of the strip is now only one-half its unfolded length. This can then be draped over your arm and carried to the wall with no difficulty.

Because door frames, corners, and the walls themselves are seldom exactly plumb (truly vertical), it is important that a plumb line (a length of string

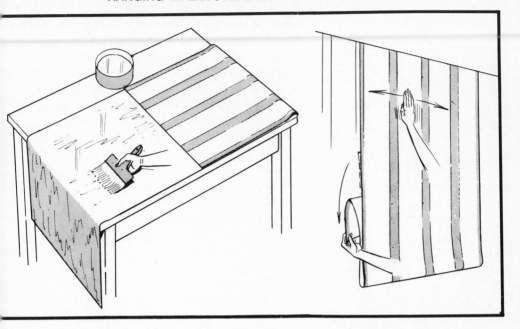

with a weight at the bottom end) be used to make certain the first strip on each wall is perfectly plumb. Succeeding strips along the same wall do not have to be checked as long as you are careful about butting each one snugly against the previous one without overlapping. However, when you come to a corner never fold a whole strip around the corner by creasing it down the middle. Instead, slice the strip with a straightedge and razor blade to make it just wide enough so that only about half an inch folds around the corner. Then use the rest of that strip to start the adjoining wall, butting the two edges together (in some cases it may be necessary to overlap them slightly if the corner is not exactly plumb). A plumb line should again be used to check the first strip on the new wall before continuing with the rest of the strips on that wall.

When hanging the wallcovering, unfold only one half at a time, starting at the top. Unfold the top half, smooth it onto the wall, then reach behind and under the folded area to unfold the bottom half and continue smoothing down to the baseboard.

Apply paste to half the strip at a time, folding it over with the pasted side on the inside.

Hang strip from the top down, smoothing and unfolding as you go.

Smoothing the wallcovering against the wall is done by rubbing firmly with a special smoothing brush, or by using a damp sponge. The sponge or brush is stroked with diagonal downward movements, working from the center out to the edges to smooth out any air bubbles. The edges are pressed down by rolling firmly with a seam roller —a small wooden or plastic roller that is sold for just this purpose.

Finally, the excess along the top and bottom of each strip is trimmed off, after which the paste that had been smeared onto the ceiling or baseboard should be washed off immediately. To make sure all paste is removed, use a sponge, and rinse it frequently with water; then sponge down the entire face of the strip to remove paste smears—especially along the edges.

When necessary to trim around window frames, door frames, or other built-ins, the simplest method is to put up the full strip first, allowing it to overlap the moldings (just as though you were working on a flat wall). After the strip is approximately in position, angular "relief" cuts are made with a sharp scissors or razor blade. These cuts are made from the edge of the strip into the corner of the molding joint so as to allow the paper or fabric to lie flat against the wall. Only after it is flat against the wall and creased against the molding's edges should the excess on top of the moldings be trimmed off.

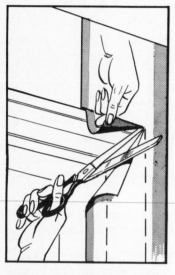

When papering around windows, hang the strip first, then make relief cuts into corner so that paper will lie flat, and cut off excess.

Chapter three

WALLS AND CEILINGS

Sooner or later you will find yourself faced with the job of patching small holes and cracks that inevitably seem to develop in the walls or ceilings of most houses and apartments. Sometimes these cracks are caused by a settling or warping of the structural beams and other lumber, in other cases there may be holes that are left when you remove pictures, shelves, or lighting fixtures. Regardless of the cause, most cracks and small holes are not especially difficult to patch neatly. However, the materials you will need and the techniques involved may vary, depending on whether your walls and ceilings are made of plaster or of gypsum board (commonly called Sheetrock, after the brand name of the original manufacturer).

PATCHING PLASTER

Fine cracks and small holes—that is, cracks up to ⅛ inch in width and holes that are not much bigger than a good sized nail—are generally filled with spackling compound. This material will stick in shallow depressions and fine openings where ordinary patching plaster would flake off. It has a soft buttery consistency which makes it easy to spread and smooth.

Spackling compound comes in two forms—as a powder which must be mixed with water before use or as a prepared paste which is ready for use from the can. Powdered spackle is slightly cheaper but you'll find the paste type a lot easier to use because you won't have to fuss with mixing or guessing at the right consistency. Paste spackling compounds usually have a vinyl or acrylic base

A wide putty knife pressed almost flat will smooth out the spackle and will press it firmly into crack or hole.

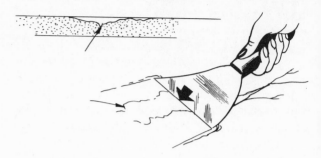

which increases their bonding strength and workability and makes it easier for you to get a smooth finish.

The tool you will need for most spackling jobs is a fairly wide (at least 3 inches), flexible putty knife with a springy blade and a sharp edge that is perfectly straight with no nicks or bends in it. A cheap quality putty knife will not have the necessary flexibility and will make it difficult for you to get a smooth finish. A putty knife that is too narrow makes it hard to do a smooth job on long cracks or on sizable holes because it does not bridge a large enough area on the wall. This makes it difficult to "feather out" the compound evenly so that it will blend in smoothly with the surrounding wall surface. As shown here, a wide, springy blade enables you to press the flat part down against the surface so that you can smooth the spackle off with the flat of the blade, rather than trying to scrape the patch smooth with only the edge of the knife.

PATCHING SMALL CRACKS

Undercut cracks with a sharp tool to insure good bond for new plaster or spackle.

Before filling cracks in a plaster wall, start by first cutting the crack out slightly so that you make it wider at the bottom (inside the crack) than it is at the surface. You may use any pointed tool for this, but one of the handiest is an ordinary beverage can opener which has a triangular-shaped blade. After you've scraped out the crack sufficiently to ensure a good mechanical "key" or bond when the patching material is applied, dust it out thoroughly with an old paint brush, then dampen the plaster on both sides of the crack with clean water.

Scoop a wad of the spackling paste out of the can with your putty knife, then smear it over the crack by wiping across it (approximately at right angles to the crack) from one side to the other. After stroking in one direction, make another stroke in exactly the opposite direction, this time pressing harder and trying to squeeze as much material into the opening as possible. In each case press hard enough to cause the blade to curve slightly so that you wipe most of the excess paste off the surface with each stroke.

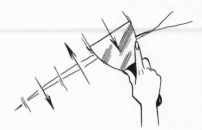

Apply the spackling paste by wiping it across the crack with the putty knife, first in one direction, then in the opposite direction.

After crisscrossing strokes several times until the length of the crack is filled and most of the excess compound scraped off, make a few more strokes almost parallel to, or at a slight angle to, the length of the crack. This should be done without applying any more material, just working with the dry blade to smooth off the surface of the patch. If done properly, the results should be a smooth finish with little or no compound left on the outside or on the wall at either side of the patch. As a result, very little sanding should be required after the patch is dry.

Nail holes and other small holes are filled in much the same way—by first smearing the compound in one direction, then crisscrossing strokes until the hole is filled completely flush with little or no excess material left on the surface. With most nail holes the hole itself will be relatively small, but extra plaster might have chipped off near the surface so that you actually may have a depression that is an inch or more in width at the surface. The hole and the chipped surface should all be filled at one time, so a wide-blade putty knife is still best for the job—a narrow one might not bridge the depression in one stroke and will tend to leave ridges on the surface, as well as increase the difficulty of achieving a smooth finish.

Spackling compound is also the material to use when you have to fill large shallow patches, as when filling in areas where thick layers of paint

Smooth off the surface of the patch with strokes almost parallel to the crack.

have peeled off so that a ridge is left where the old paint still adheres. Smooth the spackle on with the widest putty knife you have, feathering the material out so that the patch blends in smoothly on both sides. Then sand lightly to minimize any rough edges that are left, and, if necessary, apply a second, thinner layer of additional spackling compound.

LARGER CRACKS AND HOLES

For larger cracks and holes in plaster—that is, cracks which are more than ¼ inch in width and holes much larger than an ordinary nail hole—you'll have to use patching plaster to fill in most of the depression, after which spackling compound may be used for the final smoothing if needed.

For best results, deep cracks or holes should be patched in two or three layers. The first application should fill the crack about halfway to the surface, then be allowed to harden before filling the rest of the way. This is to minimize the shrinkage which usually occurs when a deep hole is filled with a single application of patching plaster. Start by first chipping away any loose crumbling material around the edges, then wet down the edges of the plaster as well as the lath (the backing over which the plaster was originally applied), if it is exposed, with clean water. Mix your patching plaster to a smooth buttery consistency, then pack it into the depression with a wide putty knife till the crack or hole is filled halfway to the surface.

If the hole is several inches across, you'll find it easier to pack the plaster around the edges first, then gradually work your way into the center until the entire depression has a layer over the bottom. If the wood or metal lath is exposed, make certain you press the wet plaster tightly against it (after dusting clean and wetting) to ensure a good bond for the patch. Make no attempt to smooth off this first layer, instead, leave it rough on the surface so that the second coat will bond more securely.

You can apply the next coat of plaster after the first coat has dried completely. Dampen the hardened plaster slightly, then spread on a new layer to bring the patch almost level with the surface. If the hole is more than 3 or 4 inches wide and you can't bridge it smoothly with an ordinary putty knife, you'll need a square metal plasterer's trowel to do the job. This will bridge a large area and will make it simpler to smooth the surface of the patch neatly so that it blends in evenly with the surrounding wall. First scoop your freshly mixed plaster out of the pan with a putty knife, using this tool to smear it over the patch, then use your wide trowel to smooth it off.

Since plaster dries fairly quickly (about 10 to 15 minutes), mix no more than you can use up in this amount of time. Once it starts to stiffen, there's no use trying to rewet it—it will have to be discarded.

For final smoothing, wet the plaster with a brush while troweling.

To get a smooth glassy finish on the final coat without having the plaster crumble under the trowel as it starts to set, there is a simple trick that all professionals use. Working rapidly, you first trowel the surface as smooth as possible before the plaster has a chance to stiffen. Then, use a clean brush (a wide paint brush works well) to re-wet the surface of the patch with plain water and drag the trowel over the surface immediately behind the brush. Hold the trowel so that the flat part is against the plaster with its leading edge raised only slightly as shown here. As you move it along, bear down hard on the rear edge and keep the surface wet to keep it from crumbling. After this is completely hard, use spackling compound if necessary to smooth off any slight depressions or irregularities that remain.

Probably the most annoying type of depression to fill is a "bottomless" hole—one which has no backing at all behind it. You'll get this kind of hole in a wall or ceiling when a light fixture or switch has been moved so that there is a hole that goes all the way through the plaster and lath with nothing behind it except a hollow space. The easiest way to fill this is to stuff in large wads of old newspaper or tightly folded and crumpled cardboard. Push the paper and cardboard in until you've packed in so much that it begins to catch on the back side of the

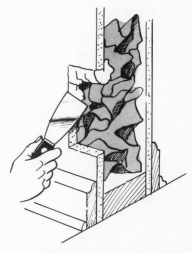

Use crumpled newspaper stuffed behind a hole to create a base for plaster application. Apply plaster around edges first.

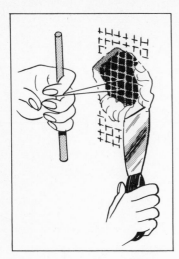

A piece of mesh with string attached to hold it in place can also provide a backing for plaster.

partition or wall. In some cases it may be easier to shove in some crumpled up pieces of wire mesh, and after this has caught in place jam crumpled newspaper on top of it. The idea in either case is to create some sort of backing inside the hole against which a first layer of plaster can be applied.

Another way to create a temporary backing is to use a piece of heavy metal mesh or a piece of corrugated cardboard as shown here. The piece of mesh or cardboard is cut slightly larger than the hole to be filled, then a piece of string or flexible wire is tied to the middle of it by punching a hole in the center and tying a knot in the back. Push the mesh or cardboard through the hole by bending it slightly to make it fit through the opening, then use the string to pull it up snugly against the back side of the plaster as shown. You can then wrap the string around a pencil or small stick and twist until it holds tightly or you can use a long piece of string which you can then tie to a piece of furniture to hold the backing temporarily in place. Cut the string off later, after the hole has been filled with plaster.

After you've "created" a temporary backing for the hole the rest is simple. Pack the plaster in around the edges of the opening so that it grips the old plaster and overlaps onto the paper, cardboard, or mesh. Don't try to fill the entire opening in one application. Instead, pack one layer of plaster around the edges so that it spreads toward the middle for about an inch or so, pushing it in hard enough so that you force it tightly against the backing. Let this dry hard, then repeat with a second and then a third layer until you eventually have the entire back of the hole covered and a patch that is level with the surrounding surface. If necessary, a final smoothing coat of spackling compound can be applied after the plaster has dried to fill in any slight depression that may develop when the plaster settles (plaster often shrinks as it dries).

REPAIRING GYPSUM WALLBOARD

Walls and ceilings that are covered with gypsum wallboard (this is known as drywall construction) seldom crack the way plaster does, but this does not mean that you'll never have to worry about making any repairs. In some cases, the joints or seams between individual wallboard panels sometimes crack or split open because the framework of the house has settled or warped, and in others, the joints were not properly filled and taped during original construction (a combination of joint cement and perforated paper tape is used in filling joints between wallboards when they are installed). Repairs may also be required because of holes accidentally created when something heavy falls against the wallboard, or when an electrical fixture is removed.

Probably the most frequent problem that you'll run across with gypsum wallboard is nail heads popping out from the surface. When wallboards are installed the nails are recessed slightly below the surface, after which joint cement is smoothed over the nail head depression to cover it. If the wrong kind or size nail has been used, or if the wall's framework settles or warps, then the nails sometimes pop back out, pushing off the compound that originally concealed them.

To permanently cure a condition of this kind, first drive the nail back in so that its head is slightly below the surface. Then drive an extra nail in a few inches above or below the old nail—only this time use an annular threaded or screw-type nail because these are more resistant to popping or pulling out. Use a nail with a large head and drive it in just deep enough so that your hammer makes a slight dimple in the face of the wallboard, but not deep enough to tear the paper facing. The depression that remains is then filled in and the nail head covered over with ordinary spackling compound—preferably with the ready-mixed paste type —using the techniques described on page 51.

If sanding is required, use only a fine grade paper and avoid sanding the paper facing on the

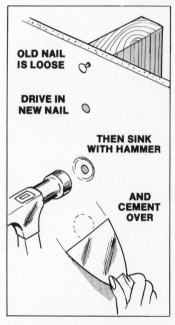

OLD NAIL IS LOOSE

DRIVE IN NEW NAIL

THEN SINK WITH HAMMER

AND CEMENT OVER

In gypsum board walls, if a nail is loose, drive in the old nail, then put in an additional nail and sink it with your hammer. Then cement over it.

wallboard surrounding the patch; this will only roughen it up and make the patch more obvious. One way to get a slick finish that will be perfectly smooth is to dip the putty knife into water after the spackle has had a chance to set for a minute or two. Then, drag the wet blade of the knife over the surface while pressing hard, and thus you'll "glaze" the patch and make it smooth enough to leave a polished finish that will need no further treatment.

Holes that go all the way through the gypsum board so that there is no backing left are filled in the same way as a "bottomless" hole in plaster (see page 53). Another way to repair a hole of this kind—especially if it's larger than 2 or 3 inches across—is to cut the damaged piece of wallboard out completely, then install a new piece as illustrated here. Use a sharp utility knife, a small utility saw, or a keyhole type saw with a pointed blade to cut the damaged piece out wide enough to expose about half of the stud (these are the vertical 2 x 4's inside the wall) on each side of the patch as illustrated. Since studs are usually spaced 16 inches apart, center to center, the piece you'll

To repair a hole in gypsum board, cut out the damaged piece with a sharp knife or small saw.

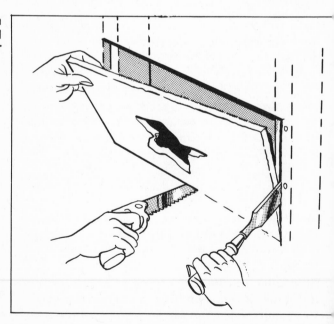

cut out will be 16 inches wide. Make it at least 8 to 10 inches high so that the piece you put in its place will be stiff enough not to buckle in the center.

Cut a new piece of gypsum wallboard (also called plasterboard) to the same size as the opening, then fasten it in place by nailing it to the partially exposed studs on each side. The cracks that are left at the top and bottom of the patch (between the new piece and the old surface) should be filled with joint cement and perforated tape.

Joint cement and tape come in a combination package in most paint and hardware stores and, as illustrated here, the application system consists of four basic steps:

1. After mixing the compound according to the directions on the package, apply it over the seam with a wide putty knife.
2. While the compound is still wet, press a length of the perforated paper tape over the seam working it into the compound until the tape is almost fully covered with joint cement.
3. Allow the compound to dry hard, then apply a second layer of just the compound over the seam to finish the job of completely covering the tape while at the same time "feathering out" the edges of the joint so the compound blends smoothly into the face of the wallboard on each side.
4. Allow this second layer to dry hard, then apply a third layer of cement over the seam to fill in any voids or rough spots that remain and to continue the job of feathering out the edges so that the seam will be invisible. For this last application you'll need the widest putty knife you can get—preferably one that is at least 6 inches across. This will simplify the job of feathering out the seam so no ridge will be visible when the compound dries (extra-wide putty knives for this purpose are available in most paint stores, or you can use a plasterer's trowel).

CERAMIC TILE REPAIRS

Walls covered with ceramic tile normally require little or no maintenance, but occasionally a tile will pop loose because of improper installation, or a structural weakness in the wall. Joints in tile walls

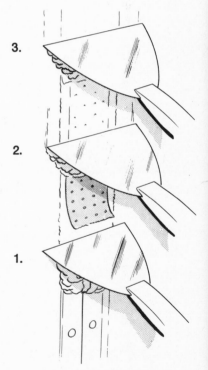

(1) Apply compound over seam first, (2) then press tape over the seam, working into the compound. (3) When it dries, add a final layer of the compound.

(between the tiles or where a wall meets the floor or tub) may also need attention due to loosening or cracking out of the grout (the compound or cement that is used to fill the joints between the tiles).

Tiles may pop out even though most of the cement or mortar is still in place. To replace them you can use any one of a number of ready-mixed tile cements which are sold in paint and hardware stores for just this purpose, or you can use one of the silicone rubber adhesives and sealants (widely sold for caulking around sinks and tubs). Start by scraping off all mortar that is still stuck to the back of the tile, then brush out loose dust or crumbling material from the recess behind the tile. Next, butter the back of the tile liberally and press it firmly into position until it sits level with the tiles on either side. Excess material that squeezes out between the joints should be scraped off immediately by using a pointed tool (a pencil with the lead point broken off works well). Remember, you don't use this cement to fill the joints *between* the tiles, only to cement the tile in place on the wall. The joints will be filled afterward with grout (see page 59).

This same kind of cement or adhesive can also be used to paste back soap dishes, paper holders, and other tile accessories that may pull loose from the wall. However, the adhesives will only work where the backing (the mortar or cement behind the tile) is still in place and relatively sound.

If you have a big hole to fill or if there is not much backing against which the fixture can be cemented, your best bet is to use a two-part epoxy cement. Epoxies are powerful adhesives that will adhere to almost anything. They come in various forms, including liquid, semipaste, and a thick puttylike mastic. For replacing a bathroom fixture the puttylike material works best. As with all epoxies, the material comes in two parts that must be mixed together immediately before use. In the case of the putty type, there will be two differently colored compounds which you knead or blend together until a uniform color is achieved.

If the hole behind a loose soap holder or other

accessory is very deep or if there is no backing at all, shove a piece of crumpled wire mesh or heavy screen wire into the opening to provide some sort of a backing for the epoxy adhesive. Next, spread epoxy on the back of the fixture, as well as on the face of the mesh or mortar that remains, then push the fixture into place until it sits in the proper position in its opening. Use strips of masking tape or pieces of string tied to something nearby to hold the fixture temporarily in place while the adhesive hardens.

Epoxy adhesives can also be used to glue back towel rod holders, glass holders, and soap dishes that break off where they project out from the wall. In this case you are better off using one of the clear liquid epoxies (they're actually amber colored). After mixing, spread the epoxy onto both halves of the broken piece, then rig up some method of taping to hold it in place until the epoxy hardens. Don't press or clamp it so tightly that you squeeze all of the adhesive out; use only enough pressure to hold it in the right position. Allow a minimum of 24 hours before removing the supports or applying any stress to the mended piece.

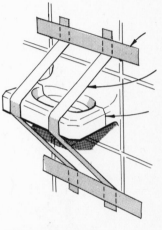

Use adhesive tape to hold soap dish in place while epoxy hardens.

GROUTING TILE WALLS

When you find it necessary to replace or install new grout in some of the joints on a tile wall, buy a prepared grout from your local paint or hardware store. This comes in either a powdered form which you mix with water before use or in an improved ready-mixed paste form which is easier to handle and generally more waterproof. Either form is smeared over the joint with your fingertip or with a rag wrapped around your finger. Pack it firmly into the joint, using a damp sponge or wet cloth to wipe off excess from the surface. The idea is to leave a slightly concave, neatly filled joint that will match the others in the wall.

A common problem with ceramic tile walls is a darkening or discoloring of the grouted joints. In many cases this is caused by mildew, not dirt, so that simple scrubbing with detergent won't restore the color. To correct this, try using an old toothbrush dipped into a household laundry bleach to clean the joints, after first scrubbing with detergent. If the darkened joints are caused by mildew, the bleach will lighten them almost immediately. In extreme cases where no amount of scrubbing with bleach and detergent will do, the only other cure is to regrout, that is, scrape out part of the old grout with a pointed tool, then apply fresh grout over all the joints as described above.

CAULKING

Frequently, in bathrooms that have ceramic tile on the walls, a joint opens up around the bathtub or sink where the edge of the tile meets the top of the fixture. Since this is usually due to a slight settling of the fixtures or floor, filling the joint with fresh grout doesn't always correct the condition permanently. In a matter of weeks the joint will open up again as the fixture settles more, because of excessive vibration in the building, or because of a structural weakness in the wall. Therefore, instead of using grout which dries hard to fill a joint of this kind, use a flexible caulking material that will "give" slightly if movement occurs.

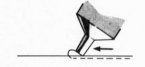

Holding the tip at a 45-degree angle and squeezing steadily, move the tube away from you. The bead should build up ahead of the nozzle (top).

A number of excellent caulking materials, sold for just this purpose, are available—some made of silicone rubber and others made with a vinyl or latex base. Both come in tubes with a special applicator tip that enables you to squeeze out a neat ribbon, much as you would toothpaste. The vinyl or latex types are a bit less expensive and are easier to apply. When squeezing any caulking material into the joint between tub and wall or between tub and floor, scrape out any of the old material that is cracked or mildewed, and be sure the joint is clean and dry. Squeeze the tube with a steady pressure, holding the tip at approximately a 45-degree angle to the surface but moving it *away* from you, following the direction in which the tube is pointing, rather than pulling it toward you (pulling it toward you tends to stretch the material and makes it harder to get a smooth uniform joint while packing the compound into the seam).

FASTENING AND HANGING THINGS ON WALLS

Unless your walls are covered with wood paneling, you can't expect to drive a nail in anywhere and have it hold when you want to hang a picture, a mirror, or a set of shelves. The walls in your house or apartment are actually hollow—that is, they are covered with plaster or gypsum board (which may vary from ⅜ to ¾ inch in thickness on each side) over a framework of 2 x 4 lumber (the 2 x 4's are called studs). The studs are supposed to be spaced 16 inches apart, center to center, but in actual practice it doesn't always work out this way—sometimes the carpenter who put up the wall was careless, in other cases the width of the wall was such that the 16-inch spacing did not work out conveniently. In any case, unless building codes were violated, the studs should not be more than 16 inches apart (center to center) and after you've located one at some point in the wall you should be able to locate another either to the left or right by merely measuring 16 inches from the first one.

Ideally, the easiest way to hang a heavy object on your walls would be to use long screws or nails driven into the studs. However, as a practical matter, this seldom works out since studs never seem to be located in just the spot where you want to hang that particular heavy mirror or set of shelves. To solve this problem there are a number of different kinds of specialized anchors which you can use—all designed for use in hollow walls (some can also be used in solid masonry).

Basically, these all work on the same principle: the fastener or anchor penetrates the wall surface (the plaster or gypsum board) so that it protrudes into the hollow space inside the wall. Then, depending on style, the anchor or shield splits and spreads apart (either when a long bolt in the center is tightened or when a screw or nail is driven through the middle) so that the device "expands" inside the wall cavity to grip against the back side of the wall surface as shown in the illustrations here.

Broadly speaking, hollow wall fasteners can be divided into three categories: metal expansion anchors, toggle bolts, and plastic anchors.

Metal expansion anchors have sleeves or shields that split apart and spread out "mushroom" style when the threaded bolt in the center is tightened. For these anchors, a hole of suitable diameter must be drilled in the plaster (unless they are the drive-in type) after which the anchor (Mollys are the best known, though not the only brand) is pushed through until the flange at the head end presses tightly against the plaster surface. The bolt in the center is then tightened and as it turns it draws the sleeve against the back side of the wall, splitting it open and causing it to lock firmly behind the wall surface. The threaded bolt can then be completely unscrewed from the wall since the mushroomed anchor will remain in position. This means that you can now push the same threaded bolt through a hole in your shelf bracket, mirror bracket, or other fixture and then install the fixture at your leisure (instead of having to hold it up against the wall while you drill the holes in the wall and insert the anchor).

There are also expansion-type metal anchors available with their own points for driving into gypsum board. These require no hole to be drilled beforehand—all you do is hammer them home, then tighten the screw or bolt in the center to lock them in place just as you would with a conventional metal expansion anchor.

Toggle bolts have spring-actuated folding wings that are hinged to a nut in the center. A long threaded bolt goes through this nut so that after a hole of the proper size is drilled in the wall, you can fold the wings and push them into the hollow space behind the plaster. The springs will then force the wings open so that as you turn the bolt the expanded wings are drawn up tight against the back side of the plaster as illustrated. Toggle bolts

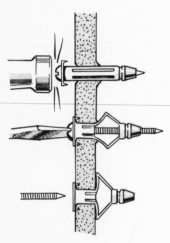

Drive-in type metal expansion anchor

of this kind will hold heavy loads, although they require a larger size hole than the expanding metal anchor type. Also you can't remove the toggle bolt once it's been tightened—if you did the wings would fall down inside the hollow wall. This means that brackets or other fixtures must be held in place and installed simultaneously with the toggle bolt (unlike anchors which you can install ahead of time).

Plastic anchors are the quickest and cheapest to use and are more than adequate for most installations where not too much weight will be supported by one anchor (for example, curtain rods, traverse rods, or shelf standards for adjustable shelving). Plastic anchors are hollow tapered sleeves, usually made of nylon, which are designed to accept long wood screws or special threaded nails through their center.

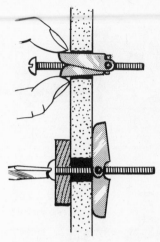

Toggle bolt

To use, first make a mark on the wall where the anchors are to be installed. This is usually done by holding the shelf standard or rod bracket up on the wall and marking locations for the holes with a pencil. Then lay the shelf standard or bracket aside and drill holes of the right size for the anchors you have purchased (the hole size will be indicated on the package). Next, push the anchor into place so that its flanged end is flush with the surface. Then, as illustrated here, the screw or nail is driven in through the hollow center. As the nail or screw penetrates, it causes the anchor to split or expand behind the plaster and against the sides of the hole so that it becomes securely anchored in the wall. This type is not only quicker to install and less expensive than a metal anchor, it has the same advantage—you don't have to hold up the bracket or fixture you're installing while drilling the holes and inserting the anchors. You merely mark the location where you want the screw to go, lay the fixture (shelf bracket, mirror hanger, etc.) aside while you drill a hole in the plaster and then insert the anchor. With the anchor in place, you can hold the fixture up and drive your screw in just as you would if you were screwing into a wood surface.

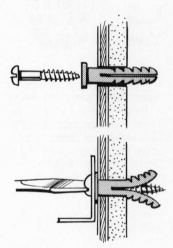

Nylon anchor

For drilling holes in plaster walls, you'll need a carbide-tipped bit which you can buy in any hard-

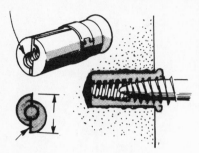

ware store. These come in various sizes, just as ordinary drill bits do, so be sure you get the size that matches the particular anchors you'll be using. You can drill in plaster with a hand drill, but the job will be easier if you use an electric drill. If your walls are made of gypsum board (Sheetrock) then you don't need a drill—you can merely punch holes with a large nail or other pointed tool.

FASTENING TO MASONRY WALLS

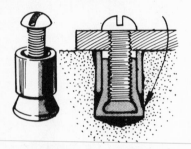

To fasten shelf brackets, cabinets, wood furring strips (1 x 2 wood strips), or 2 x 4's against a masonry surface, you can use either hardened steel nails which are made specifically for this purpose or a variety of hollow anchors which are inserted in holes bored into the masonry ahead of time. When these anchors are used, wood screws can then be driven in through the center as shown to secure the fixture or the wood to the surface.

Metal anchors for use in masonry: offset (top) takes a large screw, which expands the anchor; bottom type takes a bolt, which pulls the inner taper so it jambs inside hole when tightened.

The hardened steel masonry nails are simply hammered in like other nails are, without need for predrilling pilot holes, but it is difficult to drive them in with an ordinary hammer—a small sledge or extra-heavy impact hammer, designed for this purpose, will make the job easier. If the nails are not struck squarely they tend to break rather than bend and they are really not recommended for supporting shelves or other fixtures because they do not hold as tightly as anchors will. However, they are fine for fastening framing members such as furring strips or 2 x 4's against the surface.

Anchors for use in solid masonry may be made of either plastic, metal, or fiber. As illustrated above, they all work on basically the same principle. A hole of the size recommended is bored into the masonry, using either a carbide-tipped bit in your electric drill or a star drill and hammer (a star drill is something like a cold chisel except that it has a star-shaped blade with four cutting edges; you keep rotating it as you hammer to bore a hole into the masonry). After the hole is bored, the hollow metal or plastic anchor is tapped into it. When the

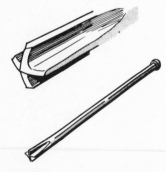

Star drill

screw—or in the case of larger anchors, the lag bolt —is driven in through the center, the anchor expands or splits and the serrated outer surface wedges firmly against the sides of the hole to lock it securely and permanently in place.

In some communities, tool rental agencies rent out special powder-actuated devices which will drive nails or threaded studs into the masonry by simply pulling a trigger. These use cartridges something like the bullets used in a gun to literally "explode" the fastener through the wood and deep into the masonry where it then holds firmly. Various types of fasteners are available: some leave a threaded stud projecting (over which a nut can be secured), while others resemble heavy nails. These tools can also be used to drive studs or nails into steel beams in places where framing must be secured to overhead beams or vertical columns made of metal.

Chapter four

DOOR TROUBLES

A door should close and latch smoothly—and open just as easily. When it doesn't, you not only have a nuisance, you also have a condition that probably will get worse until finally, after repeated banging, slamming, forcing, and muttering, you may be faced with the job of replacing the door entirely, and maybe part of the door frame at the same time.

However, there is no need to let things go this far. Most door problems are not especially difficult to correct—after you have located the source of trouble and learned what steps must be taken to eliminate it.

CORRECTING A DOOR THAT STICKS OR BINDS

When a door sticks or rubs every time you close it, don't immediately assume that you have to attack the offending edge with a plane or heavy sandpaper. In fact, trimming should be postponed wherever possible—in many cases simpler, and less drastic measures will do the trick.

One of the most frequent reasons for a door sticking or rubbing along the outside edge (the edge where the lock is located) is hinge screws that have become loose, thus permitting the door to sag outward near the top, as illustrated in the drawings on page 67. Check all of the screws that hold the hinges in place to make certain that none of them have worked loose. Use a fairly large screwdriver with a blade that fits snugly in the slot of the screw to test each one and tighten any that seem loose.

If some of the screws cannot be tightened because the wood is so badly chewed up that the threads no longer grip satisfactorily, remove the screw entirely and fill the hole with wooden toothpicks or matchsticks. Keep shoving the small sticks in, breaking each one off at the surface, until the hole is practically full of new wood. This way, when you reinsert the screw it will have something to grab on to and can be tightened securely. If the screw is badly bent, corroded, or chewed up it should be replaced with a new one at least as large as the old one.

It may happen that none of the hinge screws are loose, yet the door still sticks or rubs in one or two places along the lock edge or near the outside corners at the top or bottom of the door. In such cases there is a good chance either that one of the hinges has not been set deep enough into the wood or that a hinge has been set too deeply. When doors are installed the hinges are recessed into the wood by cutting the wood out with a chisel. These recesses are known as mortises.

To understand how improper setting of the hinges can cause trouble, study the drawings. In order for a door to open and close properly it must sit squarely inside its opening in the door frame. If it is tilted in either direction (to the left or the right when the door is fully closed) it will tend to rub in one of the corners or edges as illustrated. If the door sticks along the bottom near the outside corner (the lock edge), chances are that the lower hinge is recessed too deeply, or that the top hinge is not set in deeply enough. In either case the door is tilted away from the hinges at the top so that it rubs along the bottom or along the lock edge near the top.

Assuming that there is adequate clearance around the rest of the door, the easiest way to correct a condition of this kind is to shim out the bottom hinge by placing pieces of cardboard behind the hinge leaf. This will tend to push the lower part of the door out from the jamb, thus pivoting the door back into a square relationship with its opening so that the bottom corner is raised slightly to eliminate the rubbing.

You can insert cardboard shims behind the hinge

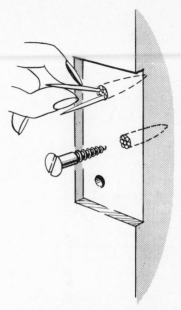

If screw cannot be tightened because hole is enlarged, force toothpicks into the hole and break them off until hole is almost filled.

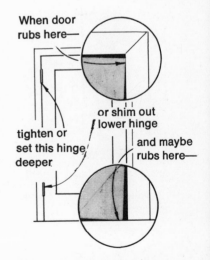

When door rubs here—

or shim out lower hinge

tighten or set this hinge deeper

and maybe rubs here—

Fixing a door that rubs

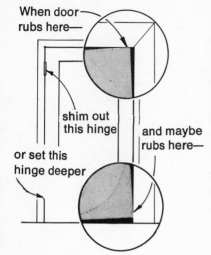

When door rubs here—

shim out this hinge

or set this hinge deeper

and maybe rubs here—

Fixing a door that rubs

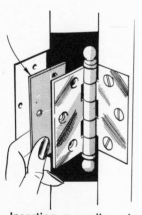

Inserting a cardboard shim behind hinge.

leaf without removing the door from its hinges. Swing the door open about 90 degrees, then prop it in this position by wedging magazines or newspapers under it to hold it in place. Remove the screws that hold the hinge leaf to the door frame, then fold that half of the hinge out of the way and slide one or two thicknesses of cardboard (cut to the proper size) into the recess behind the hinge. Screw the hinge leaf back into place and try the door again. If the condition seems better but the one or two thicknesses were not enough, you may have to insert additional pieces of cardboard to effect a complete cure. If rubbing occurs on the top edge of the door near the outside corner, you have a condition that is exactly opposite to the one just described—in other words, you need shims behind the top hinge instead of the bottom one.

It should be obvious from a study of the drawings here and on page 67 that instead of shimming out one hinge, you can get the same effect by recessing the *opposite* hinge more deeply. However, this is a job that requires removing the door and doing a bit of carpentry, so attempt to solve the problem (as long as there is a little extra clearance between the door and the frame) by shimming wherever possible. If you're in doubt as to which is the cause of the problem—one hinge set too deep or the other not set deeply enough—you may be able to get a clue by swinging the door wide open and then examining the way each of the hinges has been recessed. In a proper installation both will be set equally and the face of each hinge leaf will be flush with the wood around it.

If your examination indicates that one hinge is set much deeper than the other, your best bet is to try shimming first to raise this hinge part way out of its mortise. If, however, one hinge seems to be sticking out much further than the other, you may be faced with a job that calls for removing the hinge and chiseling out the mortise more deeply (the technique for doing this is illustrated on page 70).

If the door sticks or rubs in several different places along the whole length of the lock edge, chances are that planing or sanding will be required to trim off the extra wood in the areas where rubbing occurs. If the amount of trimming required is minor, you can probably do it without taking the door down. Prop the door open with a wedge under the bottom and do the necessary planing or trimming with a small block plane held in one hand while you steady the door with your other hand. Mark the places where the door rubs and try to trim off no more than necessary to provide about ⅛ inch clearance.

If the door seems to be rubbing or sticking along most of its length, or if rubbing occurs near the lock where you cannot trim wood off without removing and then resetting the lock (quite a job even for an experienced carpenter), your best solution is to trim the door off along the hinge edge instead—but to do this you'll first have to remove the door.

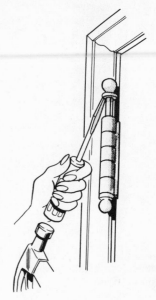

Removing a hinge pin

To take the door off, close and latch it. With a hammer and a large screwdriver drive each of the hinge pins upward until you can remove them entirely, as illustrated. Remove the bottom hinge pin first, then the top one. Next, grasp the knob and swing the door outward slowly (as though you were opening it) while gradually lifting and pulling until the hinges come apart and the door is standing on the floor. Now lay it down on its long edge so that the lock is against the floor with the hinge edge facing up toward you.

To help support and steady the door in this position while you're working on its edge, there are several things you can do: clamp one end to the side of a chair or table (use cardboard to protect the furniture against damage from the clamps), wedge one end into a corner of the room where two walls meet, clamp it to the side of another door (still in place on its hinges) which has been tightly wedged in the open position, or ask a friend to hold one end while you straddle the other end as you work. In any event, you'll find it easiest to straddle the door so that you can brace it between your legs while you're planing or resetting the hinges.

Before planing the hinge side of the door, un-

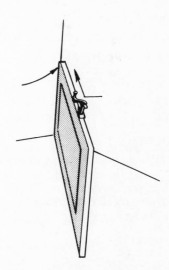

To work on the edge of a door, wedge it into a corner and plane toward the corner.

Or C-clamp the door to another door which is wedged into position.

screw the two hinge leaves and remove them so that you'll have an unobstructed edge to work on. Then plane the door down by the amount required (this should be approximated before you take the door off, but some experimentation may still be required). In most cases you'll be able to reinstall the hinges in the same recess, but if much wood has been removed, then the hinge leaf will no longer fit flush with the surface, so you'll have to deepen the mortises by cutting them with a sharp chisel.

First tap the chisel blade vertically around the outline of the mortise, then make a series of ridge-like cuts across the width of the recess by tapping the handle lightly with a hammer so you cut partway into the wood with each blow. Finish removing the excess material by moving the chisel in from the side with a sideways, shaving action. The idea is to remove no more wood than necessary to reset the hinge to its original depth, so carefully chisel small amounts of wood with each stroke. When you replace the hinge leaves, reinsert the screws in the original holes so that the hinge leaves will again line up accurately when the door is replaced.

CORRECTING DOORS THAT BIND OR WILL NOT CLOSE

This is a condition where the door resists closing unless you force it (even though there is no rubbing or sticking along the edges) and tends to

If hinge mortise needs deepening (left), make a series of crosscuts with a chisel (middle), then trim out excess by working from the side (right).

spring open if not latched securely. If you watch the hinges when the door is almost closed you will notice that they move or bend slightly toward the door as you swing it shut the last inch or two. Nine times out of ten this is due to improper setting of one or both hinges—either they have been set too deeply in their mortises (recesses) or installed so that the edge of the hinge with the hinge pin in it has been recessed deeper than the rest of the hinge.

When the whole hinge has been set too deep, the result is that the wood edge of the door meets the wood frame before the hinge is fully closed—tending to force the door open. In the second case (the hinge was not set uniformly so that the pin side is deeper than the rest of the leaf) the door is installed so that the hinges are fully closed before the door has swung all the way into its opening and before the lock engages.

Both of these problems can be solved by installing cardboard shims as described on pages 67-68. In the case of hinges that have been set too deeply, install cardboard shims cut the same width and size as the hinge leaf. In the case of a hinge that has been installed with only the pin edge too deep, use narrow pieces of cardboard that will pivot only part of the hinge out. This will tend to pivot the whole door into its opening so that its latch bolt or lock will engage easily when the hinge is completely closed. Narrow shims of this kind can usu-

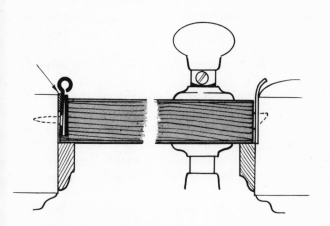

A shim half the width of the hinge leaf can be inserted without taking down the door.

If door latch is too low for strike plate hole, remove the screws and plate.

Chisel out enough wood to lower plate,

and replace in lower position.

Relocating the strike plate

ally be inserted without taking the door down and preferably without removing the hinge leaf—loosen the screws slightly, wedge the cardboard in from the outside as shown, then tighten the screws to hold the cardboard in place.

CORRECTING A LATCH BOLT OR LOCK THAT DOES NOT ENGAGE

Sometimes a door will open and close easily, but the latch bolt on the lock simply will not snap into the opening in the strike plate on the door frame. This usually is caused by the latch bolt not being quite in line with the strike plate opening—in most cases it is merely a fraction of an inch too high or too low. The easiest way to check this is to kneel down so that you are eye level with the lock, then close the door slowly to watch the action of the latch bolt (a flashlight usually helps). Any adjustment (raising or lowering) that must be made should be handled by moving the strike plate rather than the lock (the strike plate is the metal plate in the door frame into which the latch bolt fits).

If the adjustment is very slight you may get away with just taking the strike plate off, then filing the opening a little longer at the top or bottom as necessary. Otherwise, take the plate off and then remount it slightly higher or lower (fill the old screw holes with wooden matchsticks or toothpicks), depending on whether the door latch is above or below the opening. In most cases you'll have to chisel away some extra wood inside the plate opening in order to allow the latch bolt to slip through the opening.

Moving the strike plate up or down slightly will do the trick when a latch bolt doesn't engage because it's not in line with the strike plate, but occasionally, the problem is not one of vertical alignment at all. Sometimes a latch bolt will not engage its opening in the strike plate because the door just doesn't close far enough to permit the bolt to snap into place—in other words, the door hits the stop molding on the inside (the molding against which it fits when closed) before it swings far enough inward to permit the latch bolt to slide into its opening in the strike plate. There are two cures for this problem; either take the strike plate off and remount it slightly farther away from the stop molding (after the door has been closed with latch bolt engaged), or pull the stop molding off and move it farther away from the door.

CURING A RATTLING DOOR

If a door tends to rattle when closed, even if it snaps shut smoothly, the problem is caused by a condition just opposite to the one described previously. In this case, the stop molding is too far away from the closed door, thus allowing for excess movement that permits rattling. The cure for this is relatively simple: move the stop molding by prying it off and then renailing it slightly closer to the door while it is in the closed and latched position. There is also another solution—installing some type of foam-edged weatherstripping against the stop molding (see page 78) to take up the excess play when the door is closed and thus eliminate the looseness which permits rattling.

HANGING A NEW DOOR

When a door becomes so badly warped, cracked, or unsightly that the only sure cure lies in replacing it entirely, there is no reason why this too cannot be a do-it-yourself repair job. Lumberyards sell (or will custom make) wood doors in almost any size and style (flush, paneled, glazed, or ornamented) so that all you need do is measure your opening carefully and then buy a door that is slightly larger to allow for trimming and fitting, unless you can get one that fits exactly.

The door should be trimmed to its proper height by taking enough off the top and bottom so that there is about 1/4-inch clearance on the bottom and approximately 1/8-inch clearance at the top when it fits inside the frame. Usually this can be done with a saw, but if the amount is too small, it may be simpler to use a plane. The vertical edges are trimmed next, planing the door down so as to allow approximately ⅛-inch clearance at each side. In other words, the finished door will be about ¼-inch narrower than the frame into which it must fit.

After the door is trimmed to size, it is propped in place, using the strips of wood or pieces of cardboard at the bottom to raise it the required ¼-inch off the bottom. More strips of cardboard can then be wedged in at each side to center the door in its opening and to check that the required clearance has been allowed at both sides, as well as along the top and bottom. (Bear in mind that more clearance will be needed at the bottom if the floor over which the door opens is carpeted.)

A sharp knife or chisel is next used to mark the location of the hinges, lining these up exactly with the hinge mortises (recesses) in the frame—assuming, of course, that the door is being hung in a place where there originally was a door, so that the old hinge mortises in the frame are already there. The door is now taken down, propped up on edge, and the mortises cut on the edge of the door with a sharp chisel. Use the hinge leaf as a pattern to mark out the outline of the mortise, then tap lightly with the chisel while holding it vertically to score around the outline of the mortise on all three sides.

Next, start removing wood inside this outline by tapping the chisel in from the side as shown on page 70 while holding the blade at a shallow angle to the surface. Make a series of shallow cuts to avoid splitting the wood, and chisel out the mortise until it is deep enough for the hinge leaf to fit in with its surface flush with the rest of the door edge. The process is then repeated for the other hinge leaf, after which the two leaves are screwed into place in their recessed mortises. The other half of each hinge is then screwed into the original recess in the jamb or frame, after which the door can be hung by placing it in position inside its opening and tapping the hinge pins in place to join the two leaves.

A new door often calls for a new lock (in fact, many times a new door is installed simply because one wants a new lock which can't fit the openings in the old door). The simplest type of lock to install is the tubular or cylindrical lock which only requires two or three holes to be drilled in the edges and face of the door (see page 78). All locks of this type come with special templates that locate where holes must be drilled and indicate the size holes required. Detailed instructions as to installation are also included.

After the installation is complete and the door has been tested to make sure it fits and closes properly, it should be taken down for painting so that the top and bottom edges, as well as all other surfaces, can be primed with a suitable sealer to prevent absorption of moisture and future swelling or warping.

REPAIRING SLIDING DOORS

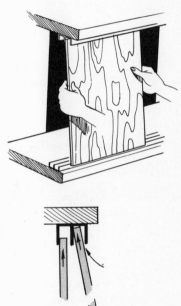

Sliding doors work on tracks. When trouble develops it's usually because a door has jumped its track. On small cabinet doors the tracks, top and bottom, may consist simply of slotted strips of wood, metal, or plastic in which the door rides. To permit removing the doors, the top track is deeper than the bottom one so that by lifting up until the bottom edge of the door clears the top of the lower track you can pull the door outward (toward you) at the bottom, then pull it down to free it.

When doors of this kind become difficult to slide, chances are either that a slight amount of lubrication is required or that some dirt has accumulated in the track to obstruct it. Use a stiff brush or narrow nozzle on your vacuum cleaner to remove dust and dirt from these tracks at regular intervals, and occasionally spray with a silicone lubricant (don't use oil—it only will attract more dirt and cake up inside the track).

Sometimes a sliding cabinet door of this kind will persist in jumping out of its bottom track every time it is moved. When this happens check to see

To remove the sliding panels, lift straight up into the top channel, swing out the bottom clear of its channel, and pull down.

if there is any foreign material in the track that is interfering with the easy movement of the door. If not, the door may be slightly too short and does not project up high enough into the top track. This may be because the doors were cut wrong to begin with, or because the top or bottom of the cabinet has warped slightly so that the tracks are now a little further apart than they were. In many cases you can cure this by removing the bottom track and putting a thin strip of cardboard or other material under it to shim it up slightly, thus bringing the tracks slightly closer together so that the doors will fit more snugly.

Larger sliding doors, such as those on closets, usually have wheels which roll inside a track at the top of the frame so that the door literally hangs from this (some older models ride with their weight resting on a track at the bottom). There is a wide variation in the styles of hardware used on sliding doors of this kind, so it is impossible to give detailed instructions for making adjustments on all of them, but a typical set of brackets and rollers is illustrated here.

Bear in mind that practically all sliding-door hardware permits some adjustment of the wheeled hangers or guides on which they ride. There usually will be a screw that permits raising or lowering individual hangers to correct a condition where the door doesn't hang square or level, or to compensate for any warping of the framework. Doors with a track at the top usually have small guides at the bottom (fastened to the floor to keep the door from swinging in or out), so check these to see that they have not been knocked out of alignment if the door seems to be rubbing or binding.

Sliding doors may also become stiff if the brackets that hold the wheels become bent or if they work loose where they are fastened to the door. If a door starts acting up, check the screws that hold the brackets in place to see if they are loose and to determine if the original adjustments have shifted or slipped enough to permit the door to sag out of alignment. Since the wheels are usually made of self-lubricating nylon, lubrication is rarely required,

Turn bolt and slide bracket up.

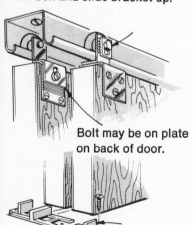

Bolt may be on plate on back of door.

Nylon clips on floor help guide door straight.

Adjusting distance between sliding door and floor

but spraying with a silicone lubricant may help if there is rubbing in the bottom guides (on doors with top tracks) or stiffness in the top guides (on doors with bottom tracks).

CURING DOOR LOCK PROBLEMS

Most door locks will last for a great many years if properly installed and normally require very little maintenance. Since they have moving parts, however, occasional lubrication will keep them from sticking and will help ensure easy opening and closing every time. Ordinary oil or grease should never be used on a lock. Instead use one of the powdered graphites or graphite-bearing oils which are designed specifically for this purpose. You can squirt this directly through the keyhole or coat the key with lubricant, then work it back and forth inside the lock a few times to spread the graphite over the inside.

Lubricating is especially important on entrance door locks which are exposed to the weather; periodic lubrication will greatly lessen the possibility of the lock becoming frozen in cold weather. If you're ever faced with the problem of opening a lock which is frozen (caused by moisture entering and freezing on the inside) the easiest way to thaw it out is to heat your key with a match or lighter flame, then work this gradually into the cylinder to melt the ice on the inside. You may have to repeat this heating process two or three times but it will eventually thaw out the lock and permit the tumbler to turn. Afterward, squirt in a little penetrating moisture-displacing lubricant to get rid of the water on the inside (this type of spray is sold in all auto supply stores, as well as in most hardware stores).

If a lock that doesn't work properly is not helped by lubrication, chances are it will have to be removed and taken to a locksmith, or possibly be replaced entirely. With most locks the procedure for removal is to first take the knobs off on each side, then remove the decorative plates or other trim through which the spindle (on which the knob

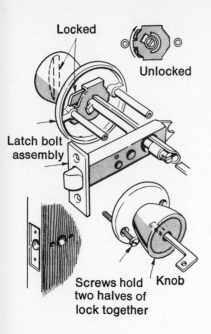

Locked

Unlocked

Latch bolt
assembly

Screws hold
two halves of
lock together

Knob

Typical interior door lock
assembly

fits) projects. Most knobs can be removed by simply loosening a setscrew on the knob, then unscrewing it, but some have a small catch on the shank of the knob that will have to be pressed down with a small screwdriver before the knob and its trim can be slid off.

Usually the inside knob and trim come off first, after which the entire assembly can be slid out from the opposite side (the side with the key). However, in some cases bolts or screws will go completely through the door to lock the two halves together so that after the inside knob has been taken off, the heads of these bolts can be removed (from the inside) in order to release the outside half of the lock.

When the knobs and spindle have been removed, the latch bolt mechanism that projects out through the edge of the door is removed next by first loosening the two screws that hold it in place, then prying it out with a screwdriver. On some models the spindle will have to be turned slightly to permit releasing the latch bolt mechanism.

After removal, the lock can be brought to a local locksmith for repair, although in many cases it will be simpler and quicker—and often just as cheap—to buy a new one instead.

WEATHERSTRIPPING DOORS

In order for a door to open and close easily it must have a certain amount of clearance or space around the edges. This creates little or no problem with most inside doors, but with doors that open to the outside or those that lead to unheated areas such as a garage or basement, spaces around the edges or along the bottom can be the cause of uncomfortable cold drafts. They also account for a great deal of heat loss from the inside during the wintertime.

To eliminate these drafts and cut down on fuel waste, every door that connects with the outside, or with an unheated area—should be sealed around its perimeter with some kind of weatherstripping. The best type is the permanent metal stripping which normally is factory installed and consists of two separate strips or channels that interlock when the door closes. If the outside doors in your house do not have this type of protection, you have two choices—you can either call in a professional to have it installed or you can buy various types of do-it-yourself weatherstripping. These are widely available in most hardware stores and lumberyards.

Most of the do-it-yourself types are not of the interlocking, all-metal variety. They are more like gaskets (similar to the kind you have around your refrigerator door) which have a resilient facing that presses against the door when it is closed to seal out drafts and keep the heat in. The resilient facing may be made of a feltlike fabric, rubber, plastic foam, or flexible vinyl, and the weatherstripping may come in either flexible rolls or rigid strips. The flexible rolls have a flange or backing so that you can install them with tacks, small nails, or adhesive. The rigid ones are made of metal or wood and look like strips of molding, which you install with nails or small screws. Both types are put up while the door is closed so that the resilient or cushioned part presses lightly against the inside face of the door when it is in the closed position. The stripping is nailed to the stop molding (the molding against

Weatherstripping for doors

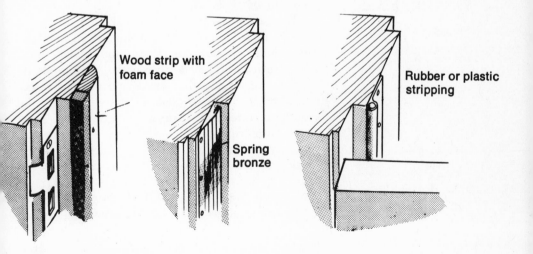

Wood strip with foam face

Spring bronze

Rubber or plastic stripping

which the door closes) along both sides of the door and across the top.

Although some of the flexible types can be installed in one continuous length by starting on one side then working up and across the top and continuing down the other side, the rigid strips will require that you cut separate strips and then miter them at the top corners to create neat joints at each side.

In addition to the gasket-type moldings which are fastened to the stop molding so that they are visible from one side of the door, there is also an all-metal spring bronze type which fits inside the jamb recess as illustrated, so that the stripping is invisible when the door is closed. As shown in the drawing, this strip is nailed to the jamb or frame along one edge only. The other edge springs out away from the frame so that it presses against the door's edge when it is in the closed position. The strips should be installed so that the unnailed free edge does not quite touch the door stop moulding, yet provides enough clearance so that when the closed door presses it flat against the jamb it still won't touch the molding. In addition to the fact that it is hidden from sight when the door is closed, another advantage of this spring bronze stripping is that it is permanent and will probably never have to be replaced.

To seal out cold drafts at the bottom there are special door bottom strips which you can purchase in almost all hardware stores and lumberyards. These consist of a metal strip with a flexible plastic "apron" or edging that projects down below the edge of the door so that it brushes against the saddle or threshold when the door is closed. Since most entrance doors open inward, it is obvious that this type of strip will have to be installed on the inside of the door so that it won't interfere with opening and closing. For doors that must clear carpets or rugs on the inside you can buy special door-bottom strips that raise up automatically when the door is opened, yet drop down to press snugly against the saddle or threshold when the door is closed. These have a projecting button or rod at

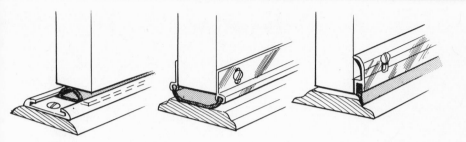

one end so that as the door swings closed this projection presses against the door jamb to force the plastic apron downward against the floor when the door is closed. As the door opens, a built-in spring raises the strip up out of the way again.

For a more permanent installation that will also be invisible when the door is closed, you can buy special metal thresholds to replace your existing saddle as shown here. These have an insert running down the middle that consists of a flexible vinyl tube or "bubble" which projects upward so that it presses against the bottom of the door when closed. In another version of this idea, there is a vinyl strip or bubble that fastens to the bottom of the door to press down against the existing saddle or threshold as shown. This eliminates the need for changing the saddle or threshold, but will usually require that a small amount be trimmed off the bottom of the door to provide the needed clearance.

Door bottom strips. Left: aluminum channel with vinyl insert fits on top of or replaces saddle. Middle: vinyl strip fastened to door's bottom edge. Right: rubber and metal strip is attached to the inside of door along bottom.

Chapter five
WINDOW PROBLEMS

A window that is stuck shut, or one that won't open without a lot of unpleasant tugging and pulling, is one of those household nuisances that no one has to live with for long—all you need are a few tools and a knowledge of what to look for in order to cure the problem.

TYPES OF WINDOWS

Residential windows come in a wide variety of sizes and styles but chances are that in your house or apartment all the windows that are designed to open will fall into one of the four broad categories illustrated: double-hung, sliding, casement, or awning type.

Double-hung windows are probably the most common type and these are the kind that have two movable sashes—an upper and a lower—which slide up and down.

Sliding windows are, as the name implies, windows that slide sideways (like a sliding door) and these may have two movable (sliding) sashes or a combination of fixed and movable sashes.

Casement windows have sash frames that are hinged at one side so they swing open and closed like a door. Since they swing outward, most models have cranks or levers to simplify opening and closing. These windows may consist of one or two movable (hinged) sashes, combined with one or two fixed sashes.

Awning windows also have hinged sash frames that swing outward but they are hinged at the top instead of the sides. Since they swing out from the bottom, they look something like an awning when open—hence the name awning windows.

DOUBLE-HUNG WINDOWS

When double-hung wood windows become "frozen," or stuck shut, the trouble usually is caused by a buildup of paint around the edges of the sash frames—in other words, paint has been carelessly applied so that it forms a seal between the sash frame and the molding or window frame next to it (this can happen on the outside or on the inside). A sash can also become jammed or stuck shut because of accumulated dirt and paint in the channel or because of excessive swelling of the wood caused by absorption of moisture from the outside.

If the trouble is caused by caked-on paint (you can usually spot this if you examine the moldings and sash frames on both sides), the first step is to break or cut the seal between the movable sash and

Window types (clockwise from top left): double-hung, sliding, casement, and awning.

To loosen a stuck sash, run blade of putty knife between window frame and sash.

the window frame by tapping a stiff putty knife with a hammer between the two as illustrated. As you force the blade of the knife in, rotate it back and forth slightly to help pry the sash frame away from the molding, then move it up and down along the length of the frame until the sash frame has been cut free from top to bottom. Repeat on the opposite side of the window, then check along the bottom where the sash slides down behind the window sill to ensure that paint hasn't become caked along this joint as well.

After the sash has been loosened and raised (or lowered if it is the top sash), use a scraper or putty knife to remove excess paint from the edge of the stop molding and the inside of the window channel so as to prevent future binding. Scrape carefully to avoid chipping or gouging, if necessary using a sheet of medium grade sandpaper to smooth the molding edges and the face of the sash frame where it contacts the molding. At the same time clean any excess dirt, paint, or other foreign material out of the window channel and then spray the inside of the channel with one of the various silicone lubricants (not oil) that are sold for this purpose in most hardware stores and lumberyards.

In some cases the wood swells so much that no amount of lubricating or forcing will permit you to move the sash frame easily. In others you are not able to get at the excess paint and dirt in order to scrape it off (for example if the paint is caked on the outside of a window which you can't reach easily). In all such cases you will have to remove the stop molding on the inside by prying it off with a chisel as illustrated on page 85. Work carefully to avoid cracking the molding, letting the nails pull through the wood so that you can pull them out afterward with a claw hammer.

After this molding has been removed, the sash should slide easily since there is nothing binding against it from the inside. If it doesn't, sand or scrape the edge of the molding that presses against the sash in order to provide added clearance before you nail it back into position. While the molding is off, scrape and clean the inner face of the sash

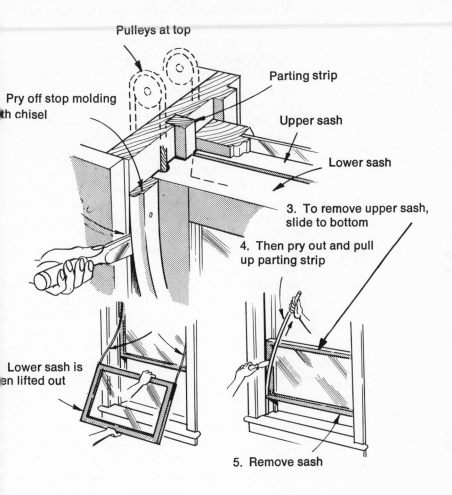

Pulleys at top

Parting strip

Pry off stop molding
th chisel

Upper sash

Lower sash

3. To remove upper sash,
   slide to bottom

4. Then pry out and pull
   up parting strip

Lower sash is
en lifted out

5. Remove sash

frame to make certain that excess dirt or paint which has accumulated along the edges will no longer be a problem.

If, after removing the stop molding, the lower sash still will not raise, it may be stuck with paint on the outside or it may be binding because the wood has swollen so that the frame is too wide for the channel in which it fits. To correct this, you'll have to take the sash out of the window so that its edges can be planed or sanded to provide additional clearance. This is not as difficult as it sounds —after the stop molding has been removed, the

To remove broken cords, the sash must be removed

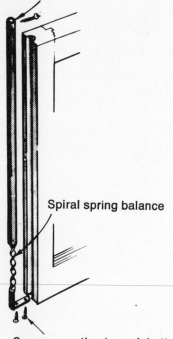

Screw to jamb top

Spiral spring balance

Screw mounting to sash bottom

Spring balance is used instead of cord or chain in modern windows.

sash can be lifted out of the window quite easily. All you have to do is unfasten the sash cords on each side (on older windows which still use sash weights) or unscrew the mechanical spring balances that hold it in place when you raise it.

This applies to the lower sash only. If it becomes necessary to remove the upper sash frame for trimming, then the parting strip will also have to be removed. This piece of molding separates the two window channels—one in which the bottom sash slides, and one in which the top sash slides. It is a square wood strip that is usually pressed into a groove in the frame during original manufacture so that you can pull it out with a pair of pliers, but be sure to avoid splitting it.

To get this strip out, lower the top sash as far as it will go, then grab the parting strip near the top of the window frame with your pliers and pull straight out while gripping firmly. On some windows there will be several nails or screws that hold this strip in place, so you may have to take these out first. Before you start to pull, check for nail heads or screw heads along the length of the strip.

As the top of the parting strip is pulled out, work your way downward pulling until the whole strip is free. In many cases the bottom rail of the upper sash frame will overlap this parting strip so that you can't pull it straight out along its full length. If so, pull the top out far enough to permit bending it past the window's frame, after which you can pull it upward and outward to free it from its groove. The top sash can then be removed quite easily after you unfasten the sash cords or spring balances at each side. Finally, plane or sand the edges to remove excess wood or caked-on paint, while at the same time cleaning out the window channel in which the window rides.

Windows that are merely stubborn—they move, but not easily—can sometimes be cured by cleaning and lubricating the channels on each side. Use a rag and a stiff brush to clean out the dirt, then spray with a silicone lubricant or rub the inside of the channel with an old candle stub. If the window has built-in metal weatherstripping in the channels, it's often a good idea to rub this metal stripping with fine steel wool before spraying on the lubricant. The steel wool will remove dirt and pitting that may interfere with the sash sliding easily.

If the double-hung windows in your home have sash cords and weights, then make certain the cords (or chains) ride up and down easily on the pulleys that are recessed into the top of the frame on each side. Spray some graphite dust (sold for lubricating locks) into the narrow space on each side of each pulley to lubricate the shaft or use one of the aerosol penetrating lubricants which are sold for lubricating locks and electronic mechanisms (available in most auto accessory stores).

When a double-hung window doesn't work properly because the sash cord is broken on either side, the best cure is to replace the cord with chain after first removing the sash from the window frame as described on page 85. After you take the bottom sash out and disconnect the cords, there should be a pocket cover or cut-out visible in the wood channel on either side. This is a removable panel that enables you to gain access to the sash weights that hang in the hollow space behind the frame. The panel or pocket cover may be held in place with one or two screws that will have to be removed first, or it may simply be a force fit. If it has never been removed from the window before, you may not be able to see it because its outline will be completely hidden by caked-on paint. If so, you may have to scrape some of the paint away from the back of the window channel to find the cover, or try tapping with a hammer until cracks appear around the edge to outline the removable cover.

Once you've found the pocket cover and removed the screws that hold it in place, pry it out with a chisel or stiff putty knife so that you can reach inside to get at the sash weights as shown. In some older houses this cover may never have been cut out completely when the window was originally assembled. If this is the case, you will have to use a keyhole saw to finish the cut so that the cover

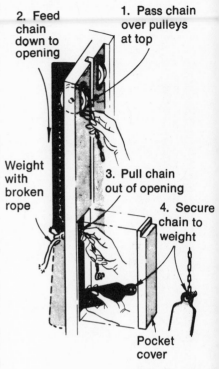

1. Pass chain over pulleys at top

2. Feed chain down to opening

Weight with broken rope

3. Pull chain out of opening

4. Secure chain to weight

Pocket cover

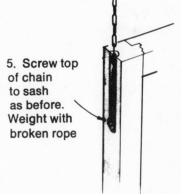

5. Screw top of chain to sash as before. Weight with broken rope

Replacing a broken sash cord with chain

can be removed. After the sash weight has been lifted out with its broken cord attached, feed new chain through the pulley at the top so that it drops down low enough to where you can reach through the pocket cover opening and grab it.

If you have trouble feeding the chain down, try tying a washer to the end to provide added weight. Attach the end of the chain inside the weight box to the top of the old sash weight, using the special hooks or clips provided. To determine the length of chain you will need for each side, you can use the old length of broken cord as a guide, or you can set the sash temporarily in place in the window frame while you measure the amount of chain needed to go up through the pulley and down inside to the weight.

After you've attached the chain to the weight, put the weight back inside its pocket in the window frame, then fasten the outside end of the chain to the side of the sash, using one or two nails to hold the chain in the cord groove. This should be done with the sash resting on the windowsill. Replace the cords on both sides with chain at this time even if only one was broken, since chances are the second one will go soon.

Now fit the sash into its channel and raise it all the way up to make certain it works freely. Check to see that with the sash as high as it will go, the weight on the inside still hangs at least 2 or 3 inches from the bottom—if not, the chain will have to be cut slightly shorter. Then replace the access panel cover for the weight pocket opening and renail the stop molding in its original position against the inside of the window frame.

You can replace cords for the upper sash in the same manner as you do for the lower sash. But remember that in order to remove the upper sash you'll have to remove the stop molding, the lower sash, and the parting strip between the two. Also, bear in mind that the weight pocket cover on each side provides access to the weights for both the upper and lower sash on each side. When reassembling, install the upper sash first, then the parting strips, then the lower sash, and finally the stop moldings on the inside.

SLIDING WINDOWS

Sliding windows seldom give much trouble, particularly if they are made of metal. Wood sliding windows will sometimes get stuck because of dried paint which has caked on around the edges, either on the inside or the outside. To free up a window of this kind, pry with a stiff putty knife and a hammer as illustrated on page 84. Then, when the window has been opened, scrape paint away from the edges or use sandpaper to smooth off the face of the frame.

All sliding windows should have their tracks lubricated regularly to keep them working smoothly, so if yours are hard to move the trouble probably can be cured by cleaning and lubricating the tracks. Use a stiff brush to remove the dirt and rub with medium-grade steel wool if the track seems pitted, corroded, or caked with accumulations of any kind. The safest and most effective lubricant to use is an aerosol silicone spray which lubricates without leaving a sticky residue (oil attracts dirt and may attack the plastic rollers on some windows).

CASEMENT WINDOWS

Casement windows which hinge at the sides may be made of wood or metal but when trouble develops it is most often due to difficulty with the levers or crank mechanism used to open and close the windows. On wood windows this will usually consist of a simple sliding rod connected by two pivots, one on the windowsill and one on the inside face of the sash frame. If the rod doesn't slide in and out easily, try lubricating it and the fittings through which it slides, as well as the two pivoting pieces to make sure they turn easily. Lightweight lubricating oil or a penetrating aerosol lubricant can be used for this. If the rod that pushes the window open seems to bind at some point, take it off and roll it on a flat surface to see if it's bent or to see if there are any sharp nicks that cause it to bind in the piece of hardware through which it slides.

Metal casement windows may also have a simple sliding rod to push them open or pull them closed, but in most there is a crank that turns a gear which in turn swings a long lever in or out to open or close the window. Sometimes this mechanism may become stiff or inoperative due to lack of lubrication, and sometimes it may have been caked with dirt and hardened lubricant so that it no longer works easily. Either way, if the crank or handle doesn't work smoothly, your best bet is to first try working some oil into the mechanism by dripping it into the joint where the handle meets the case or by reaching through the outside and squirting it in through the slot in the frame where the actuating lever comes out.

If this doesn't free it up, it's possible that the gears on the inside are worn so badly that they no longer mesh properly and the entire assembly will have to be taken apart and cleaned out. This involves removing the handle (there's a small set screw that holds it in place) and then removing the two bolts that hold the case in place against the window frame. The actuating lever on the outside is attached to the gear works so it has to come off with it, which means you'll have to detach it from the inside of the hinged sash frame. Usually this means sliding the lever along the slot in which it fits until it comes out, but in some cases it may mean unscrewing a hinged fitting which attaches the end of the arm on the sash frame.

Once the unit has been completely removed, you can flush out the inside with kerosene to remove dirt and hardened lubricant, then apply fresh grease to the inside (a white nonstaining grease is easiest to use). If the handle turns easily but the gears on the inside do not mesh properly, or if they have so much play that they don't work properly, you may have to replace the unit entirely. Building materials dealers and lumberyards who sell casement windows can order a replacement, but take the old one with you to ensure you get one that matches exactly.

Since all casement windows have hinges, stiffness can also be caused by hinges that get rusty, become caked with dirt, or need lubrication. It's a good idea to put a drop or two of lightweight machine oil on each hinge at least once a year and to scrape off rust and touch up with paint as soon as rusty spots are noticed.

Sometimes casement windows cause problems because they will not lock completely or shut tightly. Metal casements have a hook-type locking handle that reaches through a slot in the frame to engage the edge of the sash when it is fully closed. If this hook does not pull the sash tight enough against the frame, you may be able to get a snugger fit by removing the locking handle from the window (it's held in place by two screws) then placing a thin shim of cardboard or sheet plastic behind it as illustrated before you reinstall it with the two screws. This shim will tend to draw the hinged sash inward by shortening the amount which the hook protrudes on the outside so that it will pull the sash more tightly against the frame when the handle is pressed all the way down.

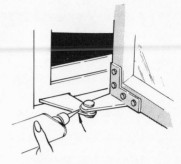

Oiling a casement hinge

Cardboard shim under handle's base tightens grips of handle when shut.

WEATHERSTRIPPING

Loose-fitting windows not only rattle noisily, they also allow cold drafts to enter and can result in a great deal of wasted heat—thus raising fuel bills much higher than necessary. To prevent this, good construction calls for weatherstripping to be installed on all windows to seal the edges and prevent leaks around the movable sash. Ideally, this should be installed during initial construction when a permanent metal seal can be recessed into the edge of the sash and the frame, but if you live in an old house or apartment that does not have this built-in protection there are ways to deal with cold drafts and wasted heat.

As described on page 78, a wide variety of weatherstripping materials, specifically designed for do-it-yourself installations, are available in local hardware stores and lumberyards. Most of those described for use on doors can also be used on

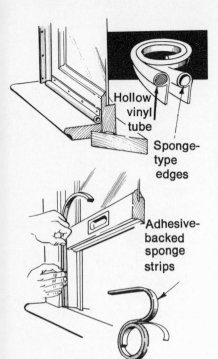

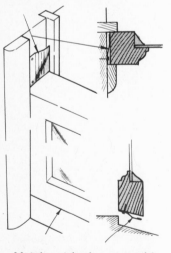

How weatherstripping is used on windows

Metal stripping provides permanent and neat weatherproofing, fitting inside window channels and under the bottom of the lower sash frame.

double-hung windows—this includes the rigid metal or wood moldings with resilient facings made of felt, rubber, plastic foam, or flexible vinyl. Nail these to the inside stop molding so that the flexible face presses against the sash—but take care not to nail them so snug against the sash as to make moving the sash up or down difficult. While any of these can be used around a lower sash, you may have trouble installing them around the upper sash on a double-hung window since these strips are often too wide to fit the space between the two sashes when the lower one is raised. However, they can be installed on the outside.

Flexible weatherstripping which you can buy in rolls or coils will probably be easiest for you to install and is most adaptable for use around windows. The principle behind all is basically the same: a resilient material or edging presses against the face of the window with enough pressure to seal out leaks without appreciably affecting your ability to slide the sash up and down. Some are installed with small nails (usually supplied with each roll of weatherstripping) while others come with an adhesive backing so that they will adhere when pressed into position.

The neatest and most permanent type of weatherstripping you can install around a window that has none is the spring-bronze metal type. This fits inside the window channels on each side as shown, and is nailed along one edge only. The free, unnailed edge springs away from the frame to press against the edge of the movable sash and thus forms an airtight seal. To seal off the bottom of the lower sash and the top of the upper sash, another piece of this metal stripping is fastened along the bottom and top so that it presses against the sill (at the bottom) or top of the frame (at the top) when the window is closed. This type of metal stripping cannot be seen when the windows are closed, and is scarcely noticeable inside the channels even when the windows are open.

To seal off windows that will seldom, if ever, be opened you can buy a stringlike putty or caulking material that can be pressed into place with your fingers (it works something like modeling clay). It never dries, so whenever you wish you can merely pull it out and even reuse it later on. This same material is also ideal for sealing leaks or openings around window-mounted air-conditioning units.

To seal casement windows that do not have factory-installed weatherstripping, the easiest material to use is an adhesive-backed plastic or rubber foam which you can buy in rolls and merely press into place around the edge of the window frame so that the sash will press against it when closed—the foam rubber or plastic acts as a gasket to help seal the openings around the edges of the sash frame. Several companies also make special U-shaped plastic channel strips which slip over the edge of metal casement windows and form a resilient gasket around the sash so that an airtight seal is formed when you close them tightly.

REPLACING A BROKEN PANE OF GLASS

A broken pane of glass is not particularly difficult to replace yourself. In fact, doing the job yourself often is easier than trying to find someone who will come promptly to do it for you. You can replace the glass without removing the sash, providing you can get at the window easily from the outside. If the window is on the second floor or where climbing to the outside might be difficult, your best bet is to remove the sash completely (see page 85).

The first thing you will have to do is remove all of the old, broken glass by pulling the pieces out gently. To avoid cutting your hands wear heavy work gloves or use several thick rags to grab hold of the glass slivers. In most cases the pieces will pull out easily, but if you run across a stubborn section rock it back and forth slowly to break the bond between the glass and the putty, then pull it straight out to remove it.

The next step is to remove all of the old, hardened putty by scraping it out with a small chisel or large screwdriver. If the putty is extra stubborn,

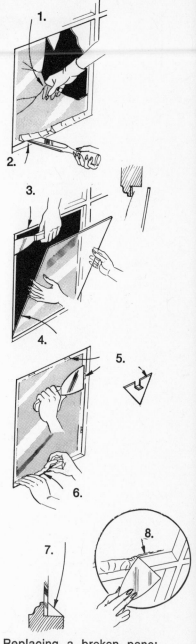

Replacing a broken pane: 1. Remove broken glass. 2. Scrape out old putty. 3. Spread thin layer of putty on wood. 4. Press new glass into place on top of putty. 5. Insert glazier's points. 6. Roll putty into strips and press in place. 7. Smooth putty into neat bevel with putty knife. 8. Wipe away curl.

you may have to tap the chisel with a hammer but work carefully to avoid gouging the molding in which the glass fits. Use a stiff brush or piece of steel wool to clean the wood thoroughly, then paint the rabbet (recess) with a coat of linseed oil or a light coat of thinned-down house paint. This coating is important to seal the wood so that when you apply fresh putty the pores will not draw all the oils out of the compound and thus leave it brittle.

Measure the opening in which the glass must fit, then have your hardware dealer cut you a new pane the right size. When measuring, remember that the piece of glass should be approximately ⅛ inch less in width and height than the actual opening, in order to allow for a small amount of clearance on all sides. Before pressing the new piece of glass into place, apply a thin layer of glazing compound to the inside of the groove around all sides. This "bed" of glazing material is necessary to ensure a water-tight seal after the glass is in place, as well as to cushion the glass and correct for irregularities in the frame. Although you can use either glazing compound or linseed oil putty, you'll find glazing compound a lot easier to work with— and it will not get as brittle as putty.

Press the glass firmly against the bed of glazing compound so it seats smoothly around all edges, then fasten it permanently in position by inserting glazier's points around the side. Glazier's points are small triangular shaped bits of metal which you can buy where you buy the glass, and small panes will usually require four to hold them properly— two on each vertical side. Larger pieces should have three or more, equally spaced along each side, as well as at least one at the top and bottom (a rule of thumb is one glazier's point every 6 or 7 inches along each side).

Remember, it is these glazier's points that are supposed to hold the glass in place, not the glazing compound, so don't leave them out. They're not hard to install, you just push them in with the end of a putty knife or a screwdriver as shown in the drawing on page 93. Some brands now have little flanges or bent-up edges which make it easy to push them into place without slipping.

With the glass secured, you're ready to finish off with glazing compound around the outside. The easiest way is to first roll the material into strips a little thinner than a pencil, then lay these into the recess around the edge of the sash, pressing them in place with your fingers. Then use your putty knife to smooth each strip into a neat bevel that runs from the edge of the sash molding up onto the glass as shown. Properly done, this should form a triangular-shaped bead that will be flush with the outer edge of the molding on the outside and will come high enough up on the glass to match the level of the wood molding on the inside. The main thing is to make certain that you pack down the compound firmly and leave no cracks or open seams into which water can seep.

The technique for glazing metal sash frames is similar to that of wood frames, except that instead of glazier's points there will be special spring clips that hold the pane of glass in place. Otherwise, use the same glazing compound (never linseed oil putty on metal sash) and "bed" the glass down with a layer of the glazing compound just as you would for wood sash.

Some metal windows don't use putty at all—the glass is held with a rubber strip or molding, which is in turn held in place by screws. Reglazing this type of window is simple—unscrew the rubber seal, remove the broken glass, then reinstall the seal on top of the new glass. Other metal windows have the glass held in place with a plastic or rubber gasket that requires a special tool to remove and reinstall it. With this type of glazing system (often used on storm sashes and storm doors) you may have to call in a professional to do the job.

REPAIRING WINDOW SCREENS

Repairs to window screens actually fall into two categories—repairs of the screen frame and repairs of the screen wire or mesh. If the frames are made of metal, chances are that they'll never need fixing —if they get badly bent or cracked complete replacement is the only cure. Window screens with wood frames sometimes do get loose or wobbly and can be easily repaired by screwing metal corner irons or corner plates onto the corners to reinforce the joints. Hammer the frame tightly together to close the joint before you install the reinforcing irons and be sure you use brass or galvanized metal pieces to avoid rust stains later on.

Repairing the screen wire is feasible as long as the tear or hole is not too big. If the screen is covered with metal wire you can patch the hole with small, ready-made screen patches, available in most local hardware stores. You can use a scrap piece of matching wire mesh that may have been left over. The patch should be larger than the damaged area and should have a few wires unraveled around the edges so that there is about a half-inch of each wire exposed. On ready-made patches these pieces of wire will be bent at right angles to the surface as illustrated, but if you're making your own patch you'll have to bend the wires yourself. First push the piece on over the hole so that the bent pieces of individual wire go through the mesh and stick out on the other side. Then, by folding these over tightly on the back you'll lock the patch firmly in place.

This type of patch won't work on plastic or fiberglass mesh, so if you have this kind of screening on your windows there are two other techniques you can use. If the hole is small, just cover it with a few dabs of clear nail polish or clear household cement, building it up in layers if necessary until the entire tear or hole is filled in. If the hole is too big for this, cut a piece of scrap mesh with scissors and cement it in place with clear household cement. For any of these patching methods to look reasonably neat, you should make every effort to line up the strands or wires on the patch so that they match the pattern on the existing mesh.

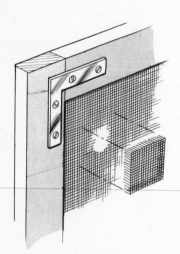

Patching a hole in metal screen wire. Note L-bracket in corner to reinforce weak joint.

INSTALLING NEW WIRE

If the screen wire is so badly torn that replacement is the only cure, your best bet is to buy new mesh made of fiberglass or plastic. This type is much easier to stretch and cut than metal mesh, and you'll never have to worry about it corroding or causing stains on the walls of your house—it will never need painting or varnishing.

When measuring for the amount you will need, remember to buy material that is at least 6 or 8 inches wider and longer than the screen frame to allow for enough excess to permit you to stretch and hold the material more easily. The excess can be cut off with scissors later.

On wooden screen frames, start by prying off the old moldings with a screwdriver or putty knife, working carefully to avoid cracking (don't worry if one piece splits—you can always buy a new length at the lumberyard). After the moldings are off, rip off the old screen wire and pull out any tacks or staples that are left. Then, with the screen frame lying flat, fold over a ½-inch "hem" at one end of the plastic mesh and staple this into place across one end of the screen frame, driving staples through the double thickness to ensure a firmer grip. If you don't have a staple gun you can probably rent one from your local hardware store or lumberyard or you could use rustproof copper tacks—but stapling is faster and much easier.

To minimize the possibility of wrinkles and to simplify stretching the plastic mesh smoothly, start stapling across the top or bottom by driving the first staple into the center and work out toward the corner in each direction. After you have one end stapled in this manner, stretch the mesh by hand as tight as you can to the other end, then drive your first staple in the center again. Now you can smooth it out by working from the center toward each of the corners, alternating staples so you drive one first to the right side of the center staple, then to the left side, then back to the right again, and so on.

After both ends have been stapled, you can

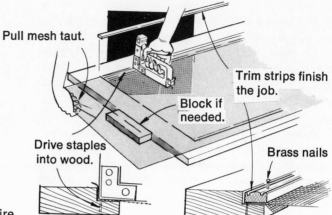

Pull mesh taut.

Trim strips finish the job.

Block if needed.

Drive staples into wood.

Brass nails

Installing new screen wire

stretch the mesh sideways and start stapling each of the long sides, again starting from the center and working out toward the corners. In all of these stretching and stapling operations you'll need excess material to give you a hand grip for pulling and holding while you staple. You'll find that the simplest method is to leave the mesh wider and longer than necessary and use the excess to provide a grip while you're working. After the wire has been stapled down around all four sides, a sharp knife and a straightedge can be used to trim off the excess (some people prefer to nail the moldings back first and trim off the excess afterward). When replacing the wood moldings, use rustproof brads if possible and touch up bare spots or new pieces with paint to protect the wood.

On metal screen frames the plastic wire mesh is held in place by a neoprene, metal, or plastic spline or strip that fits into a groove around the edge of the screen frame as illustrated here. As you can see, this wedges the plastic wire in place so no tacks or staples are needed. To replace screening on this type of frame, pry out the plastic spline first, using a screwdriver or dull putty knife. Then pull out the old screen wire and cut a new piece of screen mesh an inch or two bigger around all edges. Lay this piece in place on top of the metal screen frame, then trim off the corners of the mesh at a 45-degree angle, using a sharp knife and making this cut in such a way that it comes right across the corner of the groove in which the spline fits. The reason for trimming the material in this manner is to avoid the bunching up that would otherwise occur in each corner.

With the piece of mesh still in place on top of the frame (and the corners trimmed off), lay the spline for one of the long sides on top of the screening so that it is positioned directly over the groove into which it fits. Then use a large screwdriver or a scrap piece of ⅛-inch-thick hardboard or wood to tap the spline back into its groove, beginning at one end and working your way down along its entire length. As you force the spline back into the groove, it will press the screen mesh in with it, thus locking it securely in place.

After you've installed the spline along one side of the frame, repeat the process on the other side, only this time pull the mesh tight with one hand as you go, by grabbing the excess material on the *outside* of the spline. Then replace the spline on each of the short sides, after which you can use a sharp knife or razor blade to trim off the excess on all four sides.

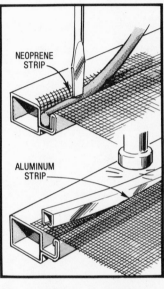

The neoprene or aluminum strip holds the mesh in place. Use a large screwdriver or hardboard to tap it into the groove.

WINDOW SHADE REPAIRS

Window shade rollers have a flat metal pin at one end that is attached to a spring on the inside of the roller. This fits into a vertical slot in one of the window shade brackets so that as you pull the shade down (unrolling it) the pin cannot turn. Since this pin is connected to a spring inside the roller, with the other end of the spring secured inside the roller, the result is that as the shade is pulled down it winds up the spring.

The spring does not immediately unwind (and thus let the shade fly back up to its original position) when you let go of it because of a small pawl-and-ratchet mechanism on the outside that catches and holds the roller in place when you let it go. When you're ready to raise the shade you give it a slight downward pull which causes the pawl to flip up out of its locked position so that the wound-up spring on the inside lets go and pulls the shade back up. The other end of the shade roller merely has a round pin which fits into a hole in the bracket to act as a pivot which supports the opposite end of the shade.

When a shade keeps unwinding by itself or doesn't have enough tension to rewind itself after you've pulled it down, it means that the spring inside the roller is not wound tight enough. The cure for this is simple: first, pull the shade down as far as it will go. Next, with the shade fully unrolled, lift the roller

Pawl keeps flat pin from unwinding.

Pulling shade down a bit drops pawl (left). Rapid raising keeps pawl loose (middle). Stopping lets pawl fall back to lock (right). Note flat pin in center is always vertical.

Remedying a sluggish shade: pull shade all the way down (left); lift roller out of brackets and roll shade up by hand (middle); replace roller in brackets (right).

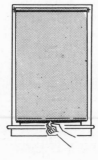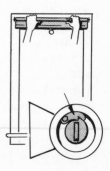

out of its brackets and then with your hands roll the fabric up around the roller as indicated in the drawing. Place the rolled-up shade back in the brackets, then pull it down slowly to see how the tension feels. If still too weak, pull it halfway down and repeat the process of lifting the shade out of the brackets and rolling it up by hand. Finally, try the shade again and, if necessary, repeat the whole process once more.

If the trouble is just the opposite—the spring is wound up too tight and has so much tension that it literally flies out of your hand every time you try to raise it, reverse the process as follows: first, raise the shade all the way up to the top. Next, lift the rolled-up shade out of the brackets, and unroll it by hand to about half its length. Finally, replace the roller in its brackets and check the tension on the shade. If it's still too tight repeat the process once more.

Sometimes a window shade will have the proper tension in its spring but will refuse to catch or stay put after you've pulled it down to the desired position. This kind of problem is caused by the fact that the pawl-and-ratchet mechanism is not engaging properly. Sometimes dirt keeps the pawl from dropping into the ratchet on the pin, while in other cases it sticks and fails to drop into place when it should.

You may be able to correct this condition by removing the shade from its brackets and then brushing out the space around the flat pin (where the pawl-and-ratchet mechanism is located) with a small stiff artist's brush or an old toothbrush. Blow out any dirt or lint that you see, then spray a little powdered graphite over the mechanism to free it up. If this doesn't work, you'll have to buy a new shade roller. They are available in all shade stores and are quite inexpensive (for average-size windows they will cost only a dollar or two).

To change rollers, first pull out the staples which hold the shade to the old roller, then restaple the fabric on the new roller. One word of caution— when stapling the fabric onto the new roller be sure you get it on straight by matching the edge of the fabric with the inked line on the wood roller. If the fabric is not perfectly straight, the shade will roll off at an angle and will not operate smoothly. If you don't have a staple gun you can use carpet tacks, but stapling is faster and easier (many stores will rent you a staple gun).

Sometimes a window shade will stick or not roll up properly even though there is nothing actually wrong with it—the trouble is in the brackets supporting the shade, rather than in the shade itself. Check to see if the brackets are bent or caked with paint or if they are loose (due to loose nails or screws). Since these brackets cost only a few cents apiece, it is always best to replace them if they look doubtful. Pay particular attention to the slotted bracket (the one that holds the flat pin). When this gets worn it won't hold the flat pin (on the end of the roller) vertical and may allow it to slip so that it lets the spring on the inside unwind—or may keep the ratchet mechanism from engaging properly when you pull the shade down.

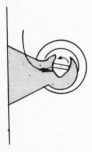

Worn bracket allows flat pin to slip or spin inside slot.

If there is too much clearance between the brackets, i.e., if the roller seems too short so that the shade always keeps falling out, then either your shade roller is too short or the brackets have been improperly mounted in the first place. If the difference is slight (say ¼ inch or less), you can correct the trouble by taking the shade off and pulling the round pin out slightly with a pair of pliers so that it projects out a bit more. You can also bend the bracket slightly or shim it out by putting a thin piece of wood or heavy cardboard behind it.

If the brackets seem too close together, so that the shade binds or rubs against them when it's unrolled, the opposite condition is causing the problem—the shade roller is a bit too long or the brackets have been mounted too close together. The cure here is either to cut the roller slightly (you do this by pulling out the round pin completely, prying off the metal cap under it, then sawing the needed amount off the end of the wood roller), or by bending or hammering the brackets outward slightly to provide a little extra clearance between them.

REPAIRING VENETIAN BLINDS

There are essentially only two problems which are likely to occur with venetian blinds: either the ladder tapes that support and tilt the slats tear or the cord which actuates the tilting or raising mechanism becomes frayed and torn. You can take care of both of these problems at home since replacement cords and prefabricated replacement ladder tapes are widely available in hardware, houseware, and department stores in most communities.

As illustrated, venetian blinds—regardless of

How venetian blinds work

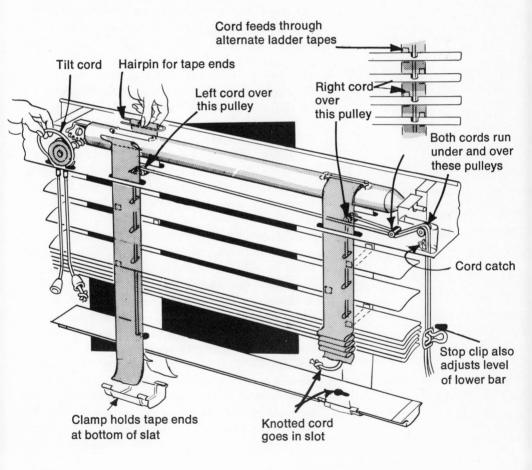

Cord feeds through alternate ladder tapes

Tilt cord   Hairpin for tape ends

Left cord over this pulley

Right cord over this pulley

Both cords run under and over these pulleys

Cord catch

Stop clip also adjusts level of lower bar

Clamp holds tape ends at bottom of slat

Knotted cord goes in slot

whether they have wooden or metal slates—are quite similar in construction and operation. The individual slats rest on horizontal strips of narrow cloth tape which are sewed to the two wider vertical strips that complete the "ladder" on each side. These tapes are fastened to the wood bar (on wood blinds) or the metal channel (on metal blinds) at the top and to the underside of the bottom bar at the lower end of the blind. On wood blinds the tape is stapled to the bottom of the wood bar; on metal blinds the tape is held in place by a spring clamp that fits over the metal bar.

To replace the tapes on the blind, lower it all the way down and unfasten the tapes from the bottom rail by pulling out the staples or prying off the clamp. Next, untie the knots at the ends of the lift cord which raise the blind (there will be one at each end of the bottom rail) so that you can pull the cords out through the top of the blind to free up all the slats. Then slide all the slats out sideways so that only the two ladder tapes will be hanging down at each end. To remove these tapes unfasten them from the top, then attach the new tapes in the same way (on wood blinds the tapes will be stapled to the tilt mechanism at the top; on metal blinds they will probably be held in place by special clips).

Replace all of the slats by positioning them across the individual ladder strips, threading the cords back through them, being careful that the cord runs down through the center so that alternate ladder strips are on opposite sides of the cord as they were originally. Pull the end of the cord through the bottom bar and retie the original knot to put the blind back in operating position.

If the lift cord is broken or frayed, you can replace it with a new one at the same time. Starting at the bottom left, thread the new cord up through the hole in the bottom bar, then up through the hole in each slat. Next, run it across the top and down through the lift cord lock-and-pulley mechanism as shown on page 103. Extend it down until it makes a loop approximately as long as the original cord, then run it back up over the second pulley and down through the slats on the right-hand side. Finish by bringing it out through the hole in the right-hand end of the bottom bar and tie a new knot after cutting it to the proper length. Restaple or reclamp the lift tapes to cover the knots in the underside of the bottom rail.

All venetian blinds have a second cord which operates the tilt mechanism to open or close the blinds. This cord simply loops over a pulley driving a worm gear that actuates the tilt tube to which the ladder tapes are attached. If this cord needs replacing, cut a new piece the same length as the old one. Thread this over the pulley (after removing the old cord) and attach the plastic or metal tassels at each end as indicated.

Chapter six

ELECTRICAL
REPAIRS

All electrical repairs can be divided into two categories—those you can safely tackle yourself and those that should be performed only by a licensed electrician. There is no definite division into which category each type of household electrical repair falls since this will depend on your own experience and ability. However, even if you've done nothing more than change a light bulb, this chapter will describe many minor and frequently encountered electrical problems that you can safely correct yourself—if you follow directions and observe commonsense precautions (such as ensuring that power has been safely shut off by removing the appropriate fuse or turning off the circuit breaker).

FUSES AND CIRCUIT BREAKERS

In every home or apartment, electric power comes in through a main service panel which normally is part of the fuse box. The current is then split into a series of separate circuits to supply power to the various lights, appliances, and electrical outlets throughout the house. Each of these individual circuits is protected by its own fuse or circuit breaker. In addition there is another, much larger fuse or circuit breaker (there may be more than one) that protects the entire service panel, through which all power to the individual circuits flows. Fuses and circuit breakers are designed to be the weakest links in the electrical system since they act as built-in safety valves for each circuit (or, in the case of the main fuse, for the entire system). If a short circuit or dangerous overload occurs in any part of the house the fuse will blow (or the circuit breaker open) before the wires in that circuit can get hot enough to melt or start a fire. The idea is to keep current flow from exceeding the safe capacity of the wires, while at the same time providing a central point at which you can exercise control and restore service (by replacing the fuse) after a "short" or overload occurs.

FUSES

In a private home the fuse box usually is located somewhere in the basement next to, or as part of, the main service entrance and the main switch that controls all power to the house. In most apartments there is a small fuse box located in or near the entrance hall, though in some older apartment houses the fuse boxes for all apartments may be located in the basement of the building. It is important that you know where the fuse box is and that each of the fuses is labeled so that you know what circuit it controls. If this hasn't already been done, you should do it at the first opportunity.

The easiest way to do this is to unscrew one fuse at a time while all lights in the house are turned on and then go around to see which lights and appliances are affected. At the same time, carry a portable lamp of some kind so that you can check each of the wall outlets to see which have no power when that particular fuse is removed. Then make a list of the rooms or receptacles controlled and post this conspicuously on or near the fuse box. Repeat this for each fuse (or circuit breaker) to give you a complete list of what is included in each branch circuit so that when and if trouble does develop you'll immediately know which fuse has to be removed. Remember that certain large appliances, such as refrigerators or washing machines, should be on their own circuit so that if your house is properly wired some fuses will actually control only the one major appliance.

The fuses normally used in home lighting circuits are of the screw-in (or plug) type pictured here. These have transparent plastic windows at the top

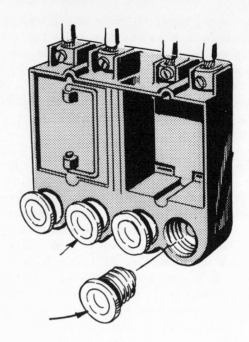

Plug-type screw-in fuses

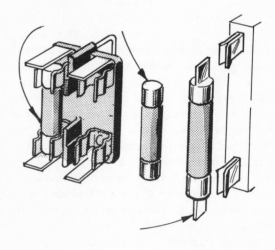

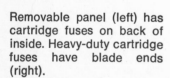

Removable panel (left) has cartridge fuses on back of inside. Heavy-duty cartridge fuses have blade ends (right).

so that you can see when one is blown—either this window will turn black or you will be able to see that the metal strip on the inside is broken (melted by the excessive current flow).

Heavier duty circuits, such as the main service entrance or the ones that supply power to a kitchen stove, hot water heater, or clothes dryer usually have cartridge type fuses instead of screw-in or plug type ones. The smaller ones (those rated below 60 amperes) have a plain metal cap at each end which snaps into spring metal clips in the box. Larger cartridge ones (above 60 amperes) have flat metal blades at each end which snap between spring clips as shown.

Unlike screw-type fuses which have transparent windows that make it easy to see when they are "blown" or burnt out, there is no quick and easy way to tell when a cartridge fuse has blown. The surest way to check is to pull the old fuse out and then replace it with a new one. Before pulling a cartridge fuse out of its socket or holder it is best first to throw the main switch so as to shut off all power. On some boxes this is not necessary because the cartridge fuses are behind a removable panel as shown on page 108—pulling this out not only removes the fuses, it also shuts off the power at the same time. However, when removing a large cartridge fuse from a box where there is no removable block, it is best to grab the cartridge in the center with a pair of pliers while wearing a dry glove. To play safe, make certain you are not standing on a damp floor (if it is damp, place a dry board down first) and be careful you don't touch any other bare wires or terminals while removing the fuse.

Because fuses have an annoying habit of "blowing" at night or on weekends when all stores are closed, and because the only way to restore power is to replace the blown fuse with a new one (after the cause of the trouble has been determined), keep several spares on hand for each size fuse in your box. Screw-in fuses have their capacity or rating stamped on top, and cartridge fuses are marked on the outside, so always check carefully before replacing one. *Never replace a fuse with one of a larger rated capacity—this is a dangerous practice that eliminates the safety factor which your fuses are designed to provide.*

For example, your common household lighting circuits will have 15-ampere fuses because this is the maximum safe current which the wires of that circuit can carry; replacing this 15-ampere fuse with a 20-ampere fuse would permit the wires to carry more current than they are really designed to handle—and this could result in dangerous overheating which might cause a breakdown of the wiring inside the walls, and might even result in fire breaking out.

CIRCUIT BREAKERS

Circuit breakers differ from fuses in that they are permanently installed switches with thermostatic controls, which cause them to switch off when an overload occurs (the overload causes overheating). They seldom if ever have to be replaced—when they are thrown to the "off" position by a short circuit or overload you can throw them back to the "on" position by simply flicking the toggle and thus resetting them (after the trouble has been corrected).

The advantages of this kind of installation are obvious—you eliminate worrying about having replacement fuses on hand and can spot the trouble instantly since the breaker's handle moves to the "off" position when a short occurs in that circuit. In addition, the circuit breaker prevents anyone from accidentally (or purposely) inserting the wrong size fuse in its place.

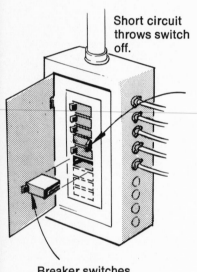

Short circuit throws switch off.

Breaker switches are removable.

Circuit breaker box

WHEN A FUSE OR CIRCUIT BREAKER BLOWS

If a household fuse blows or a branch circuit breaker shuts off shortly after you've plugged in an appliance or lamp, the trouble is caused either by a defect in that appliance or by the fact that the circuit is overloaded (i.e., appliances and lamps totaling too high a wattage are plugged in at one time). Either way, the first thing to do is unplug all portable lamps and appliances on that circuit, then replace the fuse or switch the circuit breaker back on. If it blows again immediately before plugging anything back in, the trouble is in the internal wiring or in one of the permanently wired fixtures and this is a job for a professional electrician to locate and repair.

In most cases the fuse or circuit breaker will stay on, indicating that the trouble is in one of the portable lamps or appliances that had been plugged in when the power died. Start plugging them back in one at a time to see what happens. If the fuse blows again immediately after a lamp or other appliance is plugged in, chances are that that particular lamp (or appliance) has a short in it and is causing the trouble. Or it could be that you have too many appliances plugged into that particular circuit, causing an overload on the fuse or circuit breaker. If the trouble is caused by an overload, the fuse or circuit breaker may not blow immediately—it may take anywhere from 1 to 60 seconds to blow. The cure for this is obvious—don't plug in so many appliances at the same time, or plug some into another circuit.

If all lights in the house or apartment go out at one time, this indicates that one of the main fuses has blown (unless the power supply has been interrupted in your community). This could be an overload or a serious "short" that may require the services of a professional electrician.

In homes which have circuit breakers instead of fuse boxes, the main "fuse" will also be a circuit breaker, although of much larger capacity than the individual branch circuit breakers. In this case you can safely flick the circuit breaker on again but first try to eliminate the cause of the overload if you can find it—usually by unplugging extra appliances, especially those with large wattage ratings. If this doesn't do the trick, you probably have a short circuit somewhere and should call in an electrician.

CHANGING PLUGS

When a lamp or small portable appliance of any kind fails to work, one of the first things you should suspect is a faulty plug (assuming that you've first checked to make certain the outlet is on if controlled by a wall switch and that a fuse has not blown). First wiggle the plug around in the outlet to see if it is making a good connection. If the lamp flickers or if it comes on only in a certain position then you can usually ensure a permanently good connection by removing the plug from the outlet and then bending the prongs slightly further apart. On plugs that have prongs made of a doubled-over strip of metal, best results will come from inserting a knife blade between the metal leaves as illustrated so as to spread them slightly and thus ensure a tighter fit in the wall outlet.

If the plug's prongs are badly bent, corroded, or wobbly, if the plastic or rubber cap is split, or if sparking or arcing occurs when you push it in or pull it out of the outlet—then your best bet is to replace the plug entirely. If the plug seems OK, try wiggling the wires around while pushing them in and out where they enter the plug body to see if

To ensure a good connection, spread folded metal prongs with a knife.

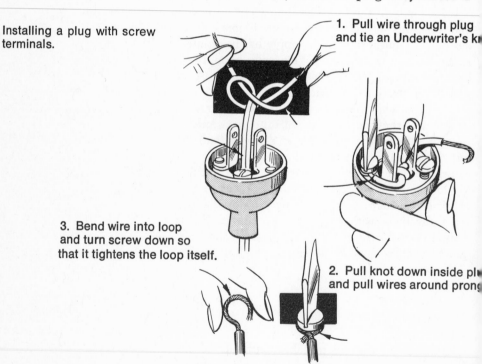

Installing a plug with screw terminals.

1. Pull wire through plug and tie an Underwriter's kr

3. Bend wire into loop and turn screw down so that it tightens the loop itself.

2. Pull knot down inside pl and pull wires around pron

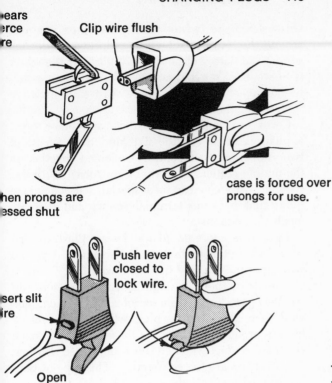

ears
erce
re

Clip wire flush

hen prongs are
essed shut

case is forced over
prongs for use.

Push lever
closed to
lock wire.

sert slit
ire

Open

Two light-duty plugs for use
with flat cords

the insulation is frayed or worn. At the same time
you can make certain that the two wires are still
solidly connected to the terminals in the plug.

If a new plug is required or if the wires look
frayed at the end and seem poorly connected, use
a pair of wire-cutting pliers to cut the wire off an
inch or two from the plug and attach a new one.
The drawings on page 112 illustrate how a conventional plug (the kind with screw terminals near
each of the prongs) is installed after first stripping
the insulation off each wire with a knife and then
feeding the wire through from the back of the plug.

Tie an Underwriter's knot in the two wires as
shown, then pull the wire back so as to draw the
knot down into the recess between the prongs. The
purpose of this knot is to take up the strain on the
cord when it is yanked—the terminal screws are only
designed to make good electrical contact, not to
hold the cord in place on the plug. The stranded

wires should be twisted tightly and then wrapped around the terminal screws in a clockwise direction so that the wire will be drawn tighter as the screw is tightened. To avoid accidental shorting, it is important to check that no bare wire ends protrude from under the terminal screws.

Cords on lamps, small radios, and other small appliances often are the flat kind that consist of two rubber-covered conductors joined together in the middle (often called rip or zip cord). With this type of wire you can use special self-connecting plugs that have no terminal screws and that are much easier to install.

Two of the more popular styles are illustrated on page 113, but note that each is connected to the wire in approximately the same way: cut the wire off square without baring the end, then separate the two parts for a distance of about ¼ inch. The wire then fits into the plug which has a set of built-in prongs that penetrate the insulation to make electrical contact when a lever is depressed or when the two parts are forced together. This type of plug is designed for light duty use only with appliances that do not draw a heavy wattage and can only be used with the flat type lamp cord or ripcord.

LAMP CORDS AND SOCKETS

If a floor or table lamp fails to light when you turn the switch on, the most obvious thing to check is the bulb. If this works, make certain that the outlet into which the lamp is plugged is "hot," i.e., that the power is on. If the outlet is controlled by a wall switch, make sure the switch is on; if not, check the fuse for that circuit to make certain it is not blown.

If the bulb and the source of power both seem all right, the next thing that should be inspected is the plug on the end of the cord. Try wiggling it around in its outlet in the wall to see if it is loose or if the light blinks, indicating that it is making poor contact. Also try wiggling the wires around while the plug is in the wall to see if this causes the light to blink or, even worse, if sparks are visible.

Needless to say, if you see sparks, pull the plug out immediately. With the plug out of the wall, see if any of the wires have worked loose around the terminal screws, or if one of the wires is broken. Also look for insulation that is badly frayed or cracked at any point and inspect the plug itself to see if it is cracked or if any of the metal prongs are loose. If so, remove the plug entirely and replace it with a new one as described on pages 113-14.

However, if the wire seems old and dried out or if the insulation seems to be worn and cracking, it's a good idea to also replace the entire length of lamp cord at the same time (a new length of lamp cord is advisable if the old cord was too short—it's never a good idea to splice wires together or to use extension cords as a permanent part of the wiring since these introduce one more possible point of failure).

Lamp cords run in one continuous length from the plug up through the base of the lamp to the lamp socket, and therefore the first step is to take apart the lamp socket so that you can disconnect the wires from that end as shown in the drawing on page 116. Make certain the plug has been pulled out of the wall to eliminate any danger of shock, then remove the shade and unscrew the bulb. Now, if you examine the side of the brass socket near the switch you will see the word "Press" embossed into the metal at one place. Wrap your fingers around the socket, then press hard with your thumb on this point. This will enable you to snap the two parts of the socket apart so that the upper half can be slid off as shown. Inside this is a cardboard insulating liner which may come off with it; if not, slide it off separately. This will expose the two terminal screws where the wires are attached.

Pull up on the socket slightly to pull the wire through the lamp base (there's usually enough slack in the wire to permit this), then loosen the terminal screws and disconnect the wires. The bottom half of the socket or cap is screwed onto the threaded end of a little pipe or tube projecting up from the lamp, and can be left as is unless you're going to change the whole socket at the same time.

You will now be able to pull the old wire out

by pulling it out from below where it enters through the base of the lamp. Before doing this, tie a heavy piece of string or light wire to the end of the old lamp cord so that as you pull the old wire out you'll pull the string down through the middle of the lamp with it. When the end of the string is

Taking apart a lamp socket

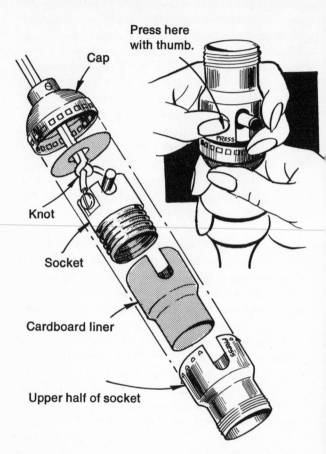

Press here
with thumb.

Cap

Knot

Socket

Cardboard liner

Upper half of socket

pulled out through the base of the lamp you can untie the old wire and tie on the end of the new length of wire so that you can pull it back through the lamp by pulling on the string from the top.

After the new cord comes up through the lamp socket's base, bare the ends by stripping off the insulation with a sharp knife for about ½ inch on each wire, then reconnect it to the terminals on the socket. Remember to twist the stranded wires tightly before wrapping them around the screw and always wrap them around in a clockwise direction so that the wires will get tighter as you tighten the screws. Now, reassemble the socket by slipping the cardboard liner in place, then slide the upper half of the socket down until it snaps into place inside the cap.

REPLACING LAMP SOCKETS AND SWITCHES

Since the switch on most lamps is part of the actual socket, putting in a new switch means replacing the entire socket. Replacement sockets are widely available in all hardware stores and are quite inexpensive, so there's no need to put up with a troublesome lamp switch for long. Remove the old one as described above and replace it with a new one.

In most cases you can leave the cap (the base of the socket that's threaded onto the top of the lamp) in place; most caps are the same size so that those on different sockets are usually interchangeable. If you wish, or if the caps don't match, you can replace the old cap with the new one by simply unscrewing it from the threaded end of the pipe after you have taken the socket apart as illustrated on page 116. On some sockets it may be necessary to loosen a small set screw first (located on the side of the cap) since this set screw "locks" the cap in place to keep it from becoming accidentally unscrewed. To install the new socket you take it apart by unsnapping the top half (see illustration), then install it in reverse order by first pulling the wires through the opening in the bottom of the new cap, and threading it onto the pipe or tube on which the old one fits. Attach the wires to the terminals on the new socket, then reassemble in place on the lamp.

When replacing an old lamp socket you can select a new one that will give you added conveniences, e.g., you can replace a conventional socket with one that will take three-way bulbs. Or, you can buy a lamp socket that has a built-in rotary dimmer switch allowing you to regulate the brightness of the bulb. Either of these come apart and can be installed just like an ordinary lamp socket.

FIXING FLUORESCENT LIGHTS

Fluorescent tubes consume only about one-third as much electricity as do incandescent bulbs of equal brightness, and, in normal use, the tube itself will last anywhere from eight to ten times as long as an incandescent bulb. However, sooner or later they will start to act up—the lamps may fail to light all the way across, they may blink unpredictably, they may work only intermittently, or they may fail to light entirely.

In most cases the trouble is not difficult to repair, providing you are familiar with the basic parts, and with the simple steps that must be taken to replace defective components. Unlike incandescent bulbs, which give off light because a filament on the inside is heated until it glows, fluorescent bulbs or tubes give off very little heat (which is why they waste much less energy). Their light comes from a phosphor coating on the inside of the tube that glows when current is applied to the cathodes at each end to create a small electric arc inside the tube ends.

All fluorescent fixtures have a ballast, which is a type of transformer that steps up the voltage sufficiently to create the arc that starts the vaporizing action inside the tube. The ballast also controls and limits current flow after the tube starts glowing. In the most common type of fluorescent fixture

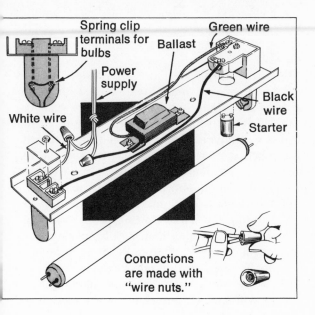

A typical fluorescent lighting fixture

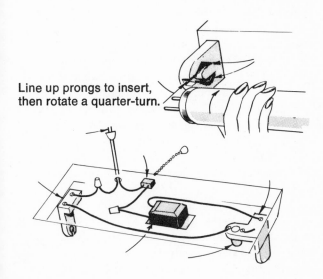

Inserting a fluorescent bulb

there is also a little device called a starter at one end (usually in one of the tube sockets). This can-shaped device is actually a thermal switch that only serves to get the tube started—it closes momentarily as the switch is turned on to send current through the filaments at each end of the tube, then

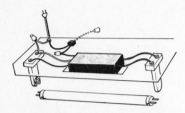

The rapid start fluorescent has no starter and special ballasts.

"cuts out" or opens. The filaments heat a mercury vapor inside the tube which causes the phosphor coating inside the glass to glow, giving off the light you see.

The newer rapid-start or "instant-start" fluorescent lamps do not have these starters—they light up almost instantly because they have special ballasts which can supply the added surge of current needed and thus eliminate the need for preheating (the function performed by a starter and the reason why conventional tubes glow at one end for a moment before the entire lamp lights up).

With all fluorescents, much more current is consumed during the initial starting phase than while the bulb is on, so rather than turn lamps on and off at frequent intervals it often is cheaper to leave them on. Frequent on-and-off switching also greatly shortens the life of both the lamp and its starter so these will have to be replaced much more often.

Probably the most frequent sign of trouble is a fluorescent lamp that blinks or flickers intermittently after it is turned on. If the tube is new, chances are that the condition will correct itself after the tube has burned for a few hours. If not, or if one or more of the tubes fail to light completely, then there are three things that are most likely causing the trouble: first, the lamp or tube is not firmly seated in the sockets at each end so that a poor contact is causing the trouble; second, the starter (if it has one) is defective; or third, the lamp or tube needs to be replaced with a new one of equal size.

To make certain that a poor connection in the socket is not causing the trouble, remove the blinking tube and then replace it while making certain that the pins are firmly seated at each end (you can do this safely with the switch on). Line up the pins first, then give the tube a quarter turn to seat it firmly. After it's in, try twisting the tube slightly back and forth to make certain the pins are all the way in and see if this cures the blinking problem.

If it doesn't, the next thing to check is the starter. This usually is located under one of the fluorescent tubes as indicated in the drawing. Since there's no easy way for you to tell if this gadget is defective, the simplest method is to replace the suspected one with a new one of equal size and capacity. If you don't have a spare on hand, you can borrow one from another fixture which is working satisfactorily.

To remove the starter you'll first have to remove the tube. Then press the starter inward and give it half a turn in a counterclockwise direction. It should now pull out easily. Put the new one in, then replace the lamp and try again. If the tube still continues to blink, or won't light at all, chances are it is wearing out and needs replacing—try inserting a new one of the same size, or test with a tube from another fixture that you know is working properly.

If a lamp must be switched off and on several times before it will stay lit, or if the filaments at each end continue to glow after the lamp is fully lighted, this usually indicates a defective starter, which should be replaced as soon as possible. Also as tubes start to wear out they gradually blacken near each of the ends. This is normal and does no harm, except for cutting down on the amount of light, but it's a good idea to keep new tubes on hand after blackening is first noticed.

Once in a great while a fluorescent lamp will not light even though tests indicate that neither the bulb nor the starter is defective. Assuming that the fuse is OK and that the switch which controls the light is not defective, chances are either that a wire on the inside has come loose or that the ballast inside the fixture needs replacing. The only way to check this is to take the fixture apart and inspect the wiring and all internal connections. If all connections are intact and all wires in good condition, take out the ballast and replace it with a new one of equal size and capacity. Before you do this be sure you pull out the fuse or shut off the circuit breaker that controls power to that fixture. After you remove the old ballast, take it with you when you go for the new one to make sure you get one that matches. The ballast is usually mounted inside the fixture's box against the back of the plate which holds the lamp sockets and it is held in place with two bolts or screws (see illustration on page 119). Before disconnecting the wire nuts or solderless connectors that hold the old wires in place, mark each wire so that you can hook the new ones up in exactly the same fashion.

There is one other rarely encountered condition which can cause fluorescent lamps to blink or glow dimly—excessively low temperatures. This may be a problem when first entering an unheated house or if fluorescent lamps are installed in unheated basements, garages, or attics. At temperatures below 50 degrees ordinary lamps may flicker, blink, or burn dimly, so special low temperature bulbs and thermal type starters are needed for locations of this kind.

Circular fluorescent fixtures are basically the same as the straight ones except that circular tubes have a four-prong socket that plugs in at one point (instead of having two prongs at each end). These come with starters or with instant-start ballasts that require no starter, and servicing them is basically the same as servicing those on conventional straight tubes.

DOOR BELL REPAIRS

When an electric doorbell or chime fails to work properly, nine times out of ten you'll find that the trouble is caused by a faulty pushbutton or a loose or corroded connection at the pushbutton, since this part of the system is often exposed to the weather. Because all home doorbells, buzzers, and chimes work on low voltages (10 to 24 volts) you can safely make most repairs without worrying about getting a shock or accidentally blowing a fuse.

When a bell, buzzer, or chime refuses to ring after the button is pushed, remove the pushbutton by unscrewing the mounting screws which hold it in place. Pull the button out from the wall, then check the connections in the back to make certain the two wires are still tightly fastened to the terminal screws on the back and that neither one of the wires is broken.

If these seem OK, disconnect the wires entirely, scrape the bare metal clean on each one with a knife blade, then touch the two bared ends together, or rub a screwdriver blade across the terminal screws. What you're doing is the same as what the pushbutton is supposed to do when it is pressed— you're closing the circuit. If touching the wires together makes the bell ring, then the trouble is in the button, so replace it with a new one.

If touching the two wires together at the button did not cause the bell to ring, then the next thing to check is to see if power (electric current) is being supplied to the bell or chimes. The two drawings here show a simplified wiring diagram of how typical household doorbell systems are wired—with only a single pushbutton for the front door, or with two pushbuttons, one for the front door and one for a back or side door. Where there is a two-button system the house will usually be equipped with a combination bell-buzzer (bell for the front door, buzzer for the back door) or with a chime giving two separate tones.

You'll note that the power for each of these systems comes from a transformer that steps down household current (110 volts) to the necessary low voltage required to operate the bell or chime. In some older houses the bell may still be powered by dry cells or batteries, but in modern homes and apartments transformers are used most frequently. The transformer is usually mounted somewhere near the main fuse box—it may be screwed directly to the side of the fuse box or it may be mounted on a separate outlet box located on or near the fuse box.

First check to see that the fuse or circuit breaker (which controls the circuit into which the transformer is wired) has not blown. The transformer has two relatively heavy wires coming out of one side which go directly into the outlet box or fuse box and are wired directly into the house current. *Be sure never to touch these wires* (known as the

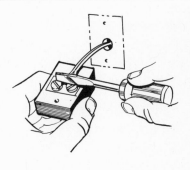

Screwdriver is used to "short out" terminals on doorbell button.

primary wires)—you can get a serious shock from this side of the transformer.

The opposite side of the transformer has two terminals or screws to which the wires for the bell system are connected. This is the secondary, low-voltage (output) side of the transformer which

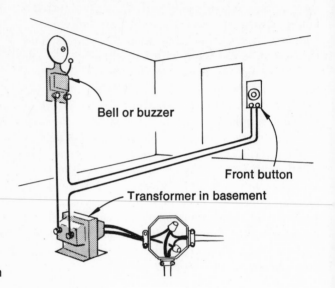

One-door bell system

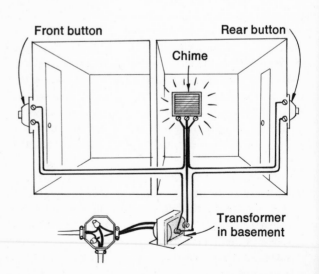

Two-door chime system

supplies the 10 or 12 volts needed for the bell. The transformer is always "on," i.e., it is always connected to the household system so that current is always flowing through the primary coil. This induces current in the secondary coil so there is always current available on the two terminal screws on the opposite side.

To check whether current is being delivered, take a small screwdriver and, holding it by the handle, rub across the terminal screws on the transformer with the blade, as shown. Small sparks will indicate that the transformer is still working and delivering current to the system. A more positive way of testing the transformer is to use a voltmeter to take a reading across the low voltage terminals, or connect a small 12-volt lamp across the terminals to see whether the lamp lights.

If the transformer is delivering current and if a previous test indicates that the trouble was not in the pushbutton, then the next most likely source of trouble is at the bell or chime itself. Take the cover off the bell or chime—sometimes it will be held on with a small screw but in most cases it's merely held with spring clips so you can remove it by prying it off.

Check to see that all wires are still firmly connected to their terminals and all screws are tight. Then inspect the mechanism of the bell or chime to see if any of the moving parts are obstructed by dirt, dust, or accumulated lint that keeps them from moving properly. Bells have a little vibrator arm with a small ball attached which acts as a hammer to ring the bell. This arm should move back and forth freely. If not, see if you can determine what's stopping it. Chimes have small plastic or metal rods that move up and down or from side to side. These strike the chime bars when the pushbutton is pressed and they should be free to move easily. If the mechanism seems caked with dust or dirt, you can usually free it up by brushing with a soft artist's brush or by blowing the lint out with the exhaust end of a vacuum cleaner, after which you should push the rods slightly, as shown.

If everything seems OK at this point, yet the

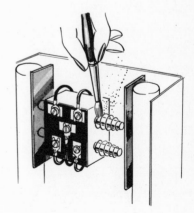

Cleaning the dust off chimes and push rod with paintbrush

bell still won't work (in spite of the fact that there seems to be nothing wrong with either the push-buton or the transformer), then it may be that the bell or chime itself is faulty and needs replacing. The other possibility is that the trouble is being caused by a break in one of the wires somewhere inside the house or in a junction point where the wires meet and are spliced together (usually in the basement almost directly under the bell or chime). If possible, look for this junction point where the wires meet and inspect each of the connections or splices. If you can't find the trouble there, or if you can't find where the break is, chances are that you will have to run new wires from the buttons to the bell or chimes, and from the transformer to the bell or chimes (follow the wiring diagrams on page 124 as a guide for this).

Chapter seven

PLUMBING REPAIRS

Clogged sinks, leaky faucets, and other minor plumbing breakdowns always seem to occur late in the evening or at the start of a long weekend when it is virtually impossible to get a plumber (or even the superintendent in an apartment house) to take care of the problem. Even if you *can* get a professional in, the bill you receive can sometimes convert the smallest plumbing job into a major financial calamity—a 10 cent washer, for example, can cost as much as $15 or $20 by the time you pay for labor and installation by a professional plumber.

Many of these small plumbing jobs are not difficult for you to tackle, providing you are reasonably familiar with the techniques involved. To avoid being caught short when the stores are closed, you will have to make certain that you have spare washers, packing material, pipe sealing compound, and a few other supplies (described later) on hand.

Because emergency repairs may call for quickly shutting off the supply of water to a particular fixture or appliance—or in some cases to the whole house or apartment—you should know exactly where the various shut-off valves are located for both hot and cold water supply lines in your home. Every house has one main valve that controls the water supply for the entire building, and its location should be familiar to everyone who lives in that house. It is most often located in the basement or utility room right next to the water meter. Locate and tag it, so that if a break occurs in one of the pipes, or if you're in doubt about exactly which supply line is affected when a sudden emergency occurs, you can quickly stop the flow of water and thus ward off a potential flood before much damage has occurred.

In addition to this main valve, every plumbing system should have additional valves located and tagged to permit shutting off the water to individual sinks, tubs, or other fixtures. In most modern homes the shut-off valves will be located directly under or behind the sink or fixture, but in others they will be in the basement or even in a closet behind a bathroom or kitchen.

To avoid the confusion that can occur when you're trying to locate the right one in a hurry, the smart thing to do is take time out now, while nothing is wrong, and find each shut-off valve in the house. Then mark each one with a prominent tag indicating to which fixture (or fixtures) it leads, and indicating exactly what line (hot or cold) it controls.

Bear in mind that in addition to water valves there may also be gas valves, steam valves, and hot water heating system valves in various locations—so make sure you tag the right ones. Ideally, every one of these should be tagged so that anyone can find the right one in a hurry when the need arises. If in doubt, it may pay to call in a plumber and have him identify and mark all the control valves—or call in a knowledgeable friend who is familiar with household utility systems.

LEAKING FAUCETS

A faucet that keeps dripping and will not shut off properly usually can be repaired simply by installing a new washer. As the drawing indicates, this washer is located at the end of the valve stem or spindle (the part to which the handle at the top is connected). As you turn the handle the stem threads its way into the faucet body until the washer presses snugly against the valve seat on the inside, thus shutting off the flow of water. If this washer is worn or of improper size and shape, it will not make a tight seal against the valve seat and will permit water to keep dripping out past it. To get at this washer when replacement is needed

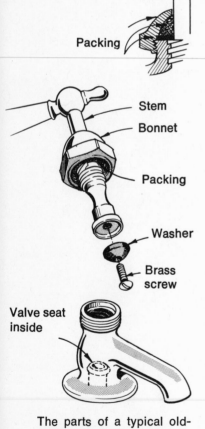

Packing

Stem

Bonnet

Packing

Washer

Brass screw

Valve seat inside

The parts of a typical old-fashioned single faucet

you'll have to take the faucet apart—a job which should give you no trouble if you take a few minutes to study the drawings in this chapter which show how the various parts fit together.

Start by first shutting off the water supply to that fixture (if you can't find the right valve, you may have to shut off the main valve for the whole house or apartment), then open the faucet until all the water drains out. Next, remove the handle. On some faucets there is a small screw at the top that has to be removed first, after which the handle can be lifted off by tapping upward from the underside. On others the screw that holds the handle in place may be covered by a decorative cap or metal cover which will have to be pried off first with a very small screwdriver or the point of a knife. Some faucets have the handle secured by a small threaded ring or collar (or in some cases a set screw) underneath the handle. Unscrewing this will then permit you to pry or pull the handle off.

After the handle is off, remove the cap-nut or chrome bonnet that fits down on top of the faucet's body and through which the faucet stem projects. This nut or bonnet is threaded onto the faucet body, as shown below, and also serves to hold the packing underneath it (the packing keeps the water from leaking up past or around the stem). On newer models there may be a rubber O-ring around the stem instead of packing, as shown in the drawing on page 131.

Some kitchen and bathroom faucets have a decorative chrome housing that fits down over the spindle to enclose the packing nut (this serves the same purpose as the cap-nut) as illustrated. On this type of faucet there will be a large flat nut which screws down on top of the bonnet or housing to hold it in place. After the handle is removed, unscrew this nut, then slide the housing up over the shaft to expose the packing nut at the bottom.

With either of the two style faucets just described, the next step is to unscrew the packing nut or cap-nut, then lift and turn out the entire valve stem or spindle. At its bottom end you'll find a small screw holding a rubber or plastic washer

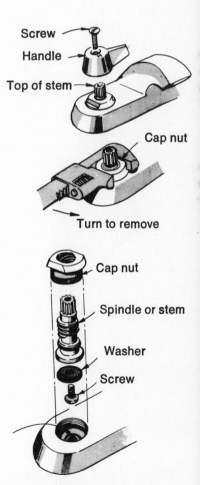

Screw

Handle

Top of stem

Cap nut

Turn to remove

Cap nut

Spindle or stem

Washer

Screw

Typical bathroom faucet

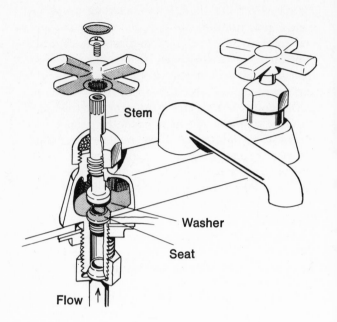

Stem

Washer

Seat

Typical kitchen faucet   Flow

in place, usually in a slight recess in the metal. To change the washer, first remove the screw holding it in place, then pry the old washer out carefully. As a rule, you'll find it easier to grip the stem or spindle with a pair of pliers while removing the screws since these screws are sometimes partly corroded or "frozen" in place.

If the screw looks chewed up, replace it at the same time you put in a new washer (brass replacement screws are usually included with the washer assortments that you buy in hardware stores). Replace the washer with a new one of the same size and shape as the old one if you want the faucet to work properly. Some washers are flat, others are tapered, and there are several different diameters or sizes in common use. If the washer is so badly chewed up that you can't identify its original shape (flat or conical), you may have to remove the other faucet on the same sink to determine the size and style needed.

Some of the newer faucet stems, instead of having the washer secured by a brass screw, will have a snap-on or "high-hat" type washer that snaps on over a protrusion at the bottom end of the stem and has no screw to hold it in place. To replace it, you simply pry the old one off with a screwdriver, then snap the new one back on in place of the old one.

The faucet is reassembled by screwing the stem or spindle back into the body, then tightening down the packing nut or cap-nut that fits over the top of the spindle. Finish by replacing the decorative chrome housing on those faucets that have one, then install the handle last. If, when you originally removed the housing, there was putty packed in underneath (often this putty will cover the packing nut so that you have to scrape it away to get at the nut), it is a good idea to replace it with fresh putty (or glazing compound) before you replace the housing.

If water seems to leak from around the stem of the faucet after it is turned on (either just below the handle or below the packing nut or cap nut) it means that the nut needs tightening, or that the faucet needs new packing under this nut. The first thing to do is to try tightening the packing nut slightly with a large flat-jaw wrench or a pair of offset channel-type pliers. If tightening this doesn't do the trick, or if you have to tighten it so much that the handle becomes hard to turn, new packing, or possibly a new rubber O-ring (if your faucet is the type that has O-rings in it) is needed.

As illustrated on page 128, the packing is under the cap nut or bonnet which also serves as a packing nut on older style faucets, but on modern faucets with decorative chrome housings around the spindle, the packing will be directly under the separate nut which is exposed after you remove the bonnet. O-rings will be located on the spindle (they fit into a groove in the spindle) near the upper end where it goes through the packing nut.

In either case, to replace the packing or O-ring shut off the water supply to the fixture, and take the faucet apart just as you would for replacing a washer. Use the blade of a small screwdriver to dig out all of the old packing (or pry off the old O-

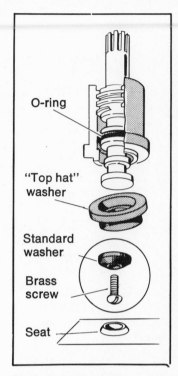

Modern stems have a rubber O-ring instead of packing—and may have a regular washer or a "top hat" washer.

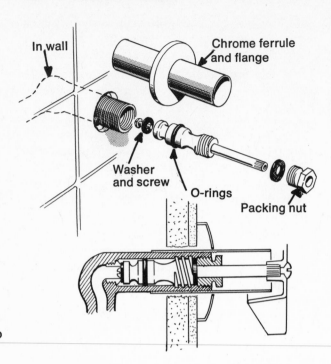

Recessed shower or tub faucet

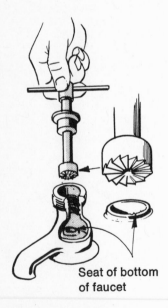

Seat of bottom of faucet

Valve-seat dressing or grinding tool

ring) and then replace with new material. Packing is sold in stringlike form which you wrap around the stem and then force back into the cavity in which it originally fit. You will need enough to fill the cavity under the packing-nut or cap-nut, but don't put so much in that you have trouble threading the nut back into place.

If a faucet continues to drip after a new washer has been inserted or if washers seem to wear out exceptionally fast, chances are that the valve seat on the inside (the metal piece against which the washer presses) is nicked or scratched. Most hardware stores sell inexpensive valve-seat grinders or dressing tools which you can use to smooth off a roughened valve seat. These have a stem or handle which you screw into the faucet in place of the original valve stem so that the grinding end of the tool bears down against the valve seat. A matching bonnet nut on this tool holds the shaft in place in the faucet body while you give it two or three turns to remove nicks or scratches on the valve's seat. After this grinding or dressing action, unscrew the tool, blow or wipe out any particles left on the inside, then replace the original valve stem and washer assembly.

SINGLE-CONTROL VALVE FAUCETS

Modern single-handle (also called single-control) faucets have only one handle that regulates the proportion of hot and cold water as well as the volume. They have no washers or washer seats that can wear down, hence there is much less of a problem with drips or leaks developing and much less over-all maintenance required.

However, single-handle faucets have some moving parts that eventually wear out and permit leaks to develop (although this may take years in normal home use), so repairs will be required sooner or later. In the earliest models this was quite often a complicated job since there were many different types in use, most requiring almost complete disassembly in order to make the needed repairs. But nowadays there are only a comparatively few styles in widespread use and the four or five large manufacturers in this field have designed their units so that the heart of each valve mechanism is an easily replaceable cartridge or ball unit that can be purchased from plumbing supply dealers when one of these faucets develops a leak.

Basically, washerless single-handle faucets differ from standard faucets (with washers) in that the flow of water is not controlled by a rubber washer pressing against a metal surface (the valve seat). Instead, there is an off-center sliding or tipping valve which is designed so that as it is moved it slides past (or tips against) an opening on the inside to open or close it (all or part-way). In one direction this valve permits more hot water to enter, in the other more cold water. Thus, in the extreme position to one side there is hot water only; to the other, cold water only.

At the same time the unit is arranged so that the valve or mixing mechanism can move in another direction—in and out or back and forth—without

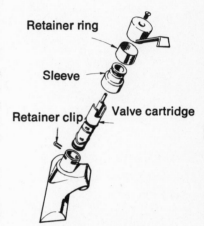

Single-control cartridge-type bathroom faucet

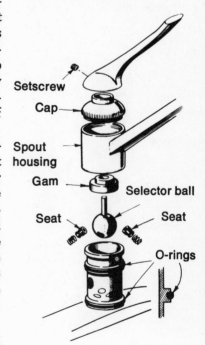

Single-control ball-type kitchen faucet

disturbing the relative amount of hot and cold water that is allowed to enter. It is this second movement that controls the total volume of water that comes out through the spout. Most units are designed so that after the temperature has been adjusted, the faucet can be shut off or the volume regulated, without affecting the temperature setting.

When a washer or packing is needed for a conventional faucet, you usually find the needed parts at your local hardware store—not so with single-control faucets. Because of the variety of brands on the market (each requiring its own parts) and because few do-it-yourselfers have occasion to repair their own single-handle faucets, parts for these units are seldom stocked by local hardware stores, unless they happen to specialize in plumbing supplies. The parts will have to be purchased from a regular plumbing supply house, the type that caters to the professional plumber. It must be kept in mind that any one of these dealers does not necessarily carry all brands—if the dealer has only Brand A single-control faucets, he will only carry Brand A's repair parts, so you may have to shop around to find the replacement unit you need.

Replacement cartridges or balls almost always come with an instruction sheet and an "exploded" view of the faucet showing how the various parts fit together and explaining how the faucet must be taken apart to remove the worn parts and install the new ones. When any of these start to drip or do not control the flow of water properly, it is the cartridge or ball assembly that must be replaced. The first step is to shut off both the hot and cold water supplies (if there are no valves for this under the sink, there should be some in the basement—otherwise the main valves will have to be shut off).

The next step is to remove the handle, usually held in place by a small screw (on some models this screw will be covered by a decorative escutcheon plate or cap). Parts should then be carefully removed in the order shown on the instruction sheet and laid out carefully, preferably in the

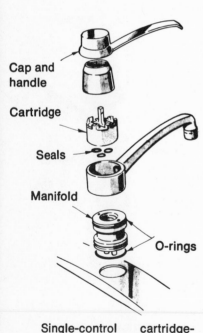

Cap and handle

Cartridge

Seals

Manifold

O-rings

Single-control cartridge-type kitchen faucet

same order, so that they can be replaced without mixing them up. Some repair kits will include rubber O-rings that should be put in at the same time, although not all models have these. On kitchen faucets it will usually be necessary to remove the spout which simply lifts off—while on bathroom fixtures this will seldom be required.

All this may sound a bit complicated to the uninitiated. However, if you have the instruction sheet or parts diagram to follow and have purchased the right parts, the job is relatively simple if you are even moderately familiar with plumbing repairs. If you don't have the diagram that originally came with the unit, write to the manufacturer or check the phone book to find the nearest distributor (a trademark or company symbol is usually engraved on the faucet).

Kitchen faucets equipped with a swivel spout will sometimes develop leaks around the base of the swiveling section but in many cases this is due to worn O-rings inside the housing. They are easily replaced by removing the handle and then lifting off the spout, but it is important that the new O-rings be exactly the same size as the old ones.

KITCHEN-SINK FAUCET SPRAYS

Faucet sprays or dishwashing spray attachments on kitchen sinks seldom give trouble, but when they do, repairs are not hard to make. Most are designed so that when the thumb lever on the spray attachment is depressed, all water should cease to flow from the spout of the faucet. However, on most models a small trickle of water from the spout will continue and is considered normal.

When little or no water is diverted to the spray head, the first thing to check is whether the aerator (the small unit that screws onto the discharge end of your sink spout) is partially or completely clogged. If it is, this causes a back-pressure that keeps the diverter valve (see page 133) from working properly. Unscrew the aerator from the faucet, then flush it out thoroughly by running water

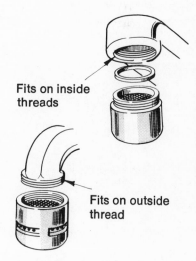

Fits on inside threads

Fits on outside thread

Two popular types of aerators

When spray
head leaks,
replace
whole head.

Save
washer
and snap
ring.

Screw into
new head unit.

Spray head for kitchen sink

through it in the opposite direction from which it normally flows (by holding it upside down under the faucet). If necessary, use a small stiff brush (an old toothbrush works fine) to scrub out the screen, and use a wooden toothpick to clean out any sediment that may have accumulated in the little holes around or above the strainer.

If the aerator is not clogged, the next thing to check is the spray head itself. Unscrew its nozzle or head and wash it out (as described for the aerator) while at the same time checking to see if any parts seem cracked or broken. If so, the simplest solution is to buy a new spray head—replacements for various types are available in most hardware stores and in all plumbing supply houses. Most are interchangeable because manufacturers have standardized hose and thread sizes.

If the spray head seems to be clean and is working satisfactorily, then check the hose itself. Look under the sink to see if it is cracked or kinked, and have someone pull it up and down while you watch from below to see if the hose kinks or catches on something when it is moved. If it shows signs of cracks or leaks, the simplest solution is to replace it with a new one (here again, replacements are readily available in plumbing-supply houses).

If these parts are working properly, yet water is still not being diverted to the spray head when the thumb control valve is depressed, the trouble must be in the diverter valve. This is a small piston-shaped valve which fits into a recess or hole at the base of the faucet, usually directly under the swing spout, although different brands of faucets vary slightly in design. The diverter valve usually can be reached by unscrewing the collar that holds the swing spout in place, then lifting off the swing spout and, in some cases, the decorative chrome housing that encloses the entire mechanism. Now, the diverter valve can be lifted or pulled out by grabbing the little stem which sticks up for just that purpose.

After the old diverter valve is removed, a flashlight should be shined down into the hole in which it fit to see if there is any dirt or foreign material on the inside. The simplest way to flush out any dirt is to turn the water on for a moment and then shut it off. Replace the diverter valve with a new one (they're quite inexpensive), making certain you install it in the same way, then reassemble the faucet. Your unit should be in working condition again.

CLOGGED SINK DRAINS

Although sinks sometimes become clogged because a foreign object is accidentally dropped down the drain, the trouble usually is caused by ignoring the fact that the sink had actually been draining sluggishly for days—or even weeks—before it finally became completely stopped up.

In kitchen sinks the majority of stoppages are caused by accumulations of grease which cake up in the trap (the U-shaped piece of pipe in the drain directly below the sink). As grease accumulates and hardens, it traps small particles of food and other solid waste such as coffee grounds, vegetable peelings, and the like, until finally a sizable obstruction builds up. Obviously, you can avoid most stoppages of this kind by not letting materials that could cause trouble go down the drain.

For example, instead of pouring waste grease or fat into kitchen sinks, pour it into a can or other container, allow to cool, then dispose along with your other garbage. Coffee grounds, food crumbs, peelings, and other solid matter should be kept out of the drain whenever possible, and the sink strainer should never be removed while the sink is in use. Anything that won't fit through the small holes in the strainer does not belong in the drain pipe.

In bathroom sinks and tubs the most common culprit is hair, combined in many cases with a build-up of soap curds. Most modern bathroom sinks have built-in metal stoppers that can be opened or closed by raising or lowering (depending on the design) a knob or handle behind the spout. The actual stopper is a metal cap that raises up into the sink when the drain is open, then closes

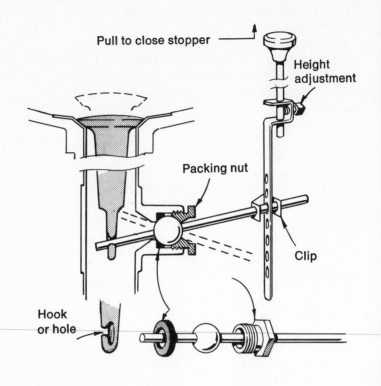

Pull to close stopper

Height adjustment

Packing nut

Clip

Hook or hole

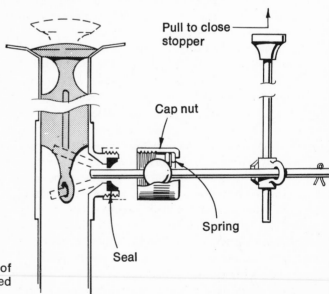

Pull to close stopper

Cap nut

Spring

Seal

Three common types of metal-stopper linkage used in bathroom sinks

down for a snug fit against the metal-rimmed drain opening when closed.

As can be seen in the drawings here, the stopper is connected by a linkage that moves it up or down when the handle at the top is moved; the end of this linkage projects into the drain pipe opening to actuate the stopper. It is in this area that hair is often trapped until it builds up to the point where it obstructs (or partially obstructs) drainage. The matted hair also serves to catch soap that sometimes cakes up and further adds to the obstruction.

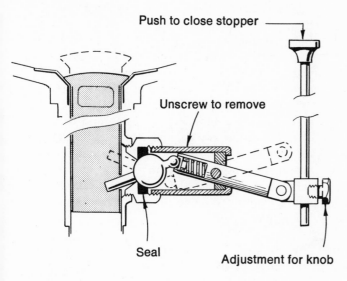

Push to close stopper

Unscrew to remove

Seal

Adjustment for knob

On most sinks the stopper can be removed simply by raising it as far as it will go, then twisting it about one-half a turn after which it should lift out. If this doesn't work, you may have to unfasten the stopper by working from below. Unscrew the packing nut or cap-nut through which the connecting arm fits (see drawings) as it enters the drain pipe, then pull out the rod with the nut that holds it in place. This enables you to lift the stopper out from the top so that you can clean off hair and lint that may have accumulated around it. Stoppers in bathtubs can be lifted out in the same way—that is, by grasping them and turning slightly to free them from the linkage.

USING CHEMICAL CLEANERS

If a sink drain acts sluggish even though there is
no hair trapped around the metal stopper—or no
grease or other foreign matter trapped around the
sink strainer—you should try a chemical drain
cleaner, following the manufacturer's directions.
(It's a good idea to use a chemical drain cleaner as
a preventive measure once every two or three
months.)

Remember that these drain cleaners are usually
quite caustic, so wear rubber gloves and be careful not to spill them anywhere except inside the
drain. They should not be used when the sink is
full of water nor should they be used in hot water.
If the fixture is already quite full, dip most of the
water out first so that you can pour the compound
directly into the drain opening without allowing it
to come in contact with the porcelain finish. Depending on the brand you're using and the extent
of the stoppage, you may have to wait several hours
for the chemical to work its way through and even
repeat the process more than once. After a gurgling
action indicates that the drain is fully open, flush
with plenty of water to rid the pipe of all remaining caustic solution.

USING A FORCE CUP

For complete stoppages or for those that can't be
cured with a chemical cleaner, the tool to use is a
rubber force cup or plunger (often called a plumber's helper). Before starting, make certain there
is at least some water in the sink—enough to cover
the rubber cup completely when it is pressed down
over the drain opening. If the problem is in a
kitchen sink, remove the sink strainer first; if it's
in a bathroom sink, remove the metal or rubber
stopper by lifting it out completely. Place the rubber cup firmly over the drain opening, while holding a damp cloth pressed tightly against the overflow opening near the top rim of the sink. This
plugging with a rag is essential—if you don't do

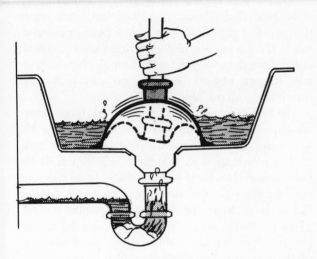

Suction created by the upward pull of the force cup is often best for removing stoppage.

it, the energy expended by the force cup will be wasted in forcing water and air out through this opening rather than down through the drain pape. Press down firmly with a hard push to create pressure in the line, and immediately jerk the handle back upward to create a suction action right after the compression stroke.

Repeat this up-and-down motion five or six times, then yank the cup from the opening to see if the water starts to drain away. Remember that in most cases the suction (up) stroke of the force cup is actually more effective in breaking up the clog than the compression (down) stroke; so place extra emphasis on yanking the handle up each time after making certain that the rim of the cup is in firm contact with the sink bottom before you start.

USING A PLUMBER'S SNAKE

If none of these methods work, the trouble may be due to the fact that the trap or drain pipe underneath or behind the fixture is clogged with something solid that will have to be physically removed

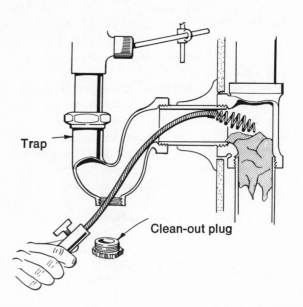

Retaining nuts

Washers

Removable U-trap

Common type of removable sink trap

by using a plumber's snake or drain auger. This is a long piece of flexible spring steel or tightly coiled wire (see illustration) that you can push down through the pipe to break up or remove obstructions. It will have a coiled spring-wire tip that is sharp enough to work its way through clogs or hook into foreign objects so that you can pull them through the drain pipe opening.

The two most common types of sink traps (these are directly below the sink and connected to the lower end of the sink's drain pipe) are shown here. Both are U-shaped so that they hold liquid at the bottom and thus keep noxious odors from escaping upward through the sink opening. Some have a clean-out plug at the bottom and some do not. The ones that don't are easily removable by loosening the two retaining nuts which hold them in place as shown. The other type of trap must be removed by unscrewing it from the pipe that projects out from the wall but the clean-out plug at the bottom usually eliminates the need for this.

Place a pail or a large pan under the trap, then

Another common type of sink trap

Trap

Clean-out plug

use a wrench to remove the clean-out plug. If there is no clean-out plug, remove the entire U-shaped piece as shown by loosening the two large retaining nuts which hold it in place at each end. Slide the nuts back up out of the way, but be sure you don't lose the rubber washers or gaskets that fit inside them. Allow all water trapped in the drain to flow out into the pail or pan that you have placed underneath, then probe the inside of the trap and up through the drain opening with the end of your snake to see if there are any obstructions.

If both the sink drain and the trap are clear, the obstruction is obviously in the pipe leading into the wall or floor, so start probing with your snake. Keep pushing it into the wall a few inches at a time, occasionally pulling it back slightly while turning or twisting the handle end. The steel snake is flexible enough to go around bends and sharp turns, although you may have to exert a little extra pressure when you come to a joint. When you feel an obstruction, maintain pressure on the end of the tool while twisting so as to cause the hook or coiled spring at the tip to bite into the clog in the pipe. This either will push it out of the way by breaking it up into small pieces that will flush through the pipe, or it will permit you to draw the object through the drain opening under the sink. As a rule, when you do feel an obstruction, it is always better to try and pull it out rather than to push it further down into the pipe. After the obstruction is removed, you can reinstall the U-shaped trap and clean-out plug, but be sure you thread the retaining nuts and the plug back on carefully since these have fine brass threads that are easily damaged by forcing if the pieces are not precisely in line.

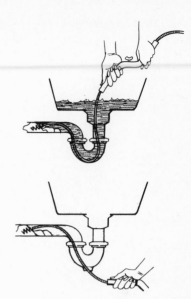

Two ways to use the plumber's snake

CLOGGED TOILETS

Toilet bowls do not have separate traps underneath them the way sinks and other fixtures do; as shown here, the trap is built in as part of the fixture. When water and other material is flushed out of

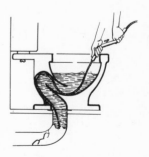

Clearing a toilet bowl stoppage with a snake

the bowl it has to run up and over a protruding lip which serves to keep a certain amount of water permanently trapped in the bottom of the bowl.

Because toilet bowls have very large drain openings which normally do not obstruct easily (it takes a sizable mass to block a toilet bowl drain), chemical cleaners are seldom effective on clogged toilets. A rubber force cup or plunger can often be used, but on some models the opening is too large or not shaped properly to permit you to cover the bottom with the bottom end of the cup. However, if the shape or design of your toilet bowl permits you to apply suitable pressure with a force cup, this usually is the easiest method to try first, following the same technique as you would on a sink drain.

For more serious toilet stoppages, a plumber's snake or drain auger is the tool you will need. Because of the built-in trap on a toilet bowl, using a snake or auger is a bit more difficult since it takes considerable pressure to force the snake into and through the trap area. Twisting steadily on the handle end while maintaining pressure on the other end will usually do the trick. But if you have trouble forcing the end of the snake or auger past the trap, slip a plastic garbage bag over your hand and your arm, then push your hand under the water and guide the tip of the snake past the inside rim of the trap. The extra pressure you can apply on the tip in this way should be enough to push the snake through. Keep feeding and twisting the snake downward until you feel the clog, then twist and pull repeatedly until you either pull the obstruction out or break it up enough to permit the water to flow out past it.

In very extreme cases, when none of these methods work, the only way to clean out the line is to remove the toilet bowl entirely so you can get at the drain pipe underneath. Unfortunately this job usually calls for the services of a professional plumber.

TOILET TANK REPAIRS

Most frequently, when the flush tank on your toilet keeps on running or fails to flush properly, the repairs required are surprisingly simple to make and may involve only the purchase of an inexpensive part. These repairs are simple if you are reasonably familiar with how a toilet tank works so that you can follow an intelligent path in locating the source of the trouble—to the uninitiated the inside of a flush-toilet tank may look like a Rube Goldberg contraption that only a master engineer would dare monkey with.

Illustrated on page 146 is the working mechanism of a typical flush-type toilet tank (the kind you probably have in your home or apartment), viewed from the front as though the front side of the tank had been cut away to give you a look at the inside. Assume that the tank is now full of water ("full" means that the water level is just below the top of the overflow tube), and follow this brief explanation of how the various parts function.

When you press down on the handle on the outside (left-hand corner), the trip lever on the inside raises, pulling the lift rods upward. This raises the rubber tank ball off its seat at the bottom and permits the water in the tank to rush rapidly out through the opening and into the bowl to flush it.

As the water level inside the flush tank starts dropping rapidly, the large metal or plastic float ball at the top drops with it. This ball is connected by means of a float arm or rod to an inlet valve (called a ballcock). As the arm drops, it automatically opens the inlet valve at the top of the ballcock and water comes rushing in to refill the tank. (To minimize splashing, this water actually comes out through the tube at the side which points down toward the bottom of the tank.) Since the rubber tank ball at the bottom is hollow and has air trapped underneath, it tends to float rapidly upward as soon as it is raised off its seat by the lift rod, even though you let go of the handle on the outside. As the water level drops, this ball falls back down until it once again sits firmly against the valve seat at the bottom—once more sealing the opening that leads out to the toilet bowl.

When the water rushing through the inlet valve starts to accumulate, it presses the tank ball down

Working mechanism of a common flush-type toilet tank

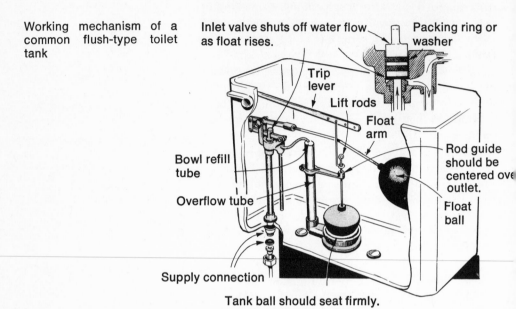

Inlet valve shuts off water flow as float rises.

Packing ring or washer

Trip lever

Lift rods

Float arm

Bowl refill tube

Overflow tube

Rod guide should be centered over outlet.

Float ball

Supply connection

Tank ball should seat firmly.

Standard ballcock action

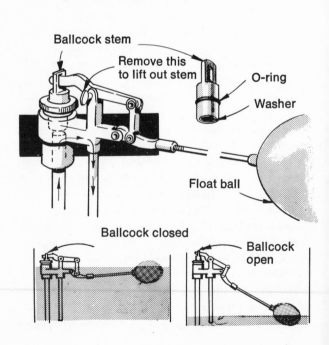

Ballcock stem

Remove this to lift out stem

O-ring

Washer

Float ball

Ballcock closed

Ballcock open

to form a tight seal which keeps the water from running back into the toilet bowl. As the water level inside the tank rises, the float ball and its arm also rise with it until a predetermined level is reached. As it rises, the float arm actuates a mechanism inside the inlet valve that shuts off the water when the tank is full and it is ready for the next flushing action.

While the tank is refilling, part of the water coming through the inlet valve is diverted through the flexible bowl refill tube so that it flows down through the overflow tube into the toilet bowl. This refills the trap in the bottom of the bowl and restores the water level inside the toilet.

WATER KEEPS RUNNING

Probably the most common toilet problem is when water continues running from the tank into the bowl after flushing is complete. When this happens, the first thing to do is take the tank cover off and look inside to see if the tank is full or empty.

If the tank is almost empty and water keeps running in without the tank ever refilling properly, chances are that the tank ball at the bottom is not seating properly against its valve seat so that water keeps leaking continuously past it into the toilet bowl. There are two things that can cause this: the rubber ball is worn, especially along the bottom and can no longer form a tight seal against the seat; or it does not seat properly because the guide rod which lifts it is not properly centered over the valve seat opening (so that when the ball falls back down it doesn't fall over the center of the valve seat).

If the ball is worn—or even if you're in doubt about it—replace it with a new one (they're cheap). This rubber ball is simply screwed onto the bottom of the lift rod, so that to replace it you just unthread the old one and screw the new one back in its place. Although you can do this while the tank has water in it, you'll probably find it easier to do if you first shut off the water supply to the tank. Most toilets

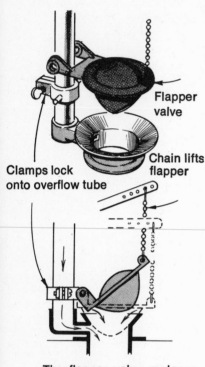

Flapper valve

Chain lifts flapper

Clamps lock onto overflow tube

The flapper valve replaces tank ball at bottom in modern toilet tanks.

have the shut-off valve located directly under the tank; if it is not there, you may have to turn off the appropriate valve in the basement. After shutting off the valve, flush the tank once to empty it so you can then work on the inside while the tank is dry.

If the original rubber tank ball seems in good condition—or if you've recently replaced it with a new one which does not seat properly, you'll probably have to move the rod guide slightly to one side or the other in order to center the ball over its seat. Most of these guides have a set screw which clamps them in place around the outside of the overflow tube (as indicated in the drawing here); so by loosening this screw slightly you can swing the guide arm left or right until the ball falls directly over the center of the valve seat when allowed to drop.

One permanent way to eliminate the problem of having to worry about alignment of the tank ball at the bottom is to replace the tank ball with one of the new flapper valves. These need no guide rods or guide arm—so remove those parts from your tank. To raise the hinged rubber flapper (which clamps around the overflow tube), attach the length of chain supplied directly to the trip lever arm as shown.

In some cases, after lifting the cover from a tank that keeps running continuously, you may find that the tank is full and the water keeps running out through the top of the overflow tube. This is caused by the inlet valve which is not shutting off as it should after the water reaches its proper level inside the tank. As a result, the water in the tank keeps overflowing into the toilet bowl through the overflow tube—either in a steady stream or in the form of a persistent trickle. When this happens, there are two things to check—the float ball and arm, or the ballcock.

To find out which one is causing the problem, try lifting up the float ball by raising it as high as it will go. If this stops the flow of water into the tank, unscrew the float ball from the end of its arm and shake it to see if there is water inside it. If there is, the ball has developed a leak and does not float up as high as it should, so you'll have to replace it.

If the ball is not leaking (it has no water on the inside) then the trouble may be caused by improper adjustment of the float arm. In other words, the arm does not allow the ball to rise high enough to shut the water off before it reaches the level of the overflow pipe opening. The simplest way to make this adjustment is to bend the float arm slightly downward near the middle (the float arm is made of soft metal so that you can bend it with your hands). Bending it downward will make it shut off sooner, thus lowering the level at which the water in the tank is maintained. Experiment with this adjustment until the float shuts off the water when its level rises almost—but not quite— to the top of the overflow pipe. Many tanks have a line drawn against the back on the inside to show the proper water level when full.

If lifting up on the float ball and arm does not shut off the flow of water from the inlet valve into the tank, the trouble is in the ballcock mechanism itself. This unit has a washer on the inside as well as one or more packing rings or O-rings that eventually wear and need replacing (see drawing on page 146). Most ballcocks can be disassembled and repaired. However, even professional plumbers agree that when trouble develops in one it usually is so old and worn that you will be better off replacing it.

One advantage of replacing the ballcock is that you can select one of the new models which are quieter, require less maintenance, and shut off more positively without leaking. Some are merely improved versions of the original ballcock concept, but at least two work on an entirely different principle—and both of these eliminate the need for the float ball and its connecting float arm which activates (closes and opens) the ballcock valve.

One of these mechanisms, made completely of plastic, has a floating cup at the top that rides up and down on the shank of the ballcock. When the toilet is flushed, this cup floats down as the water level drops, thus opening the inlet valve which fills the tank. As the tank fills, the float cup gradually rises to the top, shutting off the water flow when the tank is filled to the proper level.

The other type of ballcock replacement is a pressure-activated mechanism which does not depend on any type of floating action to regulate water level inside the tank. Located at the bottom of the tank, it contains a diaphragm that reacts to water pressure as the water level inside the tank builds up to the required height. When the water level is high enough, the diaphragm reacts to the increased pressure by shutting off the flow of water. When the toilet is flushed, the water level in the tank drops rapidly and, reacting to this, the fill valve opens to allow water to come flowing back in until the proper level is once again achieved. Like the plastic model described in the previous paragraph, there is no need for a float arm or float ball—thus there are fewer moving parts to get out of adjustment or break down.

Regardless of the type of ballcock or fill valve you decide on, replacing your old one with one of these new models is not a difficult job. Start by shutting off the valve that supplies water to the toilet tank, then flush once to empty the tank. Mop up any excess water that remains in the bottom, then disconnect the water supply connection underneath the tank (see drawing on page 146). Next, loosen the lock nut that holds the old ballcock in place on the bottom of the tank (this lock nut is a large nut on the outside of the tank), after which you can lift out the entire unit.

All new ballcocks come with instructions and fittings needed to install them, so putting in a new one is simply a matter of following the illustrated directions supplied. If the old water line connection is corroded or otherwise damaged, the simplest solution is to replace it at the same time, using one of the flexible, chrome-plated metal tubes which are sold specifically for this purpose in most hardware stores and by all plumbing-supply dealers. After the new ballcock is installed, turn the water back on and watch for leaks underneath. If necessary, tighten the nuts that hold the water line and the ballcock in place slightly until the leaks stop. Be careful not to over-tighten—excess pressure on the wrench can distort the compression fittings and make the leaks worse.

As with most other plumbing jobs around the home, it's a good idea to tackle a job of this kind on a day when the hardware stores are open so that if you need an additional part, or have trouble with fitting pieces together, you can go out to the store and get a new adapter or other needed fitting promptly.

NOISY PLUMBING

Hammering, banging, chattering, or squealing noises in your household plumbing system can be caused by many different things, but they should not be ignored. The hammering and banging cause vibration in the pipes that could eventually result in loose joints or ruptured fittings, especially if the trouble is caused by loose or missing mounting straps or clamps.

One of the most common noises is a whistling or squealing sound that you hear every time you turn on a faucet. This may be accompanied by a chattering noise that gradually disappears as the faucet is fully opened. If it only happens in one faucet and only when it's being turned on, chances are that the trouble is caused by wear inside the faucet itself. In many cases a new washer on the inside is all that's required (see page 128).

If the washer is not the cause of the trouble (i.e., the old one is still in good shape or putting in a new one doesn't stop the noise), then it is likely that the threads on the faucet spindle are badly worn or otherwise damaged so that there is an excess amount of play inside the faucet. One way to test for this is to open the faucet halfway and then try wiggling the handle around. If there is more play in this handle than there is in other faucets in the house, the spindle thread is probably worn and causing the trouble. If so, remove the spindle and stem entirely (see page 129), then take them to your local plumbing supply dealer to see if you can buy a replacement. If you can't, an entirely new faucet will have to be purchased and installed in place of the old one.

Sometimes you'll hear a chattering or banging noise in your plumbing because several of the mounting straps or supports that hold the pipes in place have worked loose. This is something you may or may not be able to fix, depending on where the trouble is. First try inspecting all of the exposed lengths of pipe in the house, especially in the basement, crawl spaces, or other unfinished areas where the pipes are easily seen. Look for any place where a pipe strap seems to have pulled loose or where you can feel sagging and vibrating when the water is running.

As a rule, water pipes should be supported at 6- to 8-foot intervals, as well as near all elbows and other fittings. You can install additional mounting blocks or supporting straps by nailing or screwing them in place against studs or beams. If the unsupported part is inside a wall, the problem is complicated by the fact that you will have to rip the wall open in order to get at the loose pipe— if you can locate the exact spot where the pipe needs more support. Unfortunately, this is not al-

Adding mounting blocks and straps to brace loose pipe

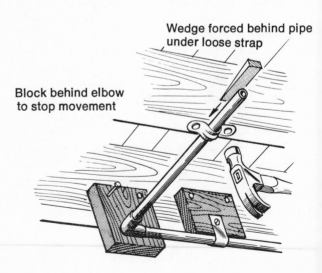

Wedge forced behind pipe under loose strap

Block behind elbow to stop movement

ways a simple task so most people elect to live with the problem as long as possible, or until major alterations are contemplated.

If the hammering or banging noise only occurs after a faucet is turned off, the problem may be caused by a condition known as "water hammer." To cure this there are special antihammer devices which can be installed (see drawings) to absorb the shock each time a faucet is shut off. (This is a problem with automatic washing machines where the water is turned on and off repeatedly by electric valves inside the machine.) Because water cannot be compressed, its momentum causes it to slam forward and bang against the pipe walls when the flow is suddenly stopped. Antihammer devices have an air chamber that acts as a pneumatic shock absorber to help absorb these shocks and provides a "cushion" of air that will soak up the extra energy created by the rushing water and thus eliminate the hammering effect that would otherwise occur.

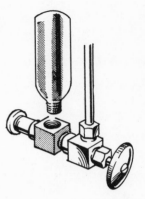

Compact antihammer chamber installs under sink.

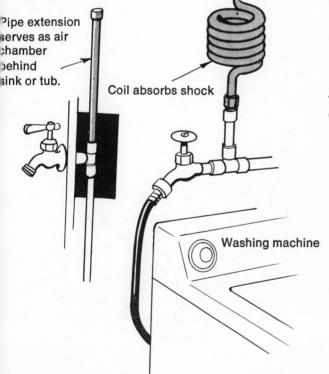

Pipe extension serves as air chamber behind sink or tub.

Coil absorbs shock

Two types of antihammer devices

Washing machine

Chapter eight

FLOORS AND STAIRS

Floors and stairs that squeak or creak every time they are walked on, or loose boards on stairs that cause people climbing or descending them to trip or fall, are great for laughs on TV or in a movie, but they can be quite unfunny in your own house or apartment. Yet it is only in comparatively few instances that major carpentry, beyond the scope of the average do-it-yourselfer, will be required to correct these annoying conditions.

SQUEAKY FLOORS

A wood floor that squeaks or creaks when someone walks across it almost invariably has one or more loose boards that move up and down when stepped upon; these boards, rubbing against each other, are what make the noise. The boards may have loosened because the beams underneath have warped, because the floor boards themselves have buckled, because some of the nails have worked loose, or because the flooring was not properly nailed and installed when the house or apartment was constructed.

To stop this noise there are two things you can do: you can lubricate the joint between the boards so that they slide against each other as they move up and down without making the rubbing noise that causes the squeaking; or you can fasten the loose boards down so they will no longer be able to move when someone steps on them.

Although the first method will get rid of the noise without actually correcting the basic cause, it will be effective in most cases. However, this cure is only temporary—the lubricant will eventually wear off and the squeaking will resume. The second method will eliminate the problem and thus cure it permanently.

If you want to try lubrication, you can use dry powdered graphite (the same kind used for lubricating locks), or a nonstaining white powdered lubricant which some hardware stores stock for use on sliding doors and windows. You could even use ordinary talcum powder. Once you've located the offending board or boards, squirt or blow the powder down between the edges of the boards (see drawing on page 156) while another person steps on and off the boards to help the material work its way into the joint. After one or two trials the squeaking should stop.

This is a temporary cure. To eliminate the problem permanently, the loose boards should be tightened by use of nails or screws in order to keep them from moving every time someone steps on them. The trick here is to drive the nails or screws in the right place, and in order to do this you must have some idea of how a typical wood floor is constructed. The drawing here shows a cross section of a typical floor. Large beams, called joists, support the flooring. Over these are (usually) two layers of boards—the subflooring which runs across the joists (either at right angles to the joists or at a 45-degree angle), and the finished flooring which is nailed down on top of this (in some cases the subflooring will be plywood instead of individual boards and in most cases there is a layer of building paper between the two).

Squeaks can be caused by loose boards in either the subflooring or the finished flooring, but in either case the procedure for curing them is the same: First locate the area where the boards are loose, then nail or screw the boards down so that they cannot move. Have someone walk around on the floor while you watch and listen, trying to determine exactly where the trouble is. Then, while your "assistant" stands on top of the loose boards (to hold them down), drive two 3-inch finishing nails in at an angle to each other so that they almost form a "V" as shown. Crossing them in this

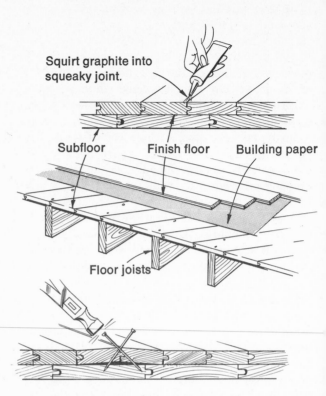

Squirt graphite into squeaky joint.

Subfloor   Finish floor   Building paper

A typical floor

Floor joists

Securing loose floor boards with finishing nails

way will make them grip better with less likelihood of their pulling out.

To avoid damaging the floor with your hammer, drive the nails most of the way in, then finish by using a nailset to drive the heads below the surface. If your floors are oak, the hardness of the wood may make it difficult to drive the nails without bending them, so drill a small pilot hole first (slightly smaller than the diameter of the nail) to facilitate hammering and to minimize the likelihood of splitting the wood.

Sometimes, instead of using nails, it is more effective to use long wood screws because screws will do a better job of pulling warped boards down into their proper position. In addition, assuming a suitable size pilot hole is drilled first, wood screws usually are easier to drive without denting or otherwise damaging the floor. However, the head of a wood screw will leave a larger mark or hole to be filled, but this usually can be concealed satisfactorily by countersinking the screw heads so that they are recessed below the surface, then filling the holes with a matching-color wood plastic or with wood plugs (short lengths of wood dowel cut off flush with the surface).

If the loose boards are in the finished floor, screwing or nailing should anchor the boards down to the subflooring so that they will no longer move. If it is the subflooring that is loose, this method will only work if you can drive your nails into one of the floor joists as shown in the drawing here, rather than through the flooring alone. If the floor is unfinished from below (e.g., the ceiling of an unfinished basement), you can locate the joists by measuring out from one of the walls on the underside of the floor, then duplicating this measurement on top of the floor.

However, if the ceiling below is finished, the simplest way to locate the joists is to tap across the surface of the flooring with a block of wood and a hammer. Keep doing this while moving the block around and you'll notice that there is a dull hollow sound in most places when you're tapping between the joists. However, when you're directly over a joist, the sound will be much more solid—this is where you want to drive your nails. Bear in mind that floor joists are usually spaced at 16-inch intervals and that the finished flooring will often run parallel to these joists, since the subflooring usually runs across them. Any holes left when the nail heads are countersunk can be filled afterward by using a colored wood plastic that matches the finish of your floor.

In those cases where the troublesome floor is on the first floor level and you can get at the floor from underneath (assuming the basement ceiling is not finished), it's easier to make the necessary repairs from below. While someone walks around on the floor above to locate the boards that are causing the trouble, watch from below to see where the subflooring moves up and down, then drive thin wooden wedges between the bottom of the floor boards and the top of the joist as shown. Coat these

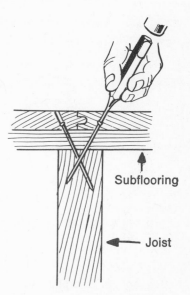

Nailset is used to drive nails below surface. For loose subflooring nails must go into joists.

Repairing a squeaky floor from underneath. Drive a wedge between the floorboards and the joist.

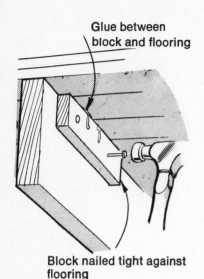

Glue between block and flooring

Block nailed tight against flooring

Support for warped sub-flooring

wedges with glue before driving them into place, and make them only thick enough to fill the space between the floor boards and the joist.

Another way to support subflooring that has warped upward away from the joists is to nail an extra block of wood along the side of the existing joists as shown. Cut a short length of 2 x 4 or 2 x 6 lumber, then, while holding it tight against the side of the joist, force it up as high as it will go before nailing it securely in place against the joist. The top edge of this will then keep the flooring from moving up and down when somebody walks across it.

If the squeaking problem is caused by the finished flooring, rather than the subflooring buckling upward, and if you can get at the floor boards from below, then the easiest way to make a repair that will be completely inconspicuous from above is to drive screws up from below. After locating the offending boards, drive screws upward through the subflooring so as to draw the finished flooring down tight. Needless to say, make certain the screws are only long enough to get a good bite in the finished flooring without completely coming through on the top side.

CURING SAGGING FLOORS

Whether due to settling of part of the house foundation, poorly located supporting posts and columns, improperly planned alterations, or simply an unusually heavy load on one of the lower floors of the house, a sagging floor can cause many problems. These include such things as interfering with proper opening and closing of windows or doors and creating large cracks in plaster walls and ceilings.

In almost every case, a sagging floor can be corrected by use of an adjustable steel jack post (also called an adjustable lolly column), properly positioned in the basement under the floor beams that are sagging. These are constructed like oversized automobile jacks with a heavy steel threaded section at the top that can be raised or lowered by turning the handle. Square steel plates at the bottom and top provide a broad bearing surface for the post when in position. Available in various sizes to accommodate different ceiling heights, these posts are sold in most lumberyards and by building materials dealers.

In order to provide a solid foundation for the post, it is important that a good footing be provided under the base. In some cases the concrete basement floor will be adequate, but it must be at least 6 inches thick and in good condition. Otherwise a hole should be chopped in the floor at the point where the post will rest, and a separate concrete footing, at least 12 inches thick, poured. As an alternative to this, it is sometimes possible to lay down two or three heavy planks at least 2 inches thick and 3 to 4 feet long; this will have the effect of spreading the load over a larger area, thus minimizing the likelihood of cracking the concrete basement floor.

Although a single jack post can sometimes be placed directly under the sagging joist, in many cases you will find that several joists are sagging, so the only way to apply the required lifting power across all of them is to place a heavy 4 x 6 timber across the bottom of the joists so that two or more jack posts can be positioned under this.

When setting up the post, it is important that it be exactly plumb (vertical), so use a carpenter's level to check in both directions. With everything in place, and with the timber at the top properly positioned under the joists, turn the screw up until slight pressure is applied and the post is securely in position. Then give it one extra half turn on the handle and *go no further at this point*.

From here on, the work has to be done very, very slowly to avoid any damage to flooring or other structural members. Most experts recommend turning the post up no more than one-half turn each week until the flooring is finally level. This will permit the beams and other structural members to settle into the new position gradually, without causing dangerous cracking or unusual stresses.

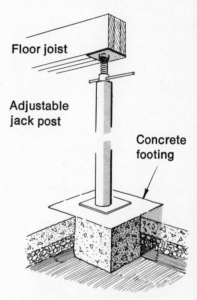

Floor joist

Adjustable jack post

Concrete footing

Footing is needed under post used to support a sagging floor.

Jacking up a sagging floor too quickly can result in cracking out large sections of plaster or flooring, or in creating stresses that will seriously weaken framing and structural members throughout the house.

SQUEAKY STAIRS

As with a wood floor, squeaks in wooden staircases are usually caused by one or more loose boards— in this case a loose tread (the part you step on). The tread may be loose along the front edge where it rests on top of its riser (the vertical piece that supports the tread), or it may be rubbing against the stringer at the sides (the stringer is the piece that runs along each side of the stairway supporting both the treads and risers).

Here again there are two ways to get rid of the noise: by lubricating with powdered graphite, talcum powder, or a similar lubricant, or by fastening down the loose piece so it can no longer move and thus rub against other members. If you decide to try a lubricant, squirt or blow it into the joints between the tread and the riser and between the tread and the stringer along the side. Step up and down on the tread a few times, then repeat the process once or twice until the noise ceases.

To tighten the loose tread and thus get rid of the problem permanently, the easiest method is to drive a few nails in from the top as indicated in the drawing. These should be driven in at an angle with alternate nails sloping in opposite directions when viewed from the front (see page 156). You'll notice that every tread overhangs the riser slightly at the front, so be sure you locate the nails far enough back so that they go into the top edge of the riser, yet not so far back that they miss it completely. The easiest way to do this is to measure under the nose of the tread to see how far it protrudes from the face of the riser; then, before driving your nails, space them about ⅜ inch further from the front so that they will be approximately in line with the center of the riser. Have someone stand on top of the tread to hold it down while you're hammering.

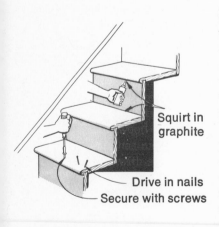

Squirt in graphite

Drive in nails
Secure with screws

Two ways to silence squeaky stairs

For an even stronger repair use long wood screws instead of nails, but drill pilot holes first. Select a drill bit that is about the same diameter as the body of the screw (without the threads) and drill through the tread into the riser. Then drill a larger clearance hole for the screw, through the tread only. Rub the tip of each screw on a cake of soap or paraffin to help lubricate the threads before you drive the screw into the hole and countersink (set it below the surface) the screw heads slightly so that you can cover them with colored wood plastic or putty.

On stairs leading to the basement, or on other stairways where the underside is open and exposed, you can make repairs by working from below. These stairs often have wedges on the bottom, where the treads fit into notches under the treads or in the stringers along the sides, and these wedges may have worked loose. If so, pry them out, coat them with glue, then hammer them back in until they are snug. While examining the underside of an exposed staircase you may also find that the bottom edge of the riser has become separated from the tread below it because of constant kicking as people walk up the stairs. To correct this, hammer the riser against the tread, then drive a few additional nails or screws through the riser and into the back edge of the tread to hold it in place.

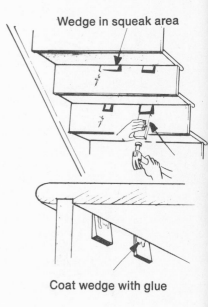

Wedge in squeak area

Coat wedge with glue

Repairing stairs from below

If your stairs squeak because one of the treads is badly split, or if the wood is so worn that the tread tends to buckle in the middle, you should replace the tread as soon as possible. On a staircase that is open on the underside you can make a fairly permanent repair by screwing one or more wood blocks or braces to the underside of the tread. However, if the staircase is inside the house, and the underside is not exposed, have a professional carpenter replace the tread completely.

If the curved front edge of one of the treads develops a split or crack, then you can usually repair it by working a little glue into the split with a knife blade or spatula. Next, drive a small brad or screw in to hold the split section back in place. If the wood is only dented, or if the split is too small to permit driving in a nail or screw, the simplest solution is to use a plane to trim off the curved front edge or nosing so as to make the damage barely noticeable. If screws or nails are used, countersink the heads slightly, then fill with matching wood plastic. Allow to dry hard, then touch up with shellac or varnish to match the rest of the tread.

REPAIRING RESILIENT FLOOR TILES

Removing a damaged floor tile (asphalt, vinyl, vinyl-asbestos, or cork) and replacing it with a new one is not an exceptionally difficult job. However, you must have on hand or be able to obtain, matching tiles. It is a good idea to buy a few extra tiles whenever a new floor is being installed. Store these where you can find them if and when the need for a patch job arises.

The trick in removing a floor tile from the middle of a floor is to do the job without causing damage to the tiles next to it. With most tiles (except for asphalt) the only tools you'll need are a sharp utility knife, a stiff putty knife, and, perhaps, a hammer. Start by scoring the tile 2 or 3 inches away from one edge, then go over this score mark or cut repeatedly until the knife has sliced all the way through. Try to make the score or cut mark as wide as possible—in some cases it's best to alternately tip the knife to one side and then the other to create a V-shaped groove. You can then insert the tip of your putty knife to pry the narrow strip off.

Using the putty knife or a chisel, and tapping with a hammer if necessary, pry off the strip of tile nearest the edge, then turn the putty knife around and wedge it under the rest of the tile by forcing it under with a hammer. Try to work across the width of the tile so that you remove it in one piece, or at least, if at all possible, in large pieces.

On asphalt tile, and on some older brands of vinyl-asbestos tile, the job will be much easier if you first soften the tile with heat. You can apply heat by working carefully with a blow torch (this is what the pros use), but this can be dangerous. The simplest and safest technique is to use an ordinary infrared heat lamp or an infrared bulb in-

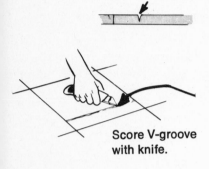

Score V-groove with knife.

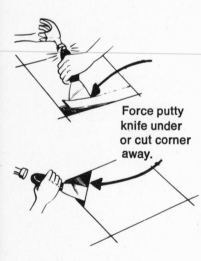

Force putty knife under or cut corner away.

Removing a damaged floor tile

serted in a portable lamp or extension cord. Keep moving the source of heat around until the entire tile is warm and pliable, then pry it up by inserting a utility knife blade along one seam to lift up a corner. A putty knife can then be used to finish the job. If you have trouble getting the corner up, try cutting the corner away first, so that you'll have a place where you can insert the blade of your putty knife.

After the old tile has been removed, it is important that you remove most, if not all, of the old adhesive if you want the new tile to lie flat and smooth. Also, make certain there is no hardened adhesive around the edges of the adjacent tiles since this will keep the tiles from butting snugly when the new tile is installed.

Before spreading adhesive for the new tile, try laying the tiles down dry first, to make certain it will lie smooth without bumps or irregularities. For best results use the adhesive recommended for that particular type of tile and spread it on with a serrated spreader (available from any tile dealer) or with a paint brush (if it is the brush-on type).

If in doubt as to which adhesive to use, select one designed for vinyl tiles—this will work with almost all resilient floor coverings. Apply it in a fairly thin layer, or the excess adhesive will ooze up around the edges. When you set the tile in place, don't slide it—line it up on edge against an adjacent tile, then drop it down flat and press firmly into place by standing on it. If any adhesive oozes up wipe it off immediately with a damp cloth.

REFINISHING WOOD FLOORS

When wood floors become so badly worn that the finish is completely gone in some places, or if the wood is stained and discolored in many areas, the only sure cure is a complete refinishing job, which involves sanding the floor down to the raw wood and applying a new finish.

If there are only a few bad spots visible it is sometimes possible to rejuvenate the floor by scrubbing these areas with steel wool and a liquid floor finish remover, then touching them up with the same finish as originally covered the floor. This system works best if the floor was finished with a penetrating sealer and wax, in which case the new material can be applied with a rag and blended in so that it is almost unnoticeable. Chances are you will see the patch to some extent if you're working with shellac, varnish, or lacquer.

SANDING OFF THE OLD FINISH

When the old finish has to be removed and the floor stripped down to the raw wood, the fastest and most effective way to do the job is to rent a floor-sanding machine from your local hardware dealer or tool-rental agent. He should rent you two machines: a large drum-type sander with its own vacuum bag attached which you'll use on most of the floor, and a smaller disk-type sander which you'll use around the edges, as well as for door saddles, stair treads, and similar small areas.

Before starting the job, remove all of the furniture, including pictures, draperies, and blinds or shades. This will save much cleaning afterwards since the sanding operation leaves a fine film of dust over everything in the room. Loose boards should be tightened by driving nails into the joints between the boards (see page 156) and any protruding nail heads in the flooring should be driven down below the surface with a nailset to avoid tearing the sandpaper or damaging the drum on the machine. To keep the dust from spreading, it's also a good idea to close all the doors leading to the room in which you're working, and to keep as many windows open as possible.

For the smoothest finish, old wood floors should be sanded three times: first with a coarse paper to remove the old finish and level off the boards, second with a medium paper to remove scratch marks left by the coarse paper, and last with a fine-grit paper that will give the wood a final smoothing and leave it ready for finishing.

As a rule, the first sanding (with coarse paper) is done at a 45-degree angle to the boards to knock off the high spots and even up the surface. The second and third sandings (with the medium and fine grit papers) should be done parallel to the grain (that is, along the length of the boards). The big drum-type floor sanders are heavy and exert quite a forward pull when in motion. To take the strain off your back the following tip might be helpful: take an old belt, loop it around your waist and tie it to the handle of the machine while you're working. This will enable you to use your whole body to hold the machine back, rather than letting the pull be exerted only through your arms and shoulders.

Since floor sanders—particularly when equipped with coarse and medium grit papers—cut into the wood very rapidly, you have to be careful never to allow the machine to stop moving while the drum is turning and in contact with the floor. Start the machine while it is tilted back (press down on the handle to do this) so that the drum is off the floor, then lower it and start walking at the same time. That way you'll avoid accidentally gouging grooves or disk-shaped marks into the floor.

Do as much as you can with the large drum sander, then finish off around the edges and in the corners with the disc sander. If there are some corners that you can't get into even with the smaller disc sander, you'll have to use a hand sander or scraper to complete the job in these areas.

After you've finished the sanding, use a vacuum cleaner, a dust mop, and plenty of rags to pick up all the dust from the floor as well as from around the baseboards, moldings, and other surfaces (you don't want any of this dust to settle on the floors while you're applying the finish).

SELECTING THE FINISH

For wood floors that have been sanded down to the bare wood, there are two basic types of floor finishes from which you can choose: a penetrating

Loop belt around waist.

Sawdust bag

Drum sander

Using a floor-sanding machine

Use a disk sander for corners and edges.

sealer that will soak into the wood and leave an "oiled type" low-luster finish with little or no surface film, or a surface coating that will form a hard glossy surface coating on the floor.

If your floors have not been sanded down to the bare wood, but merely have been scrubbed clean or partially sanded, then only a surface finish such as varnish or shellac can be used. Penetrating sealers can be applied only over raw wood, or over floors which have been previously coated with the same kind of sealers.

The penetrating sealer finishes either have a wax, oil, or synthetic-resin base and give a dull, satiny finish. Since they soak into the wood and leave no appreciable surface film, there is no coating that can scratch, crack, or peel (deep scratches will dig into the wood itself). Although the finish itself has very little gloss, a moderate gloss can be achieved by waxing and buffing.

You can buy these sealers in transparent form or in a wide assortment of wood-toned colors, varying from pine to dark walnut. Because the tinted or colored penetrating sealers actually are a combination sealer and stain, they are ideal for staining floors to a darker color while at the same time applying a finish. They wear well, have good resistance to staining and discoloration, and enable you to touch up worn areas easily—rub worn spots with steel wool, then reapply a fresh coat of the same stain-sealer.

Theoretically, if properly maintained by regular waxing and cleaning, a floor finished with penetrating wood sealer can last indefinitely since there is no building up of heavy layers—excess material is wiped off as it is applied. The sealer (colored or clear) is uniformly and liberally applied with a large paint brush or folded cloth, and the excess is wiped off with dry rags. A second coat is applied in the same way after allowing for the drying time specified by the manufacturer. The final step is applying a coat of paste wax (wait at least two or three days for this), then buffing vigorously, preferably with an electric buffing machine, to achieve the gloss desired.

Surface coatings are sold under brand names, but they generally fall into three broad categories —shellac, varnish, and lacquer or plastic finishes. All form a hard glossy surface coating with a built-up finish that some manufacturers claim needs no waxing. However, if most of these finishes are not waxed periodically they will wear more quickly in areas that get heavy traffic so that complete refinishing of the entire floor will be required that much sooner.

Shellac is the oldest and probably still the most popular of the surface coatings. It dries quickly to a clear glossy finish so that you can apply several coats on the same day (you can walk on it within an hour or two), and it darkens very little with age. It's also highly resistant to scratching and abrasion. Note, however, that if spilled water is allowed to remain on the surface for any length of time it will turn the shellac white.

Floor varnishes also give a very hard glossy finish but they are much more resistant to water damage than shellac. However, varnishes take much longer to dry, requiring several hours between coats. Thus building up a varnish finish may require keeping a floor out of service for several days. Some varnishes also tend to darken with age, but since all varnishes dry more slowly than shellac or lacquer, they are generally easier to apply. In addition, varnish builds up more quickly to a thicker and heavier film than shellac and lacquer.

Synthetic lacquer and plastic finishes give a surface coating which generally will not darken with age and which is highly resistant to staining and water damage. Some take hours to dry, while others will dry almost as quickly as shellac, but most will not give as high a gloss. Practically all of them are also somewhat thinner in body so that more coats will be required to build up a sheen equivalent to that of a shellac or varnished floor. Some also have volatile solvents which produce a strong odor while they are drying; you may find this odor objectionable.

GUIDE TO FLOOR CARE

Although maintenance procedures will vary with different types of floors, there are three general rules that apply to the care of all resilient floor coverings or tiles as well as to the care of hardwood floors:

1. Keep the floors properly protected with a thin layer of good quality wax of the type recommended for that kind of flooring.
2. Wipe up spills and dirt marks as soon as they are noticed—and before the spilled material can harden or dry on the surface.
3. Go easy on the washing. Resilient floor coverings (vinyl, linoleum, etc.) should be washed no more than absolutely necessary, and even then water should be used sparingly. Except in extreme cases, wood floors should never be scrubbed with water; instead they should be cleaned with a special cleaning wax or other non-water-base solution that is sold specifically for this purpose.

Floors of vinyl, asphalt, linoleum, cork, or similar resilient materials should be swept daily to remove surface dirt before it can be ground into the surface. When sweeping won't do the trick, the floor should be damp mopped with a dilute solution of mild detergent, not with harsh cleansers or scalding hot water. The surface should then be rinsed with clear water, wringing out the mop sufficiently to keep pools of water from accumulating (do this even if the detergent manufacturer's instructions say that no rinsing is required).

When selecting a wax for the floor, remember that there are two broad categories from which you can choose: waxes that have a solvent base and waxes that have a water base. Both are available in either liquid or paste form.

Some floors can be polished with either type of wax, but be certain that the wax is suitable for your floor covering and will not harm the finish. For example, waxes with a solvent base should never be used on asphalt or rubber tile though they are the best ones to use on wood and cork floors.

All waxes tend to clean as they polish if they are properly applied with a cloth-covered applicator. The fresh wax softens up the old wax and loosens up any dirt that may be embedded in it. This dirt is then picked up by the applicator—but cleaning action will only continue if the cloth on the applicator is changed frequently enough to keep it clean. Some combination wax-cleaners also contain special detergents or other cleaning agents mixed in with them to help remove dirt from the floor as they are applied.

Your wood floors are best maintained by periodic application of a solvent-based wax—a damp mop or sponge should be used only when it is necessary to remove a specific stain or mop up a spill. Under normal use, one of the polishing waxes (those that must be buffed) will generally stand up longer than the self-polishing kind.

When, through neglect, a wood floor or resilient-tile floor becomes so dirty and stained that simple waxing or damp mopping no longer cleans the surface, chances are that so much dirt has become embedded in the wax that you'll have to use a liquid wax remover to strip off all of the old wax. Follow the manufacturer's directions as to how to use this solution, then allow the floor to dry thoroughly and apply a thin coat of fresh wax as soon as possible. Self-polishing waxes are easier to apply but they cannot be buffed between waxing and they may, in some cases, be harder to remove if and when a complete stripping job is required.

Chapter nine

FURNITURE REPAIRS

Even though you may never plan to tackle the job of completely refinishing or rebuilding a piece of furniture, there are times when you'll find it necessary or desirable to make some minor repairs yourself, such as fixing a wobbly chair or table, curing a sticky drawer, or touching up a damaged finish. You may attempt these either because the job is too small to make it practical to call anyone in or because you just can't get someone to come in and do the work when you want them to (or the price demanded for doing the work is so high that you decide you will have to do it yourself if you want to get the job done).

This chapter will describe how to tackle some of the frequently encountered furniture problems which are simple enough for you to correct by yourself.

LOOSE JOINTS IN CHAIRS AND TABLES

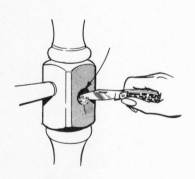

Scrape out old glue with a dull knife point.

The best way to repair a loose joint in a wobbly chair or shaky table is to disassemble the piece completely so that you can do a proper job of regluing and reassembling it—especially if the piece has several joints that are loose. As you take it apart, scrape all the old glue off the end of each rung or leg with a dull knife, then apply fresh glue and reassemble the pieces. For most indoor furniture ordinary white glue (the kind that looks milky white in the jar but dries almost clear) will do. For furniture that will take a lot of stress, or where more resistance to moisture and dampness will be required, a plastic resin wood glue should be used (this comes in powder form and must be mixed with water before use).

Except where a piece actually has broken or split, joints normally work loose because the wood tends to shrink and the end of the rung or leg no longer fits snugly in its hole, thus causing the glue to break loose. Remember that wood glues only hold if pieces fit snugly, they will not fill in voids or compensate for poorly fitted joints. Therefore, before reassembling a loose-fitting chair leg or rung, it is necessary that you take up the slack by building up the end of the shrunken piece.

There are several ways this can be done, but the simplest method is to wrap the end with closely wound linen or cotton thread coated with glue until it fits snugly. Another method that professional furniture repairmen often use is to saw a slot in the end of the rung or leg, then wedge a small piece of tapered wood, such as the end of a wood clothespin, into this slot to spread the sawed end apart slightly.

Once you've cleaned off all of the old glue and test-fitted the pieces to make certain each fits snugly into its hole or groove, coat the pieces with glue and reassemble them. Some method of clamping or applying pressure is required if you want the glued joint to hold properly and there are various types of wood clamps you can buy for this. On chair legs and large frames you'll find it easier to apply the needed pressure by using a web or band clamp, or a simple rope tourniquet which you tighten by twisting with a stick on one side. To keep the rope from cutting into and possibly damaging delicate finishes, use pieces of cardboard to pad the areas where the rope goes around a corner.

On those jobs where you find it impractical to take the piece completely apart, particularly if there is only one loose joint to worry about, you'll have to try and work glue into the crevice around the loose piece. By working gently you often can pry the joint open far enough with a small screwdriver to permit you to scrape most of the old glue out with a thin knife blade (an artist's palette knife is handy for this job) or a very narrow screwdriver. Glue can then be forced into the joint with a hypodermic-type glue injector (sold in hardware stores and

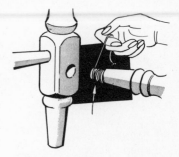

Wrap the end to be inserted with glue-coated thread to ensure a tight fit.

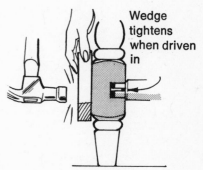

Wedge tightens when driven in

Striking a wood clamp will anchor a glued joint.

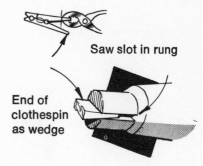

Saw slot in rung

End of clothespin as wedge

Use a small wedge to expand the end of a rung or leg to ensure a snug fit.

Stick tightens
cord when twisted

Wrap rope
around legs

Use rope tourniquet or web
clamp to apply pressure so
the glued joints set properly.

lumberyards that deal in cabinetmaker supplies), or
you may be able to run glue into the joint by positioning the piece so that the glue can work its way
in by gravity while you help poke it in with a piece
of wire or a flat toothpick.

Another trick which the pros often use is to drill
a small hole through the back side of the joint
(about ⅛ inch), then inject the glue into the cavity
through this, using one of the methods mentioned
above. The little hole which remains can be effectively camouflaged by filling with a matching colored putty stick or wood plastic.

Sometimes a chair or table will get wobbly because the frame against which the upper part of the
legs is fastened works loose, particularly in the corners. This can also happen with a table whose legs
are only braced near the top. In the case of a table,
turning it upside down generally will reveal metal
braces in the corners with a nut (or wing nut) that
locks the leg in place. On chairs there may or may
not be a similar metal brace or there may simply be
a wood-corner block that serves the same purpose.

Turn the piece of furniture upside down and try
wiggling the legs around to see where the loose
joint is. If the piece has nuts, bolts, or screws driven
through the edges of the frame, try tightening these
with a wrench or screwdriver to make certain that
all are secure. If there are wood corner blocks fastened in place with glue, you may find that one or
more of these joints has broken loose. In this case
remove the block completely, scrape off the old glue
and replace it using fresh glue and long wood
screws. If necessary, you can also add metal corner
irons or corner braces to strengthen the joint where
the frame meets the legs.

Tightening the joint where
the frame meets the legs of
a table (left) and a chair
(right).

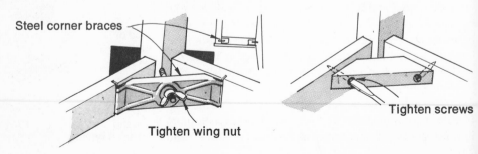

Steel corner braces

Tighten wing nut

Tighten screws

LOOSE OR BLISTERED VENEER

When veneer—which is a thin layer of wood—lifts up or blisters on a piece of furniture, it is because the glue that held it in place has crystalized and let loose. To repair it, try sliding a knife blade or spatula underneath the raised section, using it as a scraper to clean away as much of the old glue as possible or try working a small piece of sandpaper underneath, pressing down on top of it with the knife blade while you rub. After you're done, blow out any dust or dirt that remains underneath, then work white glue under the loose veneer with the tip of the blade or a cotton-tipped swab.

After you've worked glue over the area, move the loose veneer up and down a few times by pressing on the outside so as to spread the glue around uniformly. Then smooth it down and hold it in place with weights or clamps (an iron serves as an excellent weight), or even with long strips of adhesive tape wrapped around the corners of the piece. Excess glue that oozes out should be wiped away while still damp so that you don't mar the finish on the surrounding area.

If a piece of veneer is missing entirely or if bad splits are visible after you've glued the loose parts down, you may be able to patch the area with a matching colored wood plastic (sold in most paint stores). However, if the patch is sizable, the lack of grain in it, coupled with the fact that achieving an exact color match is almost impossible, will make the patch very noticeable, particularly if it's in a prominent location. In this case your best bet is to try to make a patch out of a piece of the same kind of veneer.

Veneer is still sold in some lumberyards that cater to cabinetmakers. You can also get it from several mail-order houses that specialize in selling materials to hobbyists and craftsmen in the woodworking field. If you can't find one of these sources of supply for the piece of veneer you need, or if you need such a small piece that it really doesn't pay to buy a large sheet, you may be able to cut a piece large enough to make the patch you need by "steal-

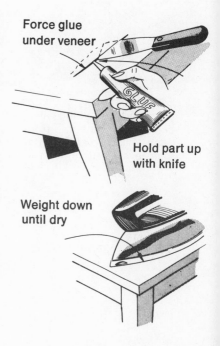

Force glue
under veneer

Hold part up
with knife

Weight down
until dry

Repairing blisters in veneer

Follow outlines of patch piece when cutting away damaged veneer (top). Sand finished patch to uniform level (bottom).

ing" it from the back of the unit or from a corner where a missing piece would be much less noticeable.

To do this, first cut out a piece of the approximate size you will need by working carefully with a sharp knife or chisel. Then pry this off with a chisel, again working carefully to avoid splitting it. Next, trim it to fit into the damaged area by laying it on top and cutting through both the new patch and the damaged veneer pieces at once to ensure a perfect fit. If you work carefully and if you try to match the direction of the grains, you often can do a surprisingly good job of making a patch that will be almost unnoticeable after you finish.

DRAWER PROBLEMS

When a drawer in a bureau or cabinet sticks or rubs each time someone opens it, try to remove it completely and then examine the slides or guide strips on the inside of the cabinet. In many cases there will be dust, dirt or other foreign matter jammed into the guides and this will interfere with free operation of the drawer. If so, clean with a stiff brush or vacuum attachment and apply lubricant to the guides as well as to the edges of the drawer itself. Paraffin (an old candle) works well, but the new silicone sprays work better and are easier to apply uniformly.

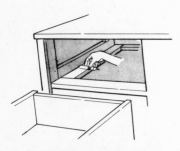

Use piece of wax or candle to lubricate drawer guides.

If lubricating both the drawer and the slides or guides does not do the trick, you may have to do some sanding or planing on those edges where rubbing occurs. Needless to say, it's easier to plane or sand the edge of the drawer rather than the guides but try to take off no more wood than absolutely necessary. Usually there will be marks to indicate where the rubbing occurs, but if not, you may be able to determine this by careful inspection underneath the partly open drawer.

In some cases binding can also occur because one or more of the guides has worked loose and is no longer in its proper position. You'll see this quickly if you shine a flashlight on the inside to

see if any of the guides seem to be out of alignment, or if any of the screws or other fasteners that
hold them in place are loose. Another thing that can
cause a drawer to become balky is when joints in
the drawer itself work loose, particularly at the
corners. When this happens, the drawer is no longer
square and will not fit smoothly between the guides.
To cure this, reglue the loose joints, reinforcing the
corners with one or two small brads if necessary,
then wrap with rope (as shown on page 172) to
form a tourniquet that will apply needed pressure
while the glue dries.

Sometimes a drawer will stick or bind because
the wood expands on humid days, so that you can
get the drawer only partway open, yet can't get it
out far enough to do the necessary planing or sanding, or even to apply lubricant on the slides. A trick
that often works when this happens is to pull the
drawer open as far as possible, then place a light
bulb (screwed into the socket at the end of an extension cord) into the drawer. To prevent scorching
the drawer, or the contents on the inside, push
flammable materials out of the way before turning
the bulb on, and make certain the bulb is inside a
wire cage of the type used on most trouble lights
or inside a metal can which has had the ends cut
out. Leaving this on for several hours inside the
drawer often will generate enough heat to dry out
and shrink the wood sufficiently to permit your pulling the drawer the rest of the way open.

On large chests and double dressers, the drawers
will sometimes fail to work properly because the
whole framework of the chest or cabinet is out of
plumb. This happens because the floor on which
the chest or dresser stands is wavy or uneven so
that the legs do not support it properly.

If you suspect a condition of this kind you can
check for it by using a carpenter's spirit level. Laid
on top of the chest the spirit level should indicate
that the chest is level from side to side as well as
from front to back. If you find that the chest is not
standing level or is twisted slightly (indicated by a
slope from front to back at one end), shim up one
of the legs by wedging thin strips of wood or heavy

folded cardboard under the low side until the top of the chest is level from side to side as well as from front to back.

BURNS AND SCRATCH MARKS

Small scratches which do not go all the way through the finish and into the wood often can be treated or colored so as to make them scarcely noticeable. In most cases all you have to do is rub with an oil-based furniture polish or cream-type polish, while in others a colored liquid scratch remover will do the trick.

White or light colored scratches on a walnut finish often can be successfully camouflaged by rubbing over the scratch with the meat of a walnut or brazil nut. This will color the scratch to match the original tone of the wood after which you can restore the luster by waxing or polishing. On dark mahogany finishes, light-colored scratches can be touched up by carefully applying a little ordinary iodine, using a small watercolor brush or cotton swab. If the iodine is too dark, thin it with rubbing alcohol to lighten it.

For other colored finishes, or where neither one of these methods will match the color successfully, you can buy small bottles of touch-up stain in a paint store. These stains are available in various colors and sometimes come with a small brush attached to the cap. If one color is not suitable as is, the different tones can be intermixed to achieve an intermediate tone. As with most other touch-ups, you should allow it to dry completely, then restore the luster by applying a light coat of paste wax or furniture polish.

Deeper scratches need filling in, in addition to staining, to make them less noticeable. Often you can do this with wax-base putty sticks or touch-up sticks, sold in various colors in most paint stores. Apply these by rubbing the stick back and forth over the scratch mark until the crevice is filled in, then scrape off the excess around the edges by working carefully with a stiff piece of cardboard or a credit card. Scratches can also be filled in by applying multiple coats of varnish with a fine pointed artist's brush or toothpick until the surface is level.

White rings of the kind often left by wet glasses or hot dishes may or may not be removable, depending on how deep they are, and on the kind of finish your furniture has. Try wiping with a rag dampened with denatured alcohol, turpentine, or lacquer thinner. Starting with the alcohol, test each one on an inconspicuous corner of the furniture before applying to the ring; some finishes will be removed by one or more of these thinners. In each case, wipe the thinner on lightly and then rub off immediately with a dry cloth. Of the three, remember that lacquer thinner acts like a remover on most finishes and if you rub too hard or allow it to stay on too long, it will remove the existing finish completely. Work carefully with this material and use it only as a last resort after you've experimented on the back or side of the piece where any damage that might occur would not be noticeable.

Another trick that sometimes works on white rings is rubbing with a rag dipped into a paste made by mixing powdered rottenstone (available in all paint stores) with a little lemon oil or ordinary mineral oil. If this removes the finish it will leave the surface dull-looking because of the abrasive action of the rottenstone, but you can restore the luster by waxing or polishing after the color is once again uniform.

Small burn marks of the kind caused by cigarette ashes or matches can almost always be removed and touched up, providing that the damaged area is not very large and the burn did not go into the wood too deeply. If the burn is very shallow and has merely scorched the finish on top, try rubbing with a dry piece of very fine (#000 or #0000) steel wool wrapped around your finger tip. Rub only the scarred area carefully, and you may be able to remove the mark without going all the way through the finish.

If this doesn't work, or if the burn mark is too deep for this treatment because the finish is

Scrape off a burn mark with a pocketknife, then refinish wood.

scorched all the way through, you'll have to scrape the finish down to the wood (and possibly into the wood if the wood is also scorched).

To do this use a pocketknife or sharp kitchen knife, holding the knife blade at a right angle to the surface as shown, then rub back and forth with very short strokes while bearing down with moderate pressure. Scrape the scorched material away until all signs of the scar are removed and then rub the spot smooth with a small piece of very fine steel wool wrapped around one finger.

To fill in the slight dent that remains, use a colored wood plastic or filler of the right shade to match your finish, unless the color of the wood underneath is very similar to the color of the finish alongside. If so, all you have to do to build up the shallow depression is apply several coats of varnish —it may take five or six—with a small brush, allowing each coat to dry hard before you apply the next one.

If you're handy with tinting colors, varnish can also be used even where the color needs darkening. To darken the varnish, add a few drops of oil color to it until it is tinted close to the shade of the finish, then build up the depression in the scarred area by brushing on successive coats of the colored varnish as described above for the clear varnish.

CLEANING AND MAINTAINING MARBLE TOPS

Although marble looks like a kind of rock or stone, it is actually a highly compacted form of limestone and will stain easily if not properly cared for. It is particularly susceptible to attack by spilled liquids that have an acid content (such as fruit juices and soft drinks) since these materials will etch the finish and ruin the gloss.

Normal maintenance of a marble furniture top consists of periodic washing with clean water and a mild detergent, followed by a rinse with clear water. The finish should then be protected by a clear, non-yellowing white wax that is buffed to a high shine and renewed whenever it shows signs of wear. To prevent staining, spilled liquids or dropped food stuffs and other foreign material should be wiped up or washed off promptly, then the wax renewed if necessary.

Stains that do not wash off easily usually can be removed by using a poultice made by mixing powdered whiting (sold in all paint stores) with a bleaching or cleaning solution—the solution depending on the type of stain to be removed. The poultice, which should have the consistency of a paste, is spread on over the stain and allowed to remain there until it draws the stain out. This may take anywhere from a few hours to a whole day, depending on the type of stain, and in some cases several applications may be required. Since the poultice only works while it is still damp, it's a good idea to keep it wet as long as possible by covering it with a sheet of thin plastic food-wrap.

Most household stains can be classified as falling into one of three over-all categories: organic stains, oil or grease stains, and rust stains.

Organic stains are usually irregular in shape and are caused by such things as soft drinks, tea, coffee, ink, tobacco, and colors leached out from wet paper or fabric left lying on the surface. To remove this type of stain first wash the surface of the marble with water, then apply a poultice made by mixing hydrogen peroxide hair bleach (sold in drug stores) with powdered whiting. After spreading it on over the stain, add a few drops of full-strength household ammonia to start the chemical action.

Oil and grease stains are usually circular in shape and tend to be darker in the center. They are caused by such materials as butter, cream, mustard, salad oil, etc. To remove these, make a poultice by mixing acetone with the powdered whiting. Amyl acetate (available from chemical supply houses) works even better; some people feel that when it is used in combination with acetone the cleaning action is even more effective.

Rust is the most stubborn of all stains to remove from marble. The stain usually follows the shape of the object causing it, and if caught promptly can sometimes be removed simply by rubbing hard with a dry rag. Otherwise, a poultice made by mixing a liquid rust remover or reducing agent (available at hardware stores and at chemical supply houses) will usually—but not always—work. If it doesn't, a professional refinishing job may be the only solution.

Regardless of the type of poultice, or the type of stain over which it is being used, you spread the paste on, cover it with a piece of plastic food-wrap to keep it from drying too rapidly, then allow it to remain there until dry. Wipe off the dried paste by scraping with a piece of cardboard, then rub hard with a dry rag. Then, if the stain is still visible, try once or twice more (stains that won't come out with two or three applications will generally have to be polished out by a professional).

After a stain has been removed, the marble often will look dull in that area and will require polishing to restore the luster. In most cases you can accomplish this by buffing with a non-yellowing white wax.

However, some stains will actually etch or eat into the finish and in these cases more drastic polishing will be required. For this a special marble polishing powder, consisting mainly of tin oxide, is used. This material is sold at some hardware stores, or it can be purchased through many marble dealers. You apply the tin-oxide powder with a pad of cloth that is first dampened with water. Then rub briskly over the dull or etched spot until a shine appears. Wipe off the powder immediately with a damp cloth, then finish by applying a light coat of white paste wax and buff to a high shine.

Chapter ten
CONCRETE AND MASONRY REPAIRS

Most people think that brick, concrete, and other masonry surfaces are permanent, stonelike materials that will last almost forever without maintenance. However, these materials do need periodic attention —mortar joints in brick walls or chimneys eventually develop small cracks or start to crumble, and concrete walls or floors sometimes crack or break in sections, so that patching is needed to keep them from further deterioration.

While it is often true that minor defects of this kind are scarcely noticeable at first, they should be attended to promptly, because eventually they may cause major breakdowns that will require expensive repairs and reconstruction to correct. Cracks and holes allow moisture to penetrate, and this hastens the deterioration process, especially in cold climates where water may freeze on the inside during the winter months. As it freezes, water expands, and this opens the cracks still further to allow more water to enter.

Fortunately, if caught in the early stages most masonry repairs are comparatively simple for the do-it-yourselfer to handle, using only a few inexpensive and readily available tools and materials.

PATCHING CONCRETE AND STUCCO

Small hairline cracks in concrete foundation walls or stucco can most easily be filled by forcing caulking compound into the crevice with a caulking gun (see page 216). Although any type of caulking can be used, the butyl- or silicone-rubber types will stand up the longest. Use a stiff brush to clean the crack out thoroughly and remove all dust, dirt, and crumbly material, then force the compound into the crevice with the caulking gun until some starts to ooze out. The excess should be smoothed off while still soft in order to create a neat looking repair.

For larger cracks (more than $\frac{1}{16}$-inch wide), you will have to use some type of patching cement rather than a caulking compound. These come in dry powdered form in bags or boxes so that all you have to do is add water. The original and least expensive form of patching cement, and the one that is still the most widely used, is the conventional cement-and-sand mixture that is suitable for most masonry jobs (available from most hardware stores, lumberyards, and building material dealers).

However, there are also special formulations available for specific purposes. For example, for laying bricks or patching mortar joints (see page 185) there is a mortar mix that has lime added to the basic cement-sand formula so as to make a more workable and waterproof mortar. For constructing something out of poured concrete, or for making sizable repairs to walks and concrete structures, there is a gravel-concrete mix which has gravel added to provide the additional bulk and strength required.

With any of these premixed dry powdered cements, it is important that the entire contents of the bag be dumped out and mixed dry before adding water. Even if only part of the bag will be used, it should all be dumped out and mixed first to ensure a uniform blend of ingredients—any material that is not needed can then be put back into the bag before adding water to the balance.

When making a patch or filling a crevice with any of these cement-and-sand mixtures, it is important that you clean the joint thoroughly to get rid of dirt and foreign matter if you want to be sure of obtaining a good bond between the old concrete and the new material. Also, widen the crack to at least ½ inch across and then undercut it with a V-shaped tool (such as a beverage can opener) or the corner of a cold chisel so as to make the crack wider at the bottom or inside than it is at the surface. This method will ensure a good mechanical bond as well as a chemical bond.

The technique of undercutting the edges of a crack or patch when filling it in with new material should also be used when making larger patches— undercutting the edges of the old concrete enables the new patch to "lock" more securely to the old material.

When mixing the dry powdered patching cement with water, it's best to follow the manufacturer's recommendations (printed on the bag or box) regarding the amount of water to be added. Always add water a little at a time while mixing continuously; it's easier to judge the consistency this way and thus avoid the danger of adding too much water (if there's not enough water it's always possible to add more—but there's no way to take out excess water once it has been added). The patching cement should be mixed to a reasonably stiff consistency that will hold its shape when mounded up, but it should not be so dry that it crumbles when spread with a trowel.

As a rule, it is best to avoid working on hot surfaces or in the hot sun since this causes the patching cement to dry too fast for a proper cure. With cement-and-sand mixtures it is important that you first wet down with a brush or rag the edges of the patch and the surrounding area of old concrete or stucco before applying the new material—this will keep the water from being drawn out of the patch too rapidly and ensure better bonding. Bear in mind that the cement will crack if not at least ½ inch thick, so make certain you cut cracks out at least this wide and that surface patches are at least this deep.

To eliminate the need for prewetting the surface and to permit applying patching cement in thin layers (as little as ⅛ inch), you can use one of the vinyl patching cements instead. These contain no sand, and cost considerably more, but they form a much stronger bond and will stick to surfaces or materials where ordinary sand-type patching cements will not.

Vinyl patching cements are ideal for resurfacing

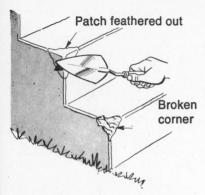

Vinyl patching cement is ideal for broken corners.

Pour water into center or add slowly with hose while mixing.

Dry ingredients are mixed first, then mounded to form a hollow in the center so water can be added gradually.

rough areas or shallow indentations in a pitted concrete floor or wall since they stick in thin layers, and furthermore, they permit feathering out the material around the edges without need for undercutting. These same qualities enable you to use vinyl patching cements for building up small broken corners on steps or walls, or filling in shallow crevices in concrete, brick, or stone.

For really large patches, such as replacing a broken or missing section in a concrete walk or patio, you'll need the gravel mix. Here again, you can buy cement-sand-and-gravel mixtures in bags of various sizes (available from lumberyards and building material dealers), so that all you have to do is add water without worrying about the proportions of dry ingredients to be mixed. However, since it's cheaper to prepare your own mixture for larger jobs, and since gravel mix is not always available in local stores here are the proportions to follow for general-purpose concrete when mixing your own: One part portland cement, two parts damp sand, and three parts gravel (these are parts by volume). Mix the ingredients thoroughly before adding water, then add enough water (approximately one-half by volume) to create a mixture that will tend to hold its shape when mounded up with a shovel or trowel yet will be moist enough to slide off a trowel when you tilt it at an angle. Be sure that it slides off, not flows off; if it flows the mixture is too wet or loose.

After first mixing the dry ingredients in a bucket or wheelbarrow, or on a flat square of plywood or hardboard, mound up the mixture and form a hollow in the center as shown here. Pour water into this hollow and gradually work the dry ingredients into the center from around the edges. Keep turning with a shovel or hoe until everything is uniformly damp or wet, then spread the material into the area being patched or filled. Be sure you poke repeatedly with the end of your shovel to push the mix into all crevices and to make certain there are no air pockets or bubbles. Spread it out to form a reasonably level surface, then let it set for 15 or 20 minutes, or until it starts to dry partially. If you want to get a slightly textured surface, suitable for walking on, smooth and level it by using a wood float (this looks like a regular plasterer's trowel except that it has a wood face instead of a metal face). A steel trowel can be used if you want an exceptionally smooth surface. Either way the idea is to get the surface level with as little troweling as possible. Excessive troweling tends to draw water and fine material to the surface and will weaken the final finish.

On any concrete patching job (except where vinyl patching cement was used) the best and strongest cure will result if the material is kept damp for at least 24 hours. This can best be accomplished by spreading burlap or straw over the surface, then sprinkling periodically with a fine spray from a hose.

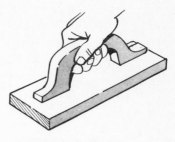

Wood float

REPAIRING BRICK AND MORTAR

One or two small cracks, or a small crumbling section of mortar in a brick wall or chimney may seem unimportant and not demanding of immediate attention. However, you should remember that this is a condition that will get worse if not attended to promptly. Repairs are actually quite simple to handle, so it would be silly to allow things to develop to the point where bricks start falling out and major repairs are required.

The procedure for repairing mortar joints—known as tuck pointing or repointing—calls for only a few basic hand tools and involves simple techniques which any do-it-yourselfer can master easily. Three steps are involved: First, scraping out the old defective mortar, or at least part of it; second, refilling the joint with fresh mortar; and third, "striking" or finishing-off the new mortar joint to match the finish or pattern of the other joints on that same wall.

Actually, the hardest part of the job is the first part—raking out the old mortar in the joints to a depth of at least ½ inch. You need to take out at least this much old mortar if you want to ensure a good bond for the fresh mortar that will be applied.

The usual method is to use a cold chisel and a hammer. Hold the chisel edgewise and use the corner of the blade to scrape out the old cement. Use the hammer only if needed, and then tap with frequent light blows while keeping the chisel moving along the length of the joint. Work carefully to avoid getting the chisel wedged between the bricks since this may split them, and don't try to remove mortar to the full depth all at once. It is a good idea to protect your eyes with goggles or safety glasses while working.

After the mortar in one section has been raked out (it's generally best to work an area of about 1 square yard at a time), use a stiff brush to clean all dust and loose material out of each joint. Then, before applying the new mortar, wet all bricks in that area by spraying with a hose or by splashing the water on with a large brush. (On very hot days you may have to do this several times before applying your mortar in order to make certain the bricks stay damp while working.)

Mortar can be purchased in dry, ready-mixed form, or you can mix your own. The ready-mixed variety is simpler and quicker to use, but if you need a lot it will cost more than starting from scratch. For those who want to mix their own (or if you have trouble locating a ready-blended mortar mix in local stores) there are two formulas you can follow. The simplest one involves using special mortar cement (also called plastic cement). With this you mix one part mortar cement with three parts of damp sand. If you can't get mortar cement, use ordinary portland cement, but here the formula calls for one part portland cement, one part hydrated lime, and four to six parts of sand.

If you are using the first formula, mix the dry ingredients thoroughly, then add water to achieve the proper working consistency—stiff enough to hold its shape when mounded up, yet plastic enough to be easily workable without sliding off the trowel when it is tilted.

If you are using the second formula which calls for hydrated lime, mix the lime with water first to form a loose putty and add this to the cement and water.

Regardless of which formula is used, the mortar should be thoroughly mixed for about five minutes to ensure a uniform wetting and blending of all ingredients. Then, after dampening the bricks again if necessary, pack the mortar firmly into each of the joints, using the tip of a small triangular pointing trowel. As a rule, it is best to fill the vertical joints in each section first, then do the horizontal joints.

To carry the mortar to the wall, professionals use a device called a "hawk," which basically is a 12-inch square sheet of metal with a wooden handle attached to the center on the underside. However, you can use a scrap piece of plywood or hardboard —make a handle for it by nailing a short length of broomstick to the center as shown here. In use, the hawk is held directly under the joint being worked on. Scoop some mortar off the hawk with the side of your trowel, then pack it into the joint with the tip. Excess mortar that falls off as you work is then caught by the hawk so that you can reuse it.

As soon as the mortar in all of the joints in one area starts to stiffen, the face of each joint should be tooled or finished to give it the same look as all the other joints in that same wall. The drawing here shows the most common joint finishes used in brick walls.

The flush joint is achieved by smoothing off the mortar with the back of your trowel; the concave joint by dragging a piece of curved pipe or tubing along each joint; the V-joint by using the point of your trowel held at a 45-degree angle to the face of the brick; the raked joint by dragging a piece of wood the thickness of the joint along the length of each joint; the weathered joint by using the side of the trowel while angling it downward; and the struck joint is achieved in the same way, except that the trowel is angled upward.

As you finish facing off the joints in each section, clean all excess mortar off the face of the brick before it dries, by scraping with your trowel or by

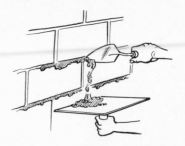

Using a pointing trowel, pack the mortar firmly into the joints.

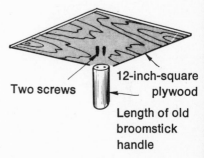

Two screws
12-inch-square plywood
Length of old broomstick handle

Constructing a homemade plasterer's hawk

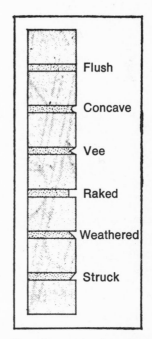

Flush

Concave

Vee

Raked

Weathered

Struck

Popular mortar joint styles

using a stiff brush dipped into water. On hot days it is best to keep the bricks and the new mortar joints damp for at least 12 hours by spraying periodically with a fine mist from your hose.

When a brick is cracked or split, the crack often is so fine that trying to pack mortar cement into the crevice usually is impractical. Nevertheless, if at all possible, this crack should be filled to keep moisture from entering and thus widening the crack and eventually making the condition worse. In many cases, the simplest way to fill very small cracks is to use caulking compound—preferably one of the silicone rubber or butyl rubber types (see page 181). However, for cracks that are more than $\frac{1}{16}$ inch wide, or for those that go through more than one brick, a more permanent repair is made by first chipping out the surface of the crack with the corner of a cold chisel or similar tool so as to make it at least $\frac{1}{4}$ inch wide. Then apply vinyl patching cement rather than a mortar cement (vinyl patching cements are described on pages 183-84).

One particularly annoying problem is when one or more bricks work loose on the corner of a stoop or wall, or along the edge of a brick-lined walk or terrace. Ordinary mortar cement must be at least $\frac{1}{2}$ inch thick to insure a good bond, and therefore the brick cannot be cemented back without first chipping out all of the old mortar—this is tricky to do without loosening more bricks or doing further damage. If the old mortar is still sound and adhering solidly, the simplest solution is to cement the one or two loose bricks back with epoxy adhesive. This bonds to brick or other masonry surfaces quite well, as long as the surface is clean and dry, and only a thin layer is required, so little or nothing will be added to the final height of the reinstalled brick. However, if the old mortar is crumbling, scrape out $\frac{1}{4}$ inch or more, then use vinyl patching cement to paste the loose bricks back in place.

DAMP BASEMENT PROBLEMS

Eliminating dampness in a basement can add considerably to the amount of living and storage space available in any house—and will add considerably to the home's resale value (few buyers will knowingly purchase a house which shows signs of dampness in the basement). Sometimes the corrective measures required will be simple, but in others a considerable amount of labor and expense may be involved.

There are several things that can cause dampness in a basement, but depending on the source of moisture, you will find that there are three principal sources: condensation, seepage, and active leakage.

The first problem, condensation, is not caused by outside moisture (that is, there is no problem with moisture coming through the walls or floor of the basement). Instead, it is caused by excessively humid air inside the basement. This excess humidity causes condensation to form on cold surfaces such as water pipes or the masonry walls themselves (these tend to stay cool because of the insulating effect of the ground on the outside). This condensation causes damp spots to form on the concrete, so that it is easy to think that moisture is actually seeping through from outside.

There is a simple way to test whether condensation is the problem. Fasten a small pocket mirror or a shiny piece of metal to the wall in the middle of a damp spot, using large strips of adhesive tape, or some type of mastic adhesive. Allow this to remain in place for 24 hours, then examine the surface. If drops of moisture form on the surface of the mirror, then the problem is condensation. However, if the surface remains dry, even though the area behind and around it is damp, then the problem is moisture that is seeping through the concrete from outside.

If condensation is the source of the moisture, the solution lies in ensuring adequate ventilation, either by opening windows more often or by installing an exhaust fan. In addition, a dehumidifier will help a great deal, and if there is a clothes dryer in the basement, make certain it is vented directly to the outside.

If the water is coming from either leakage or seepage through the concrete, the first step in correcting this is to try and eliminate as many sources of water as possible around the outside—at least close to the foundation walls.

The gutters and downspouts around the outside should not empty into the ground right next to your house. Paved areas or splash blocks under each leader pipe should carry rain water that comes down off the roof at least 4 or 5 feet away from the house foundation before allowing it to seep into the ground. Better yet, the downspout or leader should be connected to an underground pipe that leads to a storm sewer (where local codes permit) or to a dry well buried in the ground at least 10 feet away from the foundation. (A dry well is built something like a cesspool—cement blocks laid in a circular pattern to form a pit in which water can accumulate until it gradually seeps away through the bottom and sides. It can also be made by burying a large drum vertically with the top and bottom cut out, then filling the inside with large rocks before covering it.)

Another cause of water accumulating in the soil around the outside of the basement walls is poor grading of the ground around the house. Ideally, the ground should slope away from the house on all sides so that surface water drains off rapidly. If the house is on a slope and water tends to run down against it on one side, one solution is to dig a shallow, half-round ditch or trench on the high side, parallel to the house and at least 10 feet away. The ends of this ditch can then be sloped downward so that water is carried past the house on each side. For appearance and safety, the inside of this ditch can be planted with grass, or it can be filled with small stones and coarse gravel so that its surface is almost level with the surrounding soil.

After all precautions have been taken to keep outside water away from the foundation, you next turn your attention to the measures that can be taken to stop leaks in the basement walls. Seepage, the second cause of dampness, occurs when water works its way in slowly through fine cracks, small holes, or porous sections in the masonry. With this condition there will be occasional damp spots on the inside, but seldom will there be signs of water actively running in. The third condition, leakage, is when water runs in and the source is easily visible —usually a sizable crack or other defect in the masonry.

Either way, the first thing to do is to fill all cracks, holes, or other openings with hydraulic patching cement, or with one of the vinyl patching cements that will stick in fine cracks without need for cutting them out. (If water is still running or seeping, a hydraulic cement will be needed.) Both materials come in powder form that is mixed with water, but the hydraulic cement dries in just a few minutes (it should not be troweled, it is merely pressed into the opening) so only a little at a time can be mixed.

One place where water often enters is along the joint where the walls meet the concrete floor. That is because there is a natural joint here (floors and walls are poured separately) and also because hydrostatic pressure is greatest at the bottom of the wall. If this is the cause of the trouble, dampness will be first noticeable along this joint after a wet spell, though it may then spread along the wall, as well as out on the floor.

To seal this joint you can use one of two methods: First, the joint can be chipped out with a cold chisel to widen it, then the cavity filled with waterproof patching cement that is packed .in with a trowel. The second method is to use one of the various epoxy sealers that are sold for this purpose. These come in two parts (liquids) that are mixed together before use. They are liberally applied along the joint with a paint brush, carrying the sealer about 9 inches up on the wall and about 6 inches out on the floor. They also are ideal for coating fine cracks or porous areas elsewhere on the basement walls where water seems to seep through, but should be applied only when the surface is dry.

Unfortunately, one can never be sure that any of these methods of working from the inside will do the job—it depends on how porous the masonry is, and on how high the water table is in the ground around the outside (the amount of hydrostatic pressure present in the surrounding soil).

Sometimes an idea of whether interior measures will work can be obtained by speaking to others in your community, or by calling your local building-department or town engineer—he may know whether the underground water table is normally quite high. If so, chances are that interior measures will not hold back the water pressures encountered. However, if underground water levels are fairly normal and the trouble is caused primarily by porous masonry, there is a good chance that an interior waterproof coating or sealer will work. When in doubt, it sometimes pays to treat only one wall before going ahead with the entire basement.

Any attempt to seal out seepage by coating the walls on the inside will necessitate ensuring a firm bond between the sealer and the existing masonry. All loose, crumbling material should be removed with a wire brush, and in most cases all old paint or other coatings will have to be removed first. This can be done by calling a professional sandblasting contractor (if available locally) or by using a chemical paint remover (the water-wash, semipaste types work best on jobs of this kind). Some water-base paints can also be removed by mopping on a hot solution of trisodium phosphate (sold in all paint stores) and water, then scrubbing off with clean water.

The waterproofing paint or sealer is then applied according to the directions supplied by the manufacturer, after first filling all cracks and holes with vinyl patching cement—especially next to window openings and around pipes or conduits. The masonry coatings most widely sold for waterproofing basements are generally powdered, cement-base coatings that can be applied with a brush (or with a trowel in some cases, if mixed thick enough). Epoxy sealers, which work quite well in limited areas, such as floor-to-wall joints (see page 58), are also available; however, their high cost would make it impractical to use them on entire walls.

WATERPROOFING FROM THE OUTSIDE

Where conditions are severe, particularly if high water tables are a chronic problem, then interior treatment of the problem will seldom suffice. In this case waterproofing measures will have to be taken around the outside—and most of the accepted methods involve excavating around the outside to expose the foundation walls and the footing on which the foundation rests. Although expensive, and involving a great deal of labor, this may be the only sure cure and considering the amount of additional living and storage space gained, may well be worth the price.

Generally, a complete waterproofing job will then consist of two steps: application of a waterproof membrane to the outside of the foundation walls, and the installing of drain tile next to and along the footing.

The waterproof membrane can be applied to the outside of the exposed foundation walls (after first scrubbing and hosing to remove dirt and soil) by one of several methods, but the most common is to trowel on a layer of bituminous or asphalt cement, then cover this with a layer of heavy saturated building felt. Another layer of each is then applied on top of the first to complete the membrane.

To drain away the water that builds up in the soil, plastic drain tiles (actually lengths of perforated plastic pipe) at least 4 inches in diameter are then laid along the footing with individual lengths spaced about ¼ inch apart, and with strips of tar paper laid over each joint as illustrated. The

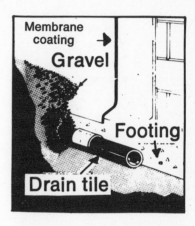

Laying drain tile along the footing

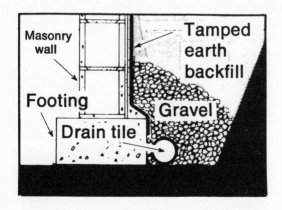

How outside of basement walls are waterproofed

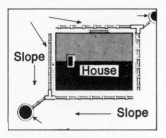

Drain tile   Dry well

Slope

House

Slope

Dry well

Drain tiles leading to dry wells are sometimes needed.

pipe should be level with the bottom of the footing (not below it) and should be pitched so that it slopes toward one corner of the house—about ½ inch for every 12 feet.

The end of this run of drain pipe should then extend past the corner of the house to empty into a dry well located at least 10 feet away from the foundation. Before replacing the soil, about 12 to 18 inches of gravel should be placed on top of this pipe to insure good drainage after the soil is replaced. When replacing the soil, extreme care should be used to prevent disturbing the drain pipe, and to avoid damaging the membrane coating applied to the walls.

Probably the most serious of all wet-basement problems is when water is forced up through the basement floor, causing possible buckling and cracking of the slab. For situations of this kind (indicating a combination of poor construction coupled with a high hydrostatic pressure) it may be necessary to dig a pit in the basement floor and then install a sump pump to carry water away to an outside drain or dry well.

Sump pumps are also used to solve other damp basement problems. They pump away water that accumulates on the floor, rather than trying to stop it at its source (or to avoid the expense of digging up around the outside when work inside had failed to improve the condition).

Another way to solve the problem of water seeping up from below—when the seepage occurs principally along the edges, next to the walls—is to chop out a trench around the inside next to the footing, then lay drain tile under the floor on the inside. This is installed as described above, then the trench refilled and cemented over.

Chapter eleven

OUTSIDE REPAIRS

Unfortunately, many homeowners pay little or no attention to the outside of their house until something goes wrong—a leak develops, paint starts peeling in large sheets, shingles start falling off the roof, or wood siding cracks and starts to rot.

One way to ward off headaches of this kind is to establish a program of regular preventive maintenance. Get in the habit of taking a slow walk around the outside of your house at least twice a year and use a ladder to check the gutters, roof shingles, and other parts not readily visible from the ground. In this way you will be able to spot minor defects before they turn into major "catastrophes" and with a few simple repairs ward off the possibility of more expensive jobs later on.

REPAIRING CLAPBOARD

When exterior clapboard wood siding splits, prompt repairs are advisable to keep water from entering and working its way in behind the wood (a frequent cause of paint peeling and a situation that can cause rotting of the wood itself). In many cases a simple repair can be made by slightly prying the cracked part open with two or three chisels or screwdrivers spaced along the length of the crack, then working glue into this crevice with a spatula or knife blade. When the entire length of the crack has been coated with glue on the inside, remove the tools that held it wedged apart, then force the crack closed by pressing up on the bottom of the board. To hold it closed, several nails are then driven in at an upward angle. Be sure you use rustproof aluminum or galvanized nails, and after countersinking these, fill the remaining holes with putty or wood plastic.

When a board is badly cracked in various places, or partially rotted so that a simple repair of this kind will not do the trick, the only solution is to cut the rotted or badly cracked section out altogether and replace it with a new piece of matching siding. Because overlapping clapboards are held in place with nails along the top edge as well as along the bottom edge (the nails along the top edge of the board actually go through the bottom edge of the one immediately above it first), you cannot pry off the old board without destroying the board above it. The usual way to remove a section is to first drive a wedge under the damaged board as shown, then slide a hacksaw blade up under this to cut off the nails that hold the damaged section in place. The end of this blade can be wrapped with tape to provide a safe grip. Then use a saw (a backsaw works best for this) to make two vertical cuts in the damaged board, one on each side of the damaged area.

After the old cracked or rotted section has been cut out and removed, a new piece of matching

Removing a badly rotted or cracked section of siding

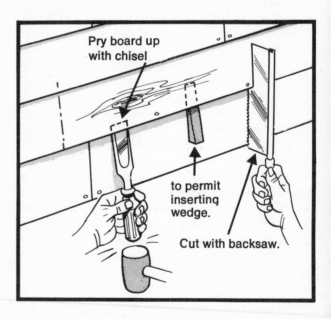

clapboard is cut for a snug fit into the opening that remains. Although not essential, it's a good idea to give this piece of wood, including the two edges, a prime coat of paint before installing it. Slide this piece up under the board above it so that its bottom edge exactly lines up with the edges of the boards on each side, then drive nails, starting along the bottom edge. Finish by driving nails along the top (the top nails will go through the board above first, just as it was in the original installation). To keep water from entering, apply caulking compound to the joints on each side where the new piece joins the old piece. Finally, apply two coats of outdoor paint to match the rest of the siding.

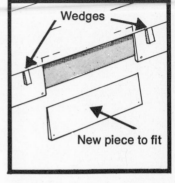

Wedges are used to pry out siding so new piece can be slid in from underneath.

REPLACING DAMAGED SHINGLES

The basic technique for replacing a split, cracked, or missing shingle is the same as that used in replacing a damaged section of clapboard, except that it is considerably simpler since you don't have to cut out the damaged section. In the case of an asbestos shingle (which is quite brittle), the simplest method is to smash what's left of the shingle with a hammer, then pull out the nails that were holding it in place. If any of the nails cannot be reached, slide a hacksaw blade underneath and cut the nails off behind the shingle. One word of caution: be careful when removing the shingle to avoid damaging those immediately above, below, or alongside it—the shingles overlap, and too heavy a blow will result in damaging more than just the one shingle you aim at.

A hacksaw blade is used to cut nails off from underneath a damaged shingle.

Wood shingles that need replacing can be removed in the same way. You can split the old pieces out with a chisel and hammer, or you can cut the nails off from underneath, then simply pull out the pieces that are left.

Regardless of the type of shingle, once the damaged one has been removed and the old nails pulled out or cut off, you make the needed repairs by sliding a new shingle in from below, then renailing it along the top and bottom as described for clapboard (page 195).

ROOF REPAIRS

Even if a roof shows no signs of a leak, it's still a good idea to inspect it at least once a year so that you can make minor repairs as soon as defects are noticed, rather than waiting until major (and expensive) breakdowns occur later on.

A simple visual inspection from up close will often disclose a damaged or missing shingle, a piece of flashing that is loose or rusted, or an open joint where roof cement is needed around a vent pipe or similar joint to keep water from entering. Wherever possible, carry out this inspection by climbing up on the roof, although you may be able to inspect some sections by standing near the top of a tall ladder resting against the eaves, or by poking your head out of a dormer or attic window.

To avoid accidents and help ensure a safe footing when inspecting your roof, climb up on a dry day when there is little or no wind, and when the temperature is cool enough so that the shingles will not be damaged by walking on them (most types get soft in hot weather, and very brittle in cold). You'll need a ladder tall enough to reach up past the eaves or gutters by at least 2 feet. Make certain you wear sneakers or soft, rubber-soled shoes while climbing. It is a good idea to have someone stand near the foot of the ladder and hold it to prevent slipping, especially when you step off the ladder to walk on the roof itself.

If you are looking for a specific leak because you have seen water stains or drips on the inside, bear in mind that the leak may not be directly over the spot where you noticed it on the inside. Water sometimes can work its way in at one point, then travel for a considerable distance along a sloping or horizontal beam before it finally drips through and stains the plaster on the inside.

If the attic is unfinished, the job of finding the leak is, of course, much simpler. By shining a bright light at the underside of the roof during a rain storm you may actually be able to trace the path of the water back to where it enters. However, if the attic is finished or if the leak cannot be traced on the inside, then your only choice is to start looking at all possible points where the water could enter above the wet spot, and at some distance to each side of it.

One of the first places that should be checked is the flashing around vent pipes, chimneys, and dormers, as well as along roof valleys and other places where the roofing material meets metal, wood, or masonry. Look for loose or open seams where the flashing material is cracked or rusted, or where the black asphalt roof cement has dried out and split, then smear a thick layer of new roof cement over these areas with a small trowel to seal all the openings. Small areas of metal flashing in roof valleys or next to dormers that have rusted or cracked often can be patched in this manner, but if there are many such rotted or rusted areas, you should call in a professional roofer to see about replacing the flashing entirely.

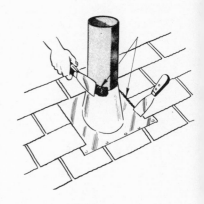

Roof cement seals open joints and cracks in the flashing around vent pipes.

ASPHALT SHINGLES

On asphalt-shingle roofs (which are by far the most common type), start by first examining all of the shingles to see if any are missing or curled upwards by the wind, or if any are cracked and split. Often, a curled shingle can be fastened back down by smearing a little asphalt roofing cement under the raised edge, then pressing it back. Nailing seldom is required, but if the shingle won't stay down, use a galvanized roofing nail (these have large heads to hold the shingle down) and cover the head with a liberal dab of roofing cement in order to prevent water seeping down through the nail hole.

If one or two shingles are missing entirely, or if they are badly cracked or split, a permanent repair can be made by sliding a sheet of aluminum or copper under the damaged shingle. Most hardware stores and lumberyards carry aluminum flashing material which they sell by the foot so all you have to do is cut it to the size needed. Before sliding the metal into place, spread a layer of roofing cement underneath, then press the metal down on top of this to bed it firmly. One or two roofing nails can then be driven into the metal to hold it

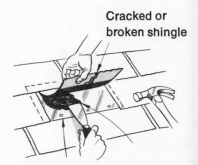

Cracked or broken shingle

More roof cement is spread over metal sheet after it is nailed down over layer of cement.

Repairing a damaged shingle with a sheet of metal

permanently, after which the nail heads should be covered with cement to prevent possible leaks later on.

When checking the shingles don't forget to check the ones that are folded along the ridge of the roof at the very top. Shingles missing along here can be replaced with pieces of heavyweight roofing felt or flashing material made of the same asphalt composition as the shingles (you can buy this, too, in lumberyards and from building material dealers). Apply roof cement over the damaged area, then cut a piece to fit and nail down on top. Finish by dabbing cement over the exposed nail heads.

ROOFS

Flat or shed-type roofs which have only a slight slope normally are covered with roll roofing instead of shingles, and are, of course, simpler to inspect and walk on since there is no steep slope to create a hazard.

Small cracks and minor defects can normally be repaired by simply troweling on a thick layer of asphalt roofing cement, spreading the material on with a small trowel after first brushing off loose dirt and foreign material. However, if the damaged area is more than a few inches across, then the section will have to be cut out and a patch applied. Use a sharp utility knife and a metal straight edge or square as a guide to cut out a rectangular section from the top layer only (roll roofing is usually applied in several layers), then pry the damaged piece off and cut a new square of heavyweight roofing felt to fit in the recess that is left.

Coat this recess with a liberal application of roofing cement, then nail the new patch into the recess as indicated, spacing nails no more than 2 to 3 inches apart around the perimeter. Next, cut another patch that is at least 4 to 6 inches larger than the original one and nail this down on top so that the second piece overlaps the first one on all sides. Be sure you apply cement under this before nailing it down, then apply additional cement over

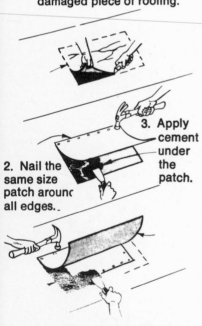

1. Cut out the damaged piece of roofing.

2. Nail the same size patch around all edges.

3. Apply cement under the patch.

4. Spread cement over the first patch and overlap.

Patching a flat roof

all the nail heads as well as around the edges of this top layer as shown above.

A problem that frequently develops on flat roofs is the formation of blisters which create a pocket where water can accumulate, particularly if the blistered section develops cracks. If the blister is not too large, the simplest solution is to slice through the middle of it with a sharp knife, cutting the top layer only. Then use a putty knife or small trowel to force roofing cement under each side of the cut and drive nails along each side to hold the blistered area down. Finish by troweling on a liberal layer of fresh cement before nailing down. Additional compound is then troweled on over the edges of this patch, making certain that all nail heads, as well as the edges of the patch, are thoroughly covered.

To keep it from drying out, and to preserve the roll roofing for a few years longer after hairline cracks and dried-out spots have developed, it's a good idea to paint on an asphalt-base roof coating every two or three years. The regular black asphalt coating is the least expensive, but a type known as aluminum-asphalt will do a much better job and will also help to reflect away the sun's heat (and thus lower air-conditioning costs) in the summer.

GUTTERS AND DOWNSPOUTS

The gutters around the eaves on the outside of your house are designed to carry rain water (and melted snow), as it flows down off the roof, safely away from the house. Thus, they help to avoid dirt streaks and stains that would otherwise develop on siding, stucco, or shingles, while at the same time minimizing the likelihood of water from the roof seeping in through cracks or open joints. In addition, the water will be carried away from the house foundation where it might otherwise cause flooding of the basement or washouts of flower beds, grass, and shrubbery located near the walls of the house.

However, gutters will only do their job properly if they are in good "operating" condition—that is, if they are unobstructed by leaves or other debris, if they have not developed cracks, leaks, and other defects that will keep them from carrying the water away as fast as it accumulates, and if they are pitched properly toward the downspouts or drainage openings so that they drain quickly and efficiently.

In areas where tall trees grow—especially if they grow near the house—the most frequent problem is clogging of the gutter by accumulated leaves and other debris. To prevent buildups of this kind you should check the inside of your gutters at least once or twice a year and clean them out before enough debris accumulates to create an obstruction. Use an old scrub brush or small whisk broom to sweep the debris into small piles, then scoop it out with a gardener's hand trowel or small hand spade. Under no circumstances should you sweep leaves or other material down into the downspouts or vertical leader pipes.

If leaves are a frequent problem, you can provide permanent protection against clogging in one of two ways—either by inserting small plastic or wire cages over each downspout opening, or by covering the entire gutter with a plastic or wire mesh that is sold in strips for just this purpose. The wire cage won't keep leaves out of the gutter, but it will keep them from being washed down into the downspout where they can cause clogging of the vertical drain pipe. Insert the cage by pushing its open end into the downspout opening as shown. Remember, however, that leaves can get so tightly packed around the cage as to prevent drainage and still cause the gutter to fill up and overflow. So even though you have a wire cage, regular inspection and cleaning are required.

The precut strips of plastic or wire mesh that cover the entire length of the gutter will do a much better job of protecting the gutters since they prevent leaves from falling in altogether. The leaves stay on top of the screen until they dry up and are blown off by the wind, or until they get washed off by cascading water coming down off the roof (the mesh slopes slightly outward away from the roof). Some of these mesh gutter protectors come with clips that snap on over the outside rim of the gutter while the other edge slips under the bottom row of roof shingles; others spring or snap into place between the upper rims of the gutter.

When gutters do not drain efficiently even though there is no clogging, chances are that they do not slope or pitch properly to ensure efficient drainage. A gutter should slope toward the downspout with a pitch that is equal to about ½ inch for every 8 feet of length (bear in mind that very long gutters may slope both ways toward a downspout at each end with the highest point being in the middle). You can check for proper slope and drainage by using a long carpenter's spirit level or by directing a hose onto the roof and observing how the gutter drains.

With wood gutters there is little or nothing you can do to correct improper slope since these are nailed to fascia boards so that repitching or resloping them would be a major carpentry job. As a rule, it is simpler to remove them completely and replace them with new metal or vinyl gutters. With metal gutters the supporting straps or hangers can get bent or pull loose, allowing the gutter to sag out of alignment. As a rule, this is not difficult to correct. Sometimes you merely have to bend one or two supporting straps, or renail one that has pulled loose from the roof edge. In other cases it may be necessary to install additional straps or hangers to replace one or two that are missing, or to provide

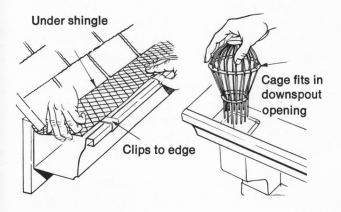

Under shingle

Clips to edge

Cage fits in downspout opening

Two methods of protecting against leaves clogging the drainpipe. The mesh strip covers the entire gutter.

Hanger strap is nailed to the roof.

Strap-type gutter support is nailed under roof shingle.

Strap clips to gutter and hanger bracket.

Hanger is nailed to facing.

This type of gutter support clips to special bracket.

additional support where the gutter dips or sags. If the gutter is supported by mounting straps which are nailed to the roof, it may be possible to renail the original straps slightly higher up where the gutter sags. If the gutter is supported by spike mounts, your best bet is to put a new one in at the low point, a few inches away from the old one after drilling a hole the proper size through the outside rim of your gutter.

Repairing gutters that have open seams, cracks, splits or rusted-out sections is important in order to prevent the condition from worsening and to contain water inside the gutter, where it belongs.

Wood gutters should be protected against rotting, cracking, and checking by having their insides coated with a waterproof sealer every year or two. Special sealers are sold for this purpose in some paint and hardware stores, or you can use ordinary roofing cement thinned with about 20 percent thinner to make brushing easier. Corner joints or seams that are open should be sealed by filling with caulking compound, preferably one of the butyl rubber or silicone rubber compounds since these stay flexible longer and will bond better than conventional caulking (see page 214 for more information about caulking).

Both of these caulking materials can also be used to seal leaky joints or seams in metal gutters. For a good bond, remember always to clean the metal surfaces thoroughly and make sure they are perfectly dry before the compound is applied.

Splits that are too big to fill with caulking in either wood or metal gutters, and rusted-out sections in metal gutters, can be repaired by using one of the special fiberglass patching kits which are put out by several companies (if you can't find them in your local hardware store, similar kits are sold in auto accessory stores for patching car bodies, and in marine stores for patching boats). When used acording to directions, these make a truly permanent repair.

Instead of one of these patching kits, you can also make a fairly long-lasting repair by using heavy-duty aluminum foil and ordinary asphalt cement. After cleaning the surface of the metal or wood thoroughly, smear a liberal coat of roofing cement over the crack or rotted section and extend it for several inches on each side. Then cut a piece of aluminum foil large enough to cover this and press it down on top of the cement. Next, smear another layer of roofing cement over the whole patch, carrying this past the foil by another inch or two. Now cut another piece of foil slightly larger than the first one and press this down on top, then finish by applying a final layer of cement over the whole area, covering all edges of the patch and feathering it out neatly on all sides so that no ridges or bumps are left.

If your gutters do not drain properly because the leaders or vertical downspouts are clogged by leaves or other debris, you may be able to unclog the vertical pipe by directing a strong stream of water down from the top to flush out the clog. Better yet, if the bottom end is accessible, work from the bottom, shooting the hose upward and pushing it up into the pipe as far as you can. If the bottom end goes underground and empties into a dry well or sewer, then you'll have to use a long plumber's "snake" to fish out the obstruction by forcing it down from the top while twisting slowly. Power-driven snakes may be required for very long runs. These are sold in many hardware stores, or you can rent them from a tool rental agency.

The vertical drain pipe that carries the water downward should always be fastened against the house wall with metal straps to keep it from sagging and to keep the upper end snug against the elbow that connects it to the gutter. If the straps pull loose, or if there are not enough of them, the downspout will pull away from the bottom of the gutter so that water comes pouring down from overhead instead of flowing down through the pipe. When this happens the pipe can be realigned in proper position and then fastened in place against the house wall with as many new straps as are necessary to support it. You can buy straps in practically all hardware stores and lumberyards. Be sure, however, that the straps you buy are made

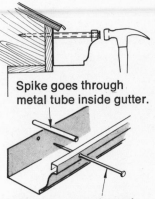

Spike goes through metal tube inside gutter.

Long spike goes through tube and into fascia board.

Spike-mounts can be added to support the gutter at low point.

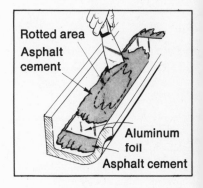

Rotted area
Asphalt cement
Aluminum foil
Asphalt cement

Wood gutters can be patched with aluminum foil and asphalt cement.

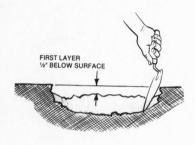

FIRST LAYER
½" BELOW SURFACE

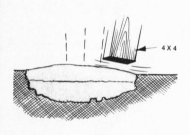

4 X 4

Patching holes in blacktop
driveways

of the same kind of metal as the leader pipe to avoid possible electrolytic or corrosive action that occurs when dissimilar metals are brought in contact with each other.

PATCHING BLACKTOP DRIVEWAYS

Blacktop driveways or walks, which are popular in many areas, require more maintenance than concrete. Fortunately, most repairs are quite simple for the do-it-yourselfer to handle.

Large cracks, holes, and broken sections are filled and patched most easily with a cold-mix asphalt material (available in paper bags in some hardware stores and from most lumberyards or building material dealers). This blacktop patching compound has fine gravel already mixed in and is ready to use as it comes. It generally is easier to work with during warm weather, but if you have to make repairs during cold weather it's best to warm the sack of patching material first by keeping it indoors overnight, preferably next to a radiator or furnace (place a sheet of plastic or several layers of newspaper under the bag to keep any asphalt that may seep through the paper bag from staining your floor).

Before applying this patching mixture, the hole or cavity being filled should be cleaned out by removing all loose crumbling edges on the old blacktop, and by cleaning out dirt and other foreign material. If the hole is more than about 3 inches deep, fill the bottom of the depression with small stones or coarse gravel until there are only about 3 inches left to fill. Using the end of a 2 x 4 or 4 x 4, tamp this gravel or rock down firmly to provide a solid foundation, then fill the hole to within about 1 inch of the top with the patching material. Using your shovel or a small spade, chop through the mix with a slicing motion to eliminate air pockets and break up lumps, then tamp down firmly again with the end of a 4 x 4. Make certain the mix is pressed firmly against the sides of the hole, as well as against the bottom.

When you've tamped this down as hard as you can, complete the patch by adding enough additional mix to bring the level up about ½ inch above that of the surrounding driveway. Now force this down as hard as you can by pounding with the end of the 4 x 4 until you force the compound down to make it flush with the rest of the surface. Instead of tamping with a 4 x 4 you can flatten the patch by driving your automobile back and forth with one wheel over the area (to keep the compound from sticking to the tire lay a sheet of plastic over the patched area first).

To help protect blacktop driveways against the ravages of sun, water, and subfreezing temperatures (which tend to break them up more rapidly), special blacktop sealers which you can easily apply yourself are available. Sold in many paint and hardware stores, as well as through most building supply dealers, these sealers generally come ready-mixed in 5-gallon cans. This quantity will cover slightly more than 200 square feet when brushed on with a large push broom (the quickest method of application). They are heavy-bodied coal-tar pitch or neoprene-base emulsions which require no heating or mixing, and which contain no flammable solvents (the most popular types are water emulsions which dry within hours and which permit easy clean-up of tools or hands by washing with water).

Before applying one of these sealers, the driveway should be swept clean of all dirt and debris and all holes, cracks, or other defects should be patched. Large cracks or holes should be patched with cold-mix as described above, but fine cracks and breaks can be patched by using the same sealer mixed with fine sand. Mix to a mudlike consistency, then work the material into the crack with the point of a small garden trowel or bricklayer's pointing trowel. Use enough to bring the patch up to the level of the rest of the driveway and allow this to dry for about 24 hours. Then proceed with the application of the sealer.

As a rule, the easiest way to apply these sealers is to pour a puddle directly onto the surface, then spread it around with a push broom, working so that total coverage will be within the rate recommended by the manufacturer. Spreading it too thin is poor economy—you will greatly shorten the life of the coating. It may help to measure out 10-foot squares (100 square feet), then cover one square at a time to insure proper coverage. Depending on the brand selected, as well as on the condition of the driveway, two coats may be required, but be sure you allow adequate drying time between coats.

REPAIRING FENCES

Like many other home maintenance projects, minor breakdowns in a fence around the outside of your house should be attended to promptly in order to ward off the need for major alterations or replacement of an entire section. Usually the first sign of trouble occurs when posts set in the ground work loose, allowing part of the fence to wobble or sag.

Posts that have been set in concrete seldom, if ever, work loose, unless the part that is underground starts to rot due to trapped moisture which causes decaying of the underground portion. This seldom happens if a rot-resistant wood, properly treated with preservative, was used, and if the concrete was deep enough to go down below the frost line. In addition, the bottom of the hole should never be filled with concrete since this will serve only to hold moisture. As indicated in the drawing, the posts should go clear through the concrete and should rest on a pile of stones or a bed of gravel at the bottom of the hole to ensure adequate drainage.

When posts that have not been set in concrete work loose, one of two simple methods can be used to firm them up: either pour concrete around the base of the post after digging the soil away down to the frost line; or reinforce the post by hammering 2 x 4 braces on each side of it and then fasten these to the post with bolts or long screws.

Pouring concrete around a loose or wobbly post

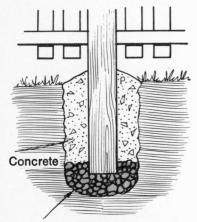

Concrete

Post rests on gravel at the bottom of the hole.

Fence post set in concrete

will provide the most permanent cure, but this requires more work and will only be effective if the post is not rotted or cracked. For best results, if possible, the post should be completely removed to facilitate digging and proper resetting, although the job can be done without removing the post by using a narrow shovel or post-hole digger and possibly a small hand spade.

In either case, the concrete should go down below the frostline to avoid heaving in freezing weather, but as indicated above, the bottom of the post should rest on gravel or stones to ensure rapid drainage.

After the hole has been dug and the post temporarily braced or wedged to make it stand absolutely vertical in both directions, 1 or 2 inches of gravel are placed in the bottom of the hole under the base of the post, after which the concrete is mixed and poured in (see page 182 for directions for mixing the concrete). A length of 2 x 4 should be used to tamp the concrete firmly into the hole and around the post to eliminate air bubbles. After this the concrete is troweled off at the surface so that it slopes away from the post on all four sides (this helps facilitate drainage).

Where posts have rotted or cracked at or below ground level, the simplest solution—short of replacing the entire post—is to reinforce it with extra 2 x 4's driven down close alongside the original 4 x 4 posts as shown. To facilitate hammering these 2 x 4's into the ground the bottom end should be beveled or cut as shown. The 2 x 4's should be driven down to almost the base of the original post and should protrude up at least 18 inches above ground to provide enough room for inserting two bolts or long screws as shown. The 2 x 4's should be hammered in snug against the post on each side, after which holes are bored for the bolts or screws. These should be galvanized to prevent rusting. For maximum protection against rotting and attack by insects, each 2 x 4 should be treated with a wood preservative such as one containing phentachloraphenol.

When a horizontal rail in a fence cracks or rots

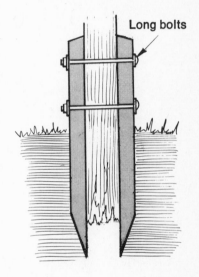

Long bolts

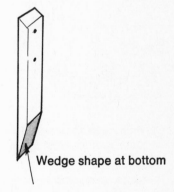

Wedge shape at bottom

Posts that have rotted or cracked below ground level can be repaired with 2 x 4 braces.

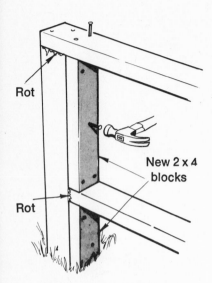

Rot

New 2 x 4
blocks

Rot

Rotting horizontal rails can be reinforced with 2 x 4 blocks.

out (usually near the end where it nails against a vertical post), the best solution is to replace that length of railing entirely. Since this may involve removing a great many pickets it's sometimes easier to reinforce the old rail by screwing a new length of 2 x 4 directly on top of the old one, making the new piece long enough to extend at least 18 to 24 inches beyond the rotted or cracked section on each side. If the rail has pulled loose from the post due to rotting in its last few inches, you can refasten it by nailing an extra block of 2 x 4 to the post directly under the end of the railing as shown here. Here again, remember to use only rustproof nails or screws as fasteners.

The gate and the end post against which it closes are the parts of a fence most susceptible to damage —children tend to climb on them and adults lean on them. To brace a hinged gate that has sagged so that it no longer is square and won't close completely, the simplest solution is to install a diagonal length of galvanized wire or chain with a turnbuckle as illustrated. When a gate sags, it's usually the outer (unhinged) end that tends to drop, so run your wire brace from the outside bottom edge to the top of the hinged edge.

To brace a wobbly end post or gate post, install a wood or metal brace from the top of the post down to the ground at a 45-degree angle as shown in the drawing. This brace is fastened to the post with screws or nails and secured to the ground by driving a stake in at a sharp angle as shown, then nailing the brace to the side of this stake. If located alongside a walk or path which goes through the gate (usually at right angles to the gate) the brace will usually be out of the way, especially if it is located on the inside next to the shrubbery or border planting where people normally don't walk.

FIGHTING TERMITES

Although ants and termites do look somewhat alike at first glance, they are actually quite different in appearance when closely examined. Termites have

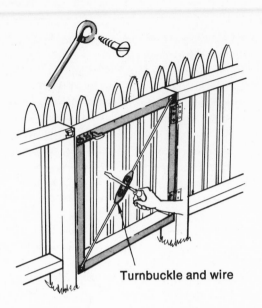

Turnbuckle and wire

A sagging hinged gate can be easily braced.

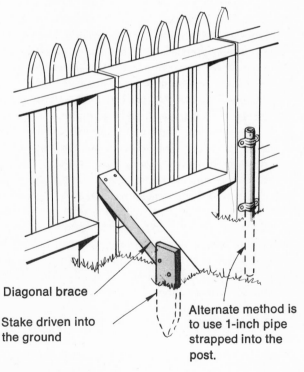

Diagonal brace

Stake driven into the ground

Alternate method is to use 1-inch pipe strapped into the post.

Two methods of bracing wobbly gate posts

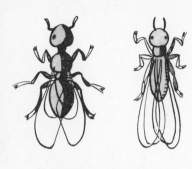

Termites (right) can be distinguished from flying ants (left) by their wings of equal length and oblong rather than hourglass bodies.

oblong bodies that are approximately of equal thickness throughout, while ants have hourglass shapes with sectioned bodies that are joined in the center by a thin wiry stem. Also, although winged ants (the kind most often confused with termites) have four wings like termites, the two back wings are shorter than the two forward ones—in termites all wings are approximately of equal length.

Termites eat cellulose which is found in buried wood, dead tree roots, and wood structural members such as fence posts, house beams, and lumber that is left lying on the ground. They will never willingly expose themselves to light and air and live in nests which usually are located in the ground around the outside of the house. They eat wood by tunneling through the wood fibers without ever breaking through to the surface, which is why their insidious work often goes unnoticed for many years. When they must travel across a surface that they cannot tunnel through in order to get to their source of food (such as metal or concrete), they will build mud tunnels or tubes along the outside of the surface to protect themselves from the drying effects of open air (they can only live in a moist environment). Where the concrete is cracked, they will build tunnels inside the cracks which are scarcely visible. Tunnels on the outside are much easier to spot, although both look like mud tubes.

Termite colonies send workers out to bring food back on a continuous basis, but these workers must return to the soil at least once every 24 hours in order to replenish their need for moisture. Once cut off from the ground, they will soon die.

Only once during its life does a termite actually leave its enclosure of tubes, tunnels, and colonies to expose itself to daylight—this is in the spring when the reproductive members sprout wings and fly out in swarms to look for a location where they can establish a new colony. During this period they will fly out in the open air on mating flights and will swarm for a few hours on a warm day until a new location is found. They then shed their wings and burrow in permanently to establish a new

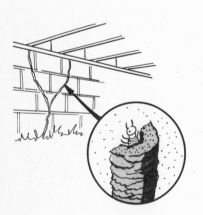

Termites will build mud tubes over surfaces they cannot tunnel through.

colony. The only evidence you will find that they are there—and frequently the first indication that termites are present—is an accumulation of discarded wings near the entrance to this new nest.

Termites can sense cellulose many feet away and will sometimes go to ingenious lengths to reach these sources of food. Not only will they build tunnels along the side of a concrete wall, they will also build mud tunnels along a length of metal pipe and even up along steel girders, in order to reach the wood which is at the other end. Once present in the ground around or under the house, the only way to get rid of termites is to poison the soil with chloradane or similar insecticide. As the termites cross this chemical barrier on their way to and from their nest they will carry the poison back to the colony where it will kill all of the other insects.

Chloradane is a highly poisonous chemical that can be harmful to humans and animals, as well as termites, so it must be used with extreme caution. It either is injected into the soil with a pressurized pumping device that forces it several feet underground, or it is poured into the soil after a trench is dug around the foundation and then mixed in with the fill as the soil is replaced. Unfortunately, simply saturating the soil around the perimeter of the house is not always enough to do a complete job—in most homes it is also necessary to pump chemicals in through holes bored through the concrete in all adjoining slabs (garages, patios, walks next to the house, etc.), as well as through holes bored in basement and crawl space floors.

Because this complete treatment often requires a lot of specialized equipment which the average homeowner does not have, and because it also involves working with poisonous chemicals which can be harmful if improperly handled, a real termite-proofing job is one which calls for the services of a licensed exterminator who will know where and how the poisonous chemical must be used. In addition, most reputable exterminators will provide an insurance-backed bond that will guarantee against recurrence of termites, although this may involve a nominal service charge for reinspecting the premises each year.

Although you can watch for signs of termite damage yourself by periodically inspecting all lumber and structural members near the ground, and by watching for mud tunnels on concrete foundation walls, if termite infestation is suspected your best procedure is to call an exterminator in to examine the premises. Most reliable firms will not charge for an inspection of this kind so you'll only run into an expense if termites are actually found (the inspector should be able to show you evidence that will prove termite activity conclusively).

APPLYING CAULKING COMPOUNDS

Every house, regardless of size and style, and regardless of what materials were used in building it, needs the protection afforded by careful application of a good-quality caulking compound to seal the seams, cracks, and open joints that are inevitable around the exterior.

Most houses use a variety of materials on the outside, and in most cases individual pieces or parts are cut to fit and assembled on the site. Since these materials expand and contract with changes in temperature, it is impossible to create a watertight fit without using some kind of semiflexible caulking compound to fill in the crevices.

Not only is caulking compound required around all window frames, door frames, and similar openings, it should also be used to seal every other joint where two different types of materials meet (wood and brick, metal and concrete, etc.), as well as to seal inside and outside corners where siding boards are joined, seams where chimneys meet roof shingles or walls, or where stoops, porches or other "add-on" structures join the house walls.

Caulking should also be applied to the joint where posts rest on wood floors or concrete slabs (porch posts, carport posts, and similar structures), as well as wherever a pipe, wire, or utility conduit of any kind goes through the house wall. This includes television antenna wires, vent pipes, electrical conduits and similar installations that call for drilling a hole in the side or roof of the house.

Caulking compounds are thick mastic materials that are designed to remain partly flexible and never harden entirely. They are available in several different formulations, the oldest type being oil-base caulking. It adheres well to most porous structural materials and can be painted over immediately with an oil paint, but it is not as durable as some of the newer types.

If the caulking compound will be painted over with a latex (water-thinned) exterior paint, then you are better off using one of the newer latex-base caulking compounds. These are more compatible with latex paint (oil-base caulking will tend to "burn through" a latex paint). You can paint over a latex caulking almost immediately, and it permits you to clean up your hands and tools by washing with running water. A third type of caulking, which was first widely used on commercial and industrial buildings, is butyl-rubber caulking. It costs more than the first two mentioned, but it will also last much longer under extreme temperatures. In addition, it will bond to metal, steel, and glass, as well as masonry (which is why it is used on large buildings where recaulking is quite expensive). Butyl rubber will remain flexible many years longer than oil or latex. However, most of these caulking compounds cannot be painted over immediately—a curing period of anywhere from several days to a week may be required before paint can be applied over them.

The most recent addition to the field is silicone-rubber caulking. This type will bond to almost anything and dries to a permanently flexible, rubbery consistency. However, some of these cannot be painted over at all, so make certain you buy one that can take paint if you will have to apply paint over it later on. The silicone-rubber caulkings cost much more than the other caulking materials, so they may be impractical for an entire house, but

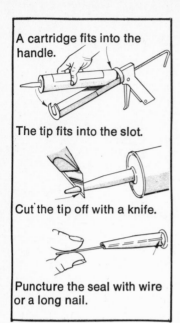

A cartridge fits into the handle.

The tip fits into the slot.

Cut the tip off with a knife.

Puncture the seal with wire or a long nail.

Half-barrel caulking gun uses cartridges with plastic tips.

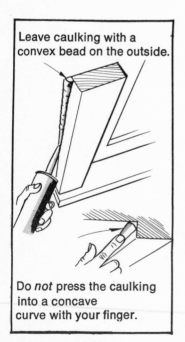

Leave caulking with a convex bead on the outside.

Do *not* press the caulking into a concave curve with your finger.

Applying caulking

they are excellent for difficult jobs such as sealing metal gutter seams, caulking around pipes that go through masonry, closing openings around air conditioners, and creating a watertight seal around electrical fixtures on the outside.

Although some caulking materials are still available in bulk, most homeowners buy them in disposable cartridges which fit into a standard half-barrel or drop-in caulking gun. These cartridges (usually made of plastic-coated cardboard) have a plastic tip or nozzle that is tapered so that you can control the size of the opening (and thus the size "bead" that will be applied) by how far back from the tip you cut the end off (the tip is closed or sealed when you buy it). The caulking gun has a trigger-actuated plunger that fits against the back of the cartridge so that as the trigger is squeezed it builds up a pressure on the inside which forces compound out through the tip.

As a general rule, you'll find you can do a neater job if you cut the nozzle tip off at an angle rather than straight across. Hold the gun so that the tip is at about a 45-degree angle to the surface, then squeeze the trigger with a steady, slow pressure while keeping the tip moving along at a uniform pace. When first starting a cartridge you'll find it necessary to run a piece of heavy wire or a long nail down through the tip to puncture the cellophane seal on the outside.

It takes a little practice to get a neat bead, but if you will remember to keep the gun moving while squeezing the trigger slowly and steadily at the same time, you'll soon learn to dispense the material in a neat, smooth ribbon of uniform thickness. Contrary to popular opinion, caulking should form a *convex* curve on the outside rather than a *concave* surface. In other words, don't smooth the caulking down with your fingertip. Instead, allow the caulking to bulge outward slightly since this is less likely to cause the material to crack when it contracts in cold weather.

When you've finished running the length of a joint with the caulking compound, pressure that has built up inside the gun will keep the material oozing out even though you've stopped pressing on the trigger. To stop this flow of compound, rotate the plunger handle so as to disengage the ratchet, then pull back slightly on the handle to relieve pressure on the inside of the cartridge.

Chapter twelve

HEATING AND AIR CONDITIONING

Although automatic furnaces and modern heating systems are surprisingly trouble-free, they do require occasional adjustment of the various controls that are built into the system, as well as periodic maintenance.

Because preventive maintenance is the surest way to avoid unexpected breakdowns, you should make certain the furnace gets an annual checkup by a professional serviceman. However, there are some adjustments that you should be familiar with and some maintenance procedures that you can attend to yourself. For example, all furnaces in an automatic heating system have at least one motor (many have several) and these usually need periodic lubrication—a few drops of motor oil applied two or three times a year. Your serviceman may take care of this once on his annual visit, but it's up to you to take care of the needed lubrication between visits. A few drops are added to the oil cups on all blowers and blower motors (in hot air systems) as well as to circulator motors or pumps in hot-water systems. If your system is oil-fired don't forget that your oil burner also has a motor and pump. Some motors have a single cup at one end, others have cups at each end.

Lubricating an oil burner motor is necessary several times a year.

Of all the controls in your furnace and heating system, the one control that everyone is most familiar with is the thermostat. This switches the furnace on and off automatically to keep the inside of the house at a comfortable temperature. The thermostat should be located where it is not subject to cold drafts, and it should never be on an outside wall since transmitted cold can cause it to call for heat when the rest of the house is comfortably warm. By the same token, never place lamps, tele-

vision sets or other heat-producing appliances anywhere near or under a thermostat—this will cause
a false reading that will make everyone in the house
feel chilly.

To conserve fuel, thermostat settings should be
turned down 5–10 degrees during the night and
the doors of unused rooms should be closed. The
thermostat can be turned down manually each
night, or a clock-controlled thermostat installed to
do the job automatically.

Poorly functioning thermostats not only fail to
keep a house as comfortable as it should be, they
also waste considerable amounts of heat by making
the house alternately too hot, then too cold. Some
will cycle on-and-off so frequently that the furnace
fails to operate at maximum efficiency and thus
wastes a great deal of fuel due to the short heating
cycles. Chances are that if your thermostat is more
than 8 or 10 years old it probably will need replacing, or at least cleaning and adjustment, so have
your serviceman inspect it the next time he comes.
If in doubt, buy a new one and replace it. This is
a job that you can do yourself since all you need
do is disconnect the old wires and then reconnect
them to the matching terminals on the new one.
(For disconnecting wiring, see Door Bell Repairs,
page 122.) Make certain you pull out the fuse or
shut off the circuit breaker that controls power to
the furnace before you start.

All automatic furnaces have an on-off limit control that keeps the circulator motor (in the case
of a hot-water system) or blower motor (in the
case of a hot-air system) from kicking on before
the water or air has been heated up sufficiently. If
the circulator (in a hot-water system) or the
blower (in a hot-air system) were to kick on immediately after the furnace came on, cold water
or air would be sent up at the beginning of each
cycle, and this would chill occupants of the house
each time the unit came on.

The high-limit switch which all furnaces contain
is designed to keep a furnace from overheating. It
usually is set so that the circulator motor or blower
motor keeps running long enough (after the ther-

mostat stops calling for heat) to dissipate the heat that's been built up and thus minimize fuel waste. If you are not already familiar with these high- and low-limit controls on your furnace, it's a good idea to ask your serviceman to point them out to you and show you how to make adjustments when and if it becomes necessary.

On a hot-water system there is another control called an aquastat that controls the temperature of the water in the boiler. In some furnaces this boiler water also serves to heat the domestic hot water (the water that comes out of your faucets). In these cases you may be able to effect fuel savings by setting your aquastat to a lower setting in the summer when no heat is required, and turning the aquastat (boiler temperature) higher only during the winter months.

HOT-AIR SYSTEMS

Hot-air systems have a motor which powers a large blower to force the heated air through ducts that carry it to various rooms in different parts of the house. In addition to lubricating both the motor and the blower as previously described, it's a good idea to check the drive belts which connect the motor to the fan. If the belt is too slack, power will be wasted; if the belt is badly worn or frayed it's liable to tear—so your best bet is to play safe and replace any belts that show signs of wear.

While checking the belt, also check the blades on the fan or blower, using a vacuum and a stiff brush to remove lint or dust that has accumulated, since this will cut down considerably on the effectiveness of the fan.

Most hot-air systems have filters which need periodic replacement or cleaning. These air filters usually are located in or near the furnace in one of the main ducts. They may be of either the disposable type which is replaced when it gets dirty, or the permanent type which can be washed or cleaned when dirty. Either way, get in the habit of checking these filters at least once a month during the heating season by holding them up to a light and looking through them. If you can't see the light clearly, the filter needs cleaning or replacement. Leaving a filter in place when it is heavily clogged with dust and dirt will cut down tremendously on the circulation of air in your system and will increase heating costs considerably. In addition, if neglected long enough, some of this dirt will get distributed throughout the ducting and will eventually become lodged in places that may be difficult or impossible to reach without expensive dismantling of some of the ducts.

HOT-WATER SYSTEMS

Radiators in hot-water systems need periodic "bleeding," usually at the beginning of each heating season. Each radiator should be completely full of water when the system is running so that it gets hot all the way across, as well as from top to bottom. Air that gets trapped in the system rises to the top of the radiator, and this keeps water from filling it completely, thus lowering its efficiency and sometimes causing a hammering or knocking noise. To prevent this, every hot-water radiator has a small vent valve built in near the top. Some of these require a special key, while others can be opened by using a screwdriver. Either way, you bleed your radiator by opening this vent valve until all air escapes and water starts to run out (catch the water with a cup if you don't want to get your floor wet) then shut the valve immediately.

As a rule, you'll have to do this at the beginning of each heating season, but you'll have to do it to each radiator (starting from the top of the house) in order to bleed the entire system. You can avoid having to perform this task by installing automatic vent valves instead of the manual-bleed type. These automatically let air escape, but not water.

Most hot-water heating systems have an expansion tank located directly above or close to the

A vent valve "bleeds" a hot-water radiator of trapped air which is preventing heat from reaching all parts of the radiator.

boiler. These tanks should be about half full of water to allow for an air cushion at the top, but they may have to be drained periodically by opening the valve which always is located at the bottom of this expansion tank. Shut off the valve that lets water into the tank from the boiler first, then drain off one or two pails of water from the bottom.

STEAM SYSTEMS

One of the most common problems with a steam system is a radiator that does not get hot all the way across because water gets trapped at one end and keeps steam from entering. In a steam-heating system, steam rises from the boiler and then condenses to water which must run back down to the boiler through gravity only. It is for this reason that steam radiators should pitch slightly towards the valve or pipe through which the steam enters. If you have trouble with a radiator not heating all the way across, the first thing to check is the little vent valve which is supposed to let cold air escape. If removing this little valve allows trapped cold air to escape so that steam finally flows out, chances are that this little valve is clogged. It sometimes can be cleaned by boiling, but since these valves are inexpensive, your best bet is to replace it with a new one.

If venting does not solve the problem, and the radiator still does not get hot all the way across—or if your radiators tend to hammer or knock every time the steam comes up—the radiator may not be pitched properly. You can check this quite easily by laying a spirit level on top to see if the radiator slopes toward the inlet valve. If it doesn't, place a small block of wood under the legs of the radiator at the far end (away from the valve) so that the radiator now pitches properly.

Another problem that can cause knocking in the pipes is sagging of one or more pipes so that a low spot occurs in which water gets trapped on its way back to the boiler and does not flow smoothly. If you can't find the source of this problem call a

Water trapped
in this end

will knock
at this end.

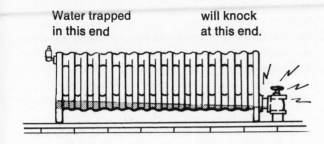

Wedge

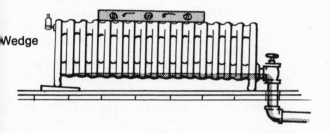

Using a spirit level, you can determine if radiator is level or sloping toward inlet valve. If not, insert a wedge to create slight slope so water can drain freely.

plumber in to check the various lines and see where the trouble is. There is one other point to remember about a steam-heating system: The radiator valve should always be opened or closed all the way—it should never be part way open, since this is a certain cause of knocking and hammering in the system.

Regardless of the type of heating system you have, remember that for maximum efficiency, radiators or registers (in the case of a hot-air system) should never be blocked or obstructed by large pieces of furniture, bulky hangings or accumulations of dust, dirt, or lint. Anything that interferes with free circulation of air in and around the heating unit (radiator or grill) is certain to cut down on the efficiency of the system and will result in unnecessarily large fuel bills as well as in uneven heating throughout your home.

IF YOUR FURNACE SUDDENLY STOPS

If your heating system suddenly stops functioning on a cold wintry day and you can't get a serviceman immediately, there are some steps you can take that may put it back in operating condition:

1. Check the fuses that supply power to the furnace to make certain that the fuse or circuit breaker controlling the burner has not blown. If the fuse or circuit breaker is OK, check the master emergency shut-off switch for your heating system to see if anyone has accidentally shut it off (some people accidentally mistake these for light switches).
2. If your furnace is oil-fired, check the oil tank to make certain you still have fuel (even if you bought some recently, a leak may have developed).
3. If your furnace is gas fired, make certain the pilot light has not gone out—this usually will shut the furnace off on safety. If the pilot light is out, follow instructions on the burner to relight it. If the pilot light goes out again, call your serviceman or utility company as soon as possible.
4. Check your thermostat to make certain that no one has accidentally turned it down below the desired temperature, nor put a source of heat close to the thermostat so that its temperature has been raised up beyond that of the surrounding room area. Turn the dial back and forth to see if you can hear it click open and closed—in other words, see if it is still operating properly.
5. If your system is a forced-air system and the burner is working but the house still doesn't get warm, first check to see if the filters are clogged. If this is not the problem, see if the fan belt has broken on the blower. If only one room won't warm up, see if the register in that room is closed or clogged by something.
6. Check the safety recycling button on the stack relay control that is attached to the smoke pipe (this is also called the primary control). This has a safety button (often red) that pops out to shut off the burner when the stack temperature or burner chamber pressure climbs beyond safe limits. Press the button in to see if this starts your burner. If it does, but then the flame goes out again in a few minutes, open your furnace door to relieve possible pressure, then try again. If the flame still goes out, check to see if the chimney or smoke pipe that connects the furnace to the chimney is clogged. If it is not, but the flame keeps going out, there is a good chance that the sensing unit in the stack probably needs cleaning. Remove the en-

tire unit from the smoke pipe—it's normally held in place with one or two setscrews—then gently clean the soot off the end of the element that protrudes into the smoke pipe.

7. If you have a steam-heating system, check the water-level indicating gauge on your boiler. If the water level is low, the furnace will cut off automatically. Filling the boiler past the halfway mark on the gauge should start it up again.

8. If you have a forced-air heating system, check the belt that drives the fan or blower—if it is broken or so loose that the blower is slipping, no hot air will be circulated and the furnace will overheat and shut off on safety. Replacing the belt (or tightening it if it is so loose that it slips) will cure this problem.

MAINTAINING ROOM AIR CONDITIONERS

Modern room air conditioners are surprisingly dependable appliances that actually require very little maintenance. Still, there are a few things you can and should do which will help keep your unit operating at peak efficiency, and which also will help prevent breakdowns in the middle of a heat spell.

Most air conditioners should be plugged into a separate electric circuit—that is, they should have their own circuit or at least be plugged into a circuit on which no other appliance is operating at the same time. If at all possible, avoid use of extension cords, especially long ones, but if one is necessary to reach an outlet make sure you use one with a heavy-gauge wire that is adequate to supply the amount of current needed. Light-gauge extension cords will cut down on the amount of current the machine receives and will lower its efficiency. In addition, low current can cause motors and compressors to overheat and often is a contributing factor in greatly shortening the life of these components.

All air conditioners have removable air filters on the inside which should be cleaned or changed periodically. Clean the permanent ones by washing them in running water, and replace the inexpensive disposable ones when they become dirty. The filter should be checked at least once a month and the best way to do this is to take it out, then hold it up and look through it at a bright light. If you can barely see the light through the filter then it needs to be cleaned (if it is of the permanent type) or replaced (if it is of the disposable type).

Before replacing the filter it's a good idea to also clean the grill on the front or side of the unit by using a soft brush and vacuum cleaner. The best way to do this is to remove the grill completely—although you can clean with the grill still in place if necessary. Use a rag to wipe off lint or greasy residue that will not come off with the vacuum, and also use a narrow nozzle on the vacuum to remove lint and dust from around the coils and fins that are visible when the grill is removed.

An air conditioner's efficiency is directly related to how effectively it moves air, and thus cleaning it is very important. Cleaning removes lint and dust that can cut down on the unit's cooling capacity; furthermore, if the dirt buildup is severe enough (and ignored long enough) it can overload the refrigerating unit dangerously and eventually will cause a serious breakdown.

Wherever possible, the outside half of the unit should also be cleaned in the same way. To understand the need for this, you must remember that an air-conditioning unit consists of two separate systems: a cooling mechanism on the inside that chills and dehumidifies the air in the room as the fan recirculates it, and a condensing unit on the outside that dissipates the heat to the outside. Thus, there are actually two sets of coils (condenser coils and evaporator coils) and two fans (one to cool each set of coils). Both sets of coils need a free flow of unobstructed air around them, and both fans need to work freely—so clean the fan blades at the same time if you can reach them.

In some models the outside can be cleaned by sliding the whole unit inside to permit reaching the outer end; in others it may be more practical to work from the outside—although a ladder may be needed. The outer grill should be wiped clean with a rag dipped into a detergent solution and the condenser drain should be checked to make certain that condensed water can run off freely on the outside.

While you're working on the outside half, inspect the metal housing to see if there are any rusty areas that need to be touched up (use a metal primer first) and also check to see if bugs or rodents have worked their way into the inside. Prune any shrubs or trees whose branches come close enough to obstruct a free flow of air past the outside, and make certain there are no fences or other obstructions close by that can cause a similar problem.

Although many modern units have sealed motors that never require lubrication, some older air conditioners do need periodic lubrication of the motors, so read the owner's manual for your unit to see where and if this is required (if in doubt write to the manufacturer).

While cleaning and lubricating, check the caulking around the outside and the weatherstripping or other seals around the inside to make certain that these form a watertight and airtight seal around all sides of the unit. Cracks or openings not only permit hot air to enter and thus add to cooling costs, if they are large enough they also may cause the machine to overwork and run at top capacity for long periods. This, too, can lead to premature breakdowns and unnecessarily large repair bills.

ADDING INSULATION

One of a homeowner's most potent weapons in his continual battle to conserve fuel in the winter, and conserve electricity (used for air conditioning) in the summer, is insulation. Adequate insulation serves to keep the heat where it belongs—inside in cold weather and outside in hot weather. Insulation not only saves on heating and air conditioning costs, it also helps to make your home more comfortable all year round.

For maximum effectiveness a house should have insulation in all of its outside walls and under the roof (or on top of the ceiling of the upper floor if the attic is unfinished). If the attic is finished, the

Airspace

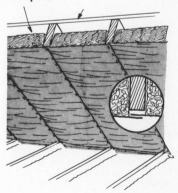

Insulation in a finished attic is applied between roof beams.

Any house should have insulation on all of its outside walls and under the roof, or on the attic floor, and on walls adjacent to unheated areas. Insulation over finished attic (top); insulation on house with flat roof (bottom).

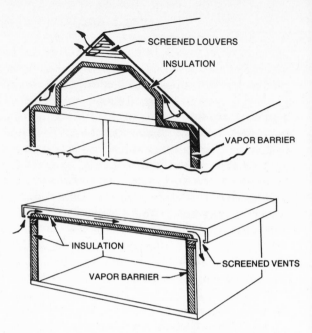

insulation should be carried up between the roof rafters and down the walls of the finished attic room as shown here. In addition, homeowners often forget that insulation is also required in walls that adjoin unheated areas, for example, a wall next to an unheated garage, or next to an unheated open porch. Insulation also is necessary under floors that have crawl spaces below, or under floors that are suspended over an unheated garage, utility room or storage room.

Bulk insulation made of rock wool or fiberglass (both are inorganic materials known as mineral wool) is the kind most often used in homes. It comes in blankets or batting, or as loose fill that can be poured into cavities (such as between beams in an unfinished attic floor) or blown into walls. Reflective insulation is made of aluminum foil in one or more layers that open up accordian-style, but it is more effective in reflecting the sun's heat away than it is in keeping a furnace's heat in, so it finds most use in warm climates where air conditioning is the prime consideration. As a rule, the thicker the insulation the more resistance it offers to the passage of heat, but this can vary with different brands and types. However, homeowners have a simple means for judging the effectiveness of comparative brands by checking their R-numbers —an industry-wide rating system that indicates each product's effectiveness. The higher the R-number, the better the insulation. Ceilings should have insulation rated at R-19 or better (this is usually 5 to 7 inches thick), while walls and floors over heated crawl spaces should have insulation rated at R-11 (3 to 4 inches thick). Adding an extra R-11 insulation to a ceiling that only has 2 or 3 inches on it now can result in a fuel saving of up to 15 percent during the heating season, and even more if a house is or will be air conditioned.

If the attic floor is unfinished, adding insulation to the top of the house is simple—merely lay fiberglass of the appropriate thickness (as indicated by the R-number on the bag) between the beams on the attic floor. If there already is some insulation in place, the extra amount needed can be laid right on top of the old material.

Insulation usually comes with a vapor barrier on one side, made of aluminum foil or a specially impregnated kraft paper. This vapor barrier should always be installed so it faces toward the warm side. In other words, on an attic floor the vapor barrier would be on the bottom; if the insulation is put up between the roof rafters the vapor barrier would face downward, toward the inside (see drawing on page 228). This paper or foil barrier has flanges that stick out along the sides so that you can staple these on the face side of the studs (in the case of a vertical wall) or rafters (in the case of overhead roof rafters). The vapor barrier is essential with all insulation since it prevents condensation from soaking into the material and thus lowering its efficiency.

If you are adding new insulation to an attic floor on top of existing insulation which already has a vapor barrier in place, try to buy the type which has no vapor barrier so that you simply can place it on top. If you do put down a second layer that has its own vapor barrier, leave the original vapor barrier intact, but cut slits or holes in the new barrier so that you do not have two barriers which will trap moist vapors between them. Either way, when installing additional insulation on an attic floor put

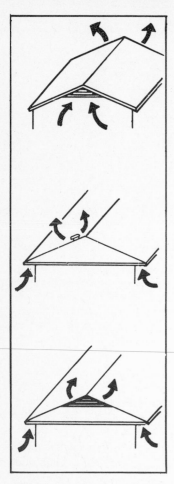

There are various ways to ventilate an attic—all allowing air to flow *above* the insulation.

it down merely by pushing it into place between the studs or rafters (it comes in various widths to fit standard spacing between beams). In lieu of this you can also put down loose fill, which is a cottony, granulated material that comes in large bags. This is poured into place on top of the old material.

The best way to insulate walls is during initial construction when blankets or batting can be stapled up between the exposed studs on the inside before the walls are finished. However, for homes that are already finished this method is obviously impractical, so the only way to add insulation at this point is to hire a professional applicator who will work from the outside. Using specialized equipment he will remove sections of siding and then blow loose fill or a special insulating foam in from the outside, after which he will replace and repair the siding so that little or no damage is noticeable.

To avoid condensation problems in attic spaces or under roofs it is important that ventilation be provided above the insulation at all times. In attics there should be at least two vents up near the peak so that air can flow in through one and out the other. Another method is to have vents along the ridges, with additional vents along the overhanging eaves at the bottom of the roof. In any event, there should be enough vents installed to provide a total of 1 square foot of free opening for every 300 square feet of attic floor area. These vents should be left open year round—in the winter to let moisture vapor escape and in the summer to let hot air out.

or add a blanket without a vapor barrier.

Use loose fill

Adding insulation on an attic floor

Vapor barrier on bottom of the old insulation.

INDEX

Adhesives, new, *viii*
Aerator of faucet, cleaning of, 135-136
Aerosol spray cans, 35-38
Air conditioners
   maintaining methods, 225-227
   sealing openings around, 93
Air filters, of air conditioners, 225-226
Alkyd-base paints, 21, 22-23
Allen wrenches, 8
Aluminum flashing, for roof repairs, 199-200
Aluminum foil
   in paint trays, 26
   and repairing gutters, 204-205
Amperes of fuses, 109
Anchors
   for hanging objects on walls, 61-62
   for use in solid masonry, 64-65
Antihammer devices, 153
Asphalt cement
   and gutter repairs, 204-205
   and roofing repairs, 200-201
Asphalt shingles, for roof repairs, 199-200
Asphalt tile. *See* Floor tiles
Attic floors, insulation added to, 229-230
Attics, ventilation of, 42
Awning windows, 82-83

Ballast of fluorescent fixtures, 118-119, 121-122
Ballcock of toilet tank, replacement for, 148, 149-151
Bar clamp, 18
Basements, damp, 189-194
Bathroom accessories, repair of, 58-59
Bathtub drains, clogged, 137-139
Belt sanders, 38
Bench plane, 12
Blacktop driveways, patching of, 206-208
Blacktop sealers, 207-208
Bleach, ceramic tile joints and, 60
Blisters, on flat roofs, 201